WILLIAM STRINGFELLOW

MODERN SPIRITUAL MASTERS SERIES

WILLIAM STRINGFELLOW

Essential Writings

Selected with an
Introduction by

BILL WYLIE-KELLERMANN

With a Homiletic Afterword by

DANIEL BERRIGAN, S.J.

ORBIS BOOKS
Maryknoll, New York 10545

Founded in 1970, Orbis Books endeavors to publish works that enlighten the mind, nourish the spirit, and challenge the conscience. The publishing arm of the Mary-knoll Fathers and Brothers, Orbis seeks to explore the global dimensions of the Christian faith and mission, to invite dialogue with diverse cultures and religious traditions, and to serve the cause of reconciliation and peace. The books published reflect the views of their authors and do not represent the official position of the Maryknoll Society. To learn more about Maryknoll and Orbis Books, please visit our website at www.maryknollsociety.org.

Library of Congress Cataloging-in-Publication Data
Stringfellow, William.
    William Stringfellow : essential writings / selected with an introduction
  by Bill Wylie-Kellermann ; with a homiletic afterword by Daniel Berrigan, S.J.
      pages   cm. – (Modern spiritual masters series)
    Includes bibliographical references.
    ISBN 978-1-62698-049-5 (pbk.)   I. Kellermann, Bill Wylie-.   II. Title.
BX4827.S84A25 2013
230–dc23
                                                            2013005192

For
Jeanie Wylie,
beloved gone to God,
author, journalist, family-maker, activist,
partner in the vocation of a marriage blessed by Stringfellow
from the Service for the Burial of the Dead,
the Book of Common Prayer:
"The One that raised Christ Jesus from the dead,
quicken your mortal bodies also."
So be it, Amen.

Contents

A Preface
Personal and Practical

Humanly speaking, this book harbors a secret yearning. Among its readers, it wants to break into the heads and hearts of a new generation of Christians—hip-hop theologians, newly monastic types, Jesus radicals, erstwhile post-evangelicals, race traitors and the anti-racist, Christian anarchists, undocumented dreamers, Gospel performance artists, urban farmers (rural ones too), dreadlocked preachers to be, revolutionary activists, nonviolent resisters, wild geese, queer believers, godly bloggers, biblico-primitivists, cradle Christians fallen away, the baptized-in-exile, young catholic workers, social justice students, a corps of volunteers ruined-for-life—these and more. Found among them are serious theologians, but also many who are hungry for something substantial and deep. A generation, raised on digital, weary of sources a mile wide and an inch deep. This book prays to be carried around in hip pocket or backpack and be passed along dog-eared hand to hand. Let it even be kindled. It prays to be in the mix of a new theological converse.

For any in that wide circle who do take their theology byte-sized, you might try beginning at the end. I have appended a "lexicon" of Stringfellow's terminology, including traditional terms for which his definitions are provocative and edifying meditations. Nearly all of his works are represented there. It serves as a snapshot of his theology and also a perfectly reasonable way into this book or any of his.

I first read William Stringfellow as a high school student in Detroit. It was the year of the 1967 rebellion. By some unaccountable providence, he had written a book for adolescents on the power of death in sex, loneliness, and identity—or more to the point, on the freedom of Christ in resurrection, vocation, and baptism. Reading *Instead of Death* (1962) was the first time I'd really thought theologically, and the light went on. When smoke and flames rose from the city, it was vocationally iconic for me because I looked upon it with the writings of Martin Luther King Jr. in one hand and those of William Stringfellow in the other. Ironically, when I put together a larger anthology of his writings two decades ago, I neglected to include a single contribution from that book. The omission is gratefully remedied in these pages.

Instead of Death was important in another way as well. Being the only volume of his republished in his lifetime, he took the opportunity not only to add pertinent chapters, but to alter the language of patriarchy, from which the earlier suffered. As elsewhere, based on this rhetorical move, I have taken the prerogative to similarly free other passages from that captivity of language.

I first heard his voice as a speaker when I was at North Central College outside Chicago. In preparation our college chaplain pressed a group of us to read *Free in Obedience* (1964), which was his first real explication of the principalities and powers. When he spoke he sat. He was ill, in considerable pain, actually dying—though radical surgery would extend his life another eighteen years. Yet his posture served only to magnify his word. He was frail but seemed to gather and focus himself with an act of pure will (or grace under pressure). And then he spoke slowly, but with a force that cut like a knife. His words possessed an incisive clarity that blew us away—especially the radical black students on campus, who had "never heard a white man talk like that before." But a few months hence and Martin Luther King would be dead. My life would be wrenched through another vocational passage involving them both.

Daniel Berrigan, Jesuit priest, prisoner, and poet (not to mention Stringfellow's dear friend) introduced a group of us to him at Union Theologocal Seminary in New York. Berrigan is necessarily a presence in this volume as well. He'd already urged us in the reading of *Ethic for Christians and Other Aliens in a Strange Land* (1974), and now in that same year he brought greetings in connection with a plan they'd hatched to mentor a new generation of disciples in an "underground seminary." We were to be part of the new generation. And my vocation passes inexorably through that series of mentored biblical gatherings.

An Ethic for Christians, I confess, is the book which has more than any other shaped my own life and ministry. That explains, only in part, why it is so prominent in the selection of these essentials. Judging his "most important and influential book" is a pointless endeavor, but I do assess it so. Witness the work of Walter Wink built in part on its foundation. It is, however, more than any other, the book from which the theme of this volume arises. Therein, empire is named both Babylon and America; there the powers that be are made a spectacle, and there the sacramental ethic of living fully human is uttered.

I am already asked how the present volume differs from the earlier anthology I edited, *A Keeper of the Word: Selected Writings of William Stringfellow* (Eerdmans, 1994). There is to be sure a certain overlap. That selection, however, was broader, more comprehensive, and tended to reflect more the range or changing terrain of his thought. This volume, including the introductory essay, is more focused—essential in the sense of getting to the heart. It also has in mind this present moment and the generation called to address it.

It humbly prays to be of service in the work and witness of human living.

Gratitudes

Thanks be to God . . .

For William Stringfellow being William Stringfellow, nothing more and nothing less;

For Daniel Berrigan, who introduced us, who uttered the homiletic afterword, who made Bill indictable, and who loved him as dearest friend;

For Gary Lueck and Larry Bouldin, who also introduced me to him in earlier ways and places;

For Scott Kennedy, of blessed memory and so presente, who has held with Jim Wallis the Stringfellow Trust honoring Bill's legacy;

For Word and World, within that legacy, and for its recent crop of mentored movement activists, including many Stringfellow devotees—among them Liz Nicolas, Danielle Miller, Matt Carson, Chris Grataski . . . indeed all;

For Lydia Wylie-Kellermann, who transcribed much of this book and as a child was heard to mutter, shaking her head, "Stringfellow, Stringfellow, Stringfellow";

For friends and companions, resisters and activists, pastors and academics, who have read and commented or otherwise encouraged this project, Liz McAllister and the Atlantic Life Community, Joyce Hollyday, Ched Myers, Elaine Enns, Laurel Dykstra, Denise Griebler, Carol Ann McGibbon, Dody Finch, Jim Perkinson, Lily Mendoza, Theresa Tensuan, Timothy Van-Meter, Kyle Lambelet, Nathan Schneider, Arthur Boers, Jeremy Kenward, Garreth Higgins, Kirk Laubenstein, Carl Gladstone, Paul Perez;

For Stringfellow scholars who honor their vocation, especially Uncas McThenia and Anthony Dancer;

For Robert Ellsberg of Orbis Books, who dogged me for years to deliver this book and who holds to the Word amid a babel of publishing powers;

For Maria Angellini and the Orbis staff, skilled in the arts of production, marketing, and otherwise serving to please authors, editors, and dear readers.

For bloggers who keep the Stringfellonian conversation alive, underground and in the cloud—among those known to me: Glenn Jordon, Myles Werntz, crookedshore, and The Mockingbird's Leap;

For Ed Spivy, stand-up comic and art designer, whose photo of Bill graces the cover;

For Walter Wink (presente), whose magisterial work on the powers was seeded by Stringfellow's own;

For the students and faculty of worthy institutions that have welcomed the teaching of this material: Whitaker School of Theology, Ecumenical Theological Seminary, Marygrove Social Justice Masters program, and the Seminary Consortium for Urban Pastoral Education;

For the Louisville Institute, which provided a Pastoral Study Grant toward the space and solitude necessary for such a project;

For the Rare and Manuscript Collections at Cornell University, who keep forty-four boxes of Stringfellow's papers safe and accessible;

For Wipf and Stock Publishers, Eugene Oregon, bless them, who have brought all of Stringfellow's books back into print. (All the quotations from his books in this volume are used with their gracious permission. www.wipfandstock.com.)

For the people of St. Peter's Episcopal in Detroit, who hear Stringfellow's life and testimony now and again in my preaching, even in my ministry;

For beloved friends in Detroit who struggle these days against lawless authority and occupation government, who rebuild a city in exile from below—too many to name, though with too few pastors, to wit: Charles Williams, David Bullock, Edwin Rowe, Maurice Rudd, David Murray;

For the calling to live humanly toward the end of empire, and grace so to do. Amen.

Sources
and Abbreviations

BOOKS BY
WILLIAM STRINGFELLOW

BPA   *The Bishop Pike Affair* (New York: Harper & Row, 1967).

CAJ   *Count It All Joy* (Grand Rapids: William B. Eerdmans, 1967).

CO   *Conscience and Obedience* (Waco, TX: Word Books, 1977).

DGS   *Dissenter in a Great Society* (New York: Holt, Rinehart, and Winston, 1966).

DL   *The Death and Life of Bishop Pike* (Garden City, NY: Doubleday, 1976).

EC   *An Ethic for Christians and Other Aliens in a Strange Land* (Waco, TX: Word, 1973).

FO   *Free in Obedience* (New York: Seabury Press, 1964).

ID   *Instead of Death* (New York: Seabury Press, 1963); 2nd ed. (New York: Seabury Press, 1976); see also *BPA* and *CAJ*).

IG   *Imposters of God: Inquiries into Favorite Idols* (Washington, DC: Witness Books, 1969).

MPE   *My People Is the Enemy* (New York: Holt, Rinehart and Winston, 1964).

PPF   *A Private and Public Faith* (Grand Rapids: William B. Eerdmans, 1962).

PS   *The Politics of Spirituality* (Louisville: Westminster
            Press, 1984).

SB   *A Second Birthday* (Garden City, NY: Doubleday,
            1970).

SF   *A Simplicity of Faith: My Experience in Mourning*
            (Nashville: Abingdon, 1982)

ST   *Suspect Tenderness: The Ethics of the Berrigan
            Witness* (New York: Holt, Rinehart, and Winston,
            1971).

The above list is by original publisher. Nearly all of Stringfellow's
books are back in print, published by Wipf & Stock in Eugene,
Oregon. All book selections are used by permission of Wipf &
Stock Publishers, www.wipfandstock.com.

BOOKS ABOUT
WILLIAM STRINGFELLOW

AKW   Kellermann, Bill Wylie-, ed., *A Keeper of the Word:
           Selected Writings* (Grand Rapids: William B. Eerd-
           mans, 1994).

ASL   Dancer, Anthony, *An Alien in a Strange Land*
           (Eugene, OR: Cascade Books, 2011).

PJPL   Slocum, Robert Boak, ed., *Prophet of Justice,
           Prophet of Life* (New York: Church Publishing,
           1997).

RCEL   McThenia, Andrew W., Jr., ed., *Radical Christian
           and Exemplary Lawyer* (Grand Rapids: William B.
           Eerdmans, 1995).

WSAAP   Dancer, Anthony, ed., *William Stringfellow in Ang-
           lo-American Perspective* (Hampshire, UK: Ashgate,
           2005).

Introduction

Living Humanly
toward the End of Empire

The Spiritual and Wordly Ethics
of William Stringfellow

*In the face of death, live humanly. In the middle of chaos,
celebrate the Word. Amidst babel . . . speak the truth.*
— EC, 142

William Stringfellow, theologian and advocate, would take wry
and ironic delight to find himself included in a series on Modern
Spiritual Masters. To be sure, he would smile at certain of the
company in which he is included, but he was openly wary of
"spirituality," especially the privatized, justified, and commodi-
fied guises it takes in U.S. culture. Many today identify themselves as "spiritual, but not religious." His first book, *Private and
Public Faith* (1962), includes a frontal assault on the assorted
idolatries of religion as confronted by the Gospel. Problem is,
he pinpointed many of the same idolatrous mechanisms at work
in the spiritualities which would supplant institutional religion.

At the same time, his final book just a year before his death,
The Politics of Spirituality (1984), truly a capstone, was a thin
little volume that included taking on the blasphemies of the
Reagan era in the spirited light of justification and holiness.
At such he was indeed a master. Count it a tract on sanctifica-
tion, in all its social dimensions. Once his general qualms on

1

"spirituality" were named and set aside, and once he'd named the task as pursuit of *biblical* spirituality, he was free to celebrate the Holy Spirit as the faithfulness of the Word not only to his own life, but to history and the very life of all creation.

Why Now?

In a time of environmental collapse, endless war, the breakdown of fundamental structures, the most important question we are facing is: What does it mean to be human? Or, in such a time as this, what is living humanly? That was Stringfellow's question, to be sure, though he put it in a variety of ways.

> I believed then, as I do now, that I am called in the Word of God—as is *everyone* else—to the vocation of being human, nothing more and nothing less. I confessed then, as I do now, that to be a Christian means to be called to be an exemplary human being. And, to be a Christian *categorically* does not mean being religious. Indeed, all religious versions of the Gospel are profanities. Within the scope of the calling to be merely, but truly, human, any work, including that of any profession, can be rendered a sacrament of that vocation.   (*SF,* 126)

Bill Stringfellow wrote theology in the concrete. In the moment. Incarnate. Some of his works are specifically autobiographical theology, written virtually as they were lived. They were storied accounts of his own humanity. *My People Is the Enemy* (1964) narrates his work as a street lawyer in East Harlem. *A Second Birthday* (1970) testifies to his survival of unremitting pain and radical surgery. And *A Simplicity of Faith* (1982) recounts his grief over the death of his "sweet companion," Anthony Towne. Stringfellow regarded them as comprising an autobiographic trilogy, each turning on a vocational crisis. He wrote theology in the first person. Virtually all his books have personal stories woven in. By ordering all such material it would even be possible to compile something of a passable autobiographical anthology.[1]

---

1. I have done something of this sort, though briefly, in *AKW*.

Moreover, the historical moment and incumbent political regimes were often close in the background or explicitly under theological critique. Because his analysis was radically biblical and biblically radical, his was no party line dissent. The Reagan administration is already mentioned. *Dissenter in a Great Society* (1966) unmasks the mythologies of the Lyndon Johnson era and reflects the freedom struggle. *An Ethic for Christians and Other Aliens in a Strange Land* (1973) was written against the lawlessness of the Nixon regime, as was *Suspect Tenderness* (1971), though it tells a specific tale of nonviolent resistance.

You would think this would render his writing time-bound. But no. For a couple of reasons. One was that he saw into things so deeply that his writing ends up being remarkably prescient. It was prophetic in the most conventional meaning of the term. Whether he's writing about the assault on creation, the ubiquity of surveillance, the spiritual intransigence of racism, the contempt of corporations for human life, the commercial and political bondage of the churches, or the technological determinism of military policy, we scratch our heads in astonishment and say, "He wrote this forty years ago?"

The other reason is that in each of these moments, whether personal or historical, he is listening for the Word of God. He discerns and recognizes. The reader is drawn in to listen and recognize as well. We are urged to discern the Word in our own life and times. He was quite explicit about his intent in this regard.

> The theological exploration of biography or the theological reconnaissance of history are apt, and even normative, styles because each is congruent with the definitive New Testament insight and instruction: *the Incarnation.* . . . This historic, incarnate activity of the Word of God signifies the militance of the Word of God, both in cosmic dimensions of space and time and in each and every item of created life, including *your* personhood and *your* biography or mine. It is this same basis of the Christian faith that is so often diminished, dismissed, omitted, or ignored when theology is rendered

> in abstract, hypothesized, propositional, or academic
> models. . . . So, I believe, biography (and history), *any*
> biography and *every* biography, is inherently theologi-
> cal, in the sense that it contains already—literally by vir-
> tue of the Incarnation—the news of the Gospel whether
> or not anyone discerns that. *We* are each one of us par-
> ables.   (*SF,* 19–20)

Parables of the Word. This phrase, Stringfellow's own, is emblematic of his incarnational theology. In this view everyone's story is necessarily theological because it reveals the presence of the Word of God, recognized or not, in the life and personhood of a human being. In fact, he took "vocation" to be essentially the name of that personal recognition. Stringfellow's spiritual-ity, as well as his ethics, may rightly be called vocational. By the Word present in our lives we are called firstly (and finally) to be fully and freely ourselves—who we are uttered in the Word of God to be.

For the subtitle of his book on Harlem, he employed a phrase related to a living parable: "an autobiographical polemic." That too is evocative. By it I believe he meant to suggest that not only is the Word inherent in our lives, but the "powers-that-be" as well. They are active characters in the drama of history and our own lives. This is so whether we acknowledge and resist them, or succumb to their wiles. Stringfellow saw the narrative of his own self-accounting as yet another engagement which carried the struggle a step further, affecting again the exposure of the powers. This too is biblically apropos. A Gospel, for example, is the good news of Jesus' open confrontation with the rulers and authorities, which is itself—in the retelling of proclamation—a frontal assault on their rule.

Sketch of a Human Life

Born April 26, 1928, William Stringfellow grew up on the other side of the tracks in Northampton, Massachusetts, where his father worked in the textile mills and knew the labor and economic turbulence of the thirties. "We were poor," he wrote, but (in contrast to black folk) "I could 'pass.'" Theologically precocious, he was taken under wing by a local clergyman who so pressured him for the priesthood that he reacted by deciding to be forever a layperson. "I would be damned if I would become a priest."

Because of its debate program he went to Bates College in Maine, where he was active in campus as well as public politics, already aspiring to political office. His theology was deepened by involvement in the Student Christian Movement and in particular by attending, in the summer of 1946, the World Conference of Christian Youth in Oslo, Norway. There he was touched by confessional witnesses from the anti-Nazi resistance as well as students from Latin America and the Far East. He titled his report, "Does the World Hate America? What an Innocent Learned Abroad."

Thus began a hectic schedule of speaking and conferencing in which he was becoming, as he later saw it, a "professional Christian," even a "pharisee." In 1950 he studied for a year at the London School of Economics, where he "died to political career," in fact to having any career at all. Thereafter he was drafted and spent two years in Germany as a supply sergeant with NATO forces.

He returned home to study law at Harvard, though he was hardly a model law student, taking seminary courses, speaking, teaching debate at Tufts University, and organizing conferences on Theology and the Law. He'd somehow expected that justice might be a suitable topic for consideration in law school. "Alas it was seldom mentioned, and the term itself evoked ridicule, as if justice were a subject beneath the sophistication of lawyers."

On Labor Day 1956, promptly demonstrating his rejection of upward-mobility, he moved to Harlem to do street law. There he encountered the racial crisis and was drawn into the freedom struggle. He'd come initially at the behest of the East Harlem Protestant Parish, cutting edge of the urban ministry movement, but within a couple of years he resigned, essentially over what he saw as the lack of Bible study, theology, and lay participation.

During the latter Harlem years he became severely lonely, and began drinking "enthusiastically," as he put it. He was not above speaking drunk and once made a Baltimore headline as a "missing theologian" when he failed to show as speaker for a dinner at Johns Hopkins. His life was becoming dissolute and even desperate. In the book for adolescents, he named loneliness the "most caustic, drastic, and fundamental repudiation of God." However, the same chapter ended: "Love yourself: that means your final acceptance of and active participation in God's love of you. . . . If you love yourself you will become and be one who can love another. . . . And when you love others—tell them so—celebrate it—not only by some words but by your life toward them and toward the whole world (*ID*, 25, 33–34).

As he was finishing the book, he fell in love with Anthony Towne, and they moved into an apartment on the Upper West Side, which became something of a theological "salon." It was a high-traffic destination, a stopping place for ecclesiastical visitors, a crash pad for the lost and lonely, a center for organizing forays into the church, a location for hosting fundraisers, and not a few parties. Stringfellow and Towne shared a common love for the circus and spent part of a summer following one in a station wagon. A book was always intended. They saw in it a parable of the reconciled community, in all its human and creaturely diversity, a veritable image of the "kindom."

In 1962, he sat as the youngest member of a panel, the only one not academically trained in theology, which questioned Karl Barth, the great Swiss biblical theologian. His questions were all politically alert: concerning the Confessing Church struggle in Germany, the interpretation of Romans 13 (be subject to the State), the quiescence of the churches, and the meaning of the "principalities and powers." He was blessed and made notorious when Barth, pointing at Stringfellow, turned toward the audience and said, "Listen to this man."

However, he was booed the following year at the first National Conference on Religion and Race when he called the event "too little, too late, and too lily white." He also named racism a demonic power that enslaves human beings and argued that the only issue at hand was baptism—the sacramental unity of all humanity before God.

His subsequent book, *Free in Obedience* (1964), was his first developed treatment of "the powers," bringing them back onto the map of Christian social ethics.

In 1967, in a move toward slower environs, Stringfellow and Towne resettled on Block Island just off the coast of Rhode Island. Not yet overdeveloped, it was a quiet community where their life of hospitality could continue in a more monastic vein. They called their place "Eschaton"—the end of the world, which is its true beginning.

The move was prompted by a gathering health crisis. In India on a Student Christian Movement trip Stringfellow had contracted hepatitis. He'd missed law school graduation for gall bladder surgery. Now he suffered a long misdiagnosed ailment that caused excruciating pain. The remedy proved to be a risky and life-threatening surgery to remove his pancreas. It would leave him for the duration a total diabetic with all the degenerative effects.

In 1970 he and Towne were indicted for "harboring a fugitive," when Daniel Berrigan, the Jesuit poet, was arrested by the FBI at their home. Berrigan had been convicted with eight others for burning draft files as a liturgical protest against the Vietnam War, but rather than submitting to sentence had gone underground. Stringfellow's recovery was still fragile. "They're trying to kill him!" said Anthony. The indictment was eventually quashed.

The two of them had also been friends with Episcopal bishop James Pike, chronicling and standing by him in his honest-to-God heresy trial. When Pike's passion for Jesus led him trackless into the Judean wilderness, where he died, Bill and Anthony went to Israel/Palestine to research a biography, which they co-wrote.

On the eve of Richard Nixon's second inauguration, using an ancient rite, Stringfellow prayed a public exorcism of the president, which he considered an act of pastoral care, though he quietly took some credit when the presidency unraveled through Watergate.

Over the years Stringfellow cofounded a number of "institutes" only to leave them when they became too clericized, or professionalized, or overinstitutionalized. In the mid-seventies he and Berrigan pulled together an underground resistance "seminary" doing Bible study and action planning in a series of anarchic weekends. During this time his book *An Ethic for Christians and Other Aliens in a Strange Land* became a handbook for the nonviolent resistance movement, in jail and out. The "seminary" waned, but its influence remains.

He stayed active as an Episcopalian, consulting with and aiding, for example, the first wave of women to be ordained as priests in the church. When William Wendt of Washington was charged in 1976 with allowing one of them to celebrate Eucharist at his church, Stringfellow served as his canonical lawyer.

Because of his ailments it was always assumed that Bill would go first, but Anthony died suddenly and unexpectedly in 1980, precipitating for Stringfellow yet another vocational crisis. In the year following he reorganized his life while actively mourning the death of his beloved, a partner in virtually everything. He wrote his most beautiful book, *A Simplicity of Faith,* chronicling two loves—for Anthony and for their Island home.

In the years following, the degenerative consequences would mount: stroke, insulin shock, circulatory deficits, retinal deterioration—more. He lived with these in a kind of radical freedom, as though they were assaults of death to be resisted with a resurrected humanity. He continued to write and speak, through pain and weakness. "My head is still working," he would say laconically.

At the age of fifty-six he died. His hospital room was hung with circus posters from his collection. His ashes were buried with Anthony's on a bluff overlooking the Atlantic. Close on a wall is a plaque that reads, "Near this cottage the remains of William Stringfellow and Anthony Towne await the resurrection." Alleluia.

Connecting the Margins: Seminary, Sanctuary, and Streets

Stringfellow occupied that liminal space which is triangulated by the academy, the church, and the movements for social transformation. He lived precisely at that intersection, bridging margin to margin.

Though he was not an academically trained theologian, at least not by degree and certification, he knew the seminary scene and lived a mendicant existence speaking in schools of theology across the country. His books were hardly systematic—more akin to tracts of theological polemic, provoking the church and its schools. Even though his biblical work on the principalities and powers effectively altered the landscape of theological ethics, he was never fully welcomed or credited within the academy, but lived at its edge.

Churchwise, he was a lifelong if "reluctant" Episcopalian, representing for years the denomination (until perfunctorily removed) on a commission of the World Council of Churches. He did not hesitate to address and intervene in the processes of the church's General Convention, goading it to movement, functioning as a canonical lawyer—and yet here too he was also something of a provocative *persona non grata* in the denomination. A critic from within. He joined the East Harlem Protestant Parish, but found it too clericized and, as it were, "established." He thought it nothing short of providential that the edifice of St. Ann's on Block Island had been swept into the sea by a hurricane, thereby freeing the congregation from the burden of its building to worship authentically in homes. Even in the monastic margins of solitude he clung to the church through Scripture and Prayer Book.

As for the "streets," he walked them first in East Harlem, where he'd ventured after graduating from law school. It was from there that he improvised "street law," heard tell of the principalities and powers from neighborhood residents, and summoned the church into the freedom struggle. He participated in Island politics, on behalf of the poorer residents and against the environmental and economic assaults of overdevelopment. At that same time he penned the theological handbook *(EC)*, which found its way into jails and prisons, guiding the nonviolent resistance movement.

Whether he lived in the Divinity School dorm while attending law school, a walk-up studio in East Harlem, a seedy penthouse on the Upper West Side, or a hilltop house on Block Island, the triangle's margin was the location wherein he lived and moved.

De-mythologizing America vs. Imperial Hermeneutics

> The task is to treat the nation within the tradition of biblical politics—to understand America biblically—not the other way around, not (to put it in an appropriately awkward way) to construe the Bible Americanly.
>
> *(EC, 13)*

This task was longstanding, even lifelong, for William Stringfellow.[2]

Recall: returning from Oslo as a college student disabused of naïveté, he found himself asking whether the world in fact hated America. In that wonderment began his reading of America biblically.

In the 1960s when it was everywhere the theological rage to de-mythologize the scriptures, he turned matters on their head, using the scriptures to de-mythologize the nation.[3] He read LBJ's Great Society, however laudable by intent, as an idol, little more than a mythic cover for indifference to race and poverty at home

---

2. Though he refers specifically to the United States, what follows will employ his otherwise chauvinist term "America."

3. "The Great Society as a Myth," *Dialog 5*, Autumn 1966, 252–57.

and sanction for militarism abroad. He tore the cover off. It was actually in this connection that he first employed the eighteenth chapter of Revelation, summoning people of conscience "to come out" of empire.

Then in the 1970s, under the Nixon regime, those same apocalyptic texts, in particular the Babylon passages, came to full development in his theological writing. By their lights, it was not wickedness in high places that was significant (though he acknowledged that aplenty), but the demonic possession of the nation which he named. If imperial moments may be tagged by presidential administration, it is empire itself which remains at issue. In the 1980s he saw the pretense of America to be a holy nation most openly articulated. In that period the mythology of the "justified" nation sanctioned nuclearism, the open emergence of first strike technology and, thereby, policy.

> Blasphemy occurs in the existence and conduct of a nation whenever there is such profound and sustained confusion as to the nation's character, place, capabilities, and destiny that the vocation of the Word of God is preempted or usurped. Thus the very presumption of the righteousness of the American cause as a nation is blasphemy. (*PS*, 63)

Reading America biblically meant summoning the nation to repentance and confessing this blasphemy.

Notice above that "to understand America biblically" entails also the apparent converse: "*not* the other way around, *not* (to put it in an appropriately awkward way) to construe the Bible Americanly."

The Word must be defended, as it were, from the powers. Stringfellow acknowledges the aggressions of what might be termed "imperial hermeneutics." His task involves resisting the subtle and overpowering grasp of empire, which lays claim to the text, seizing the book, for its own. *Not* to read the Bible Americanly. Empire, and American empire in particular, is very aggressive in its captivity and construal of the scriptures. It is an

interpretive arrogance which is virtually an assault on the Word
of God. Need it be said that this is a violence inseparable from
that done to Iraqi or Afghani children, say, as much as to the
people of our own land. In Stringfellow's words:

> To interpret the Bible for the convenience of Amer-
> ica . . . represents a radical violence to both the charac-
> ter and content of the biblical message. It fosters a fatal
> vanity that America is a divinely favored nation and
> makes of it the credo of a civic religion which is directly
> threatened by, and hence, which is anxious and hostile
> toward the biblical Word. It arrogantly misappropriates
> the political images from the Bible and applies them to
> America, so that America is conceived as Zion: as *the*
> righteous nation, as a people of superior morality, as
> a country and society chosen and especially esteemed
> by God.[4]

One can only imagine Stringfellow's response to the bald
theological claims of George W. Bush. Consider certain remarks
backdropped by the Statue of Liberty.

> Ours is the cause of human dignity, freedom guided by
> conscience and guarded by peace. This ideal of America
> is the hope of all mankind. That hope drew millions to
> this harbor. That hope still lights our way. And the light
> shines in the darkness. And the darkness will not over-
> come it. May God bless America.[5]

This echoing of the Christological preface to John's Gospel, this
uttering of messianic blasphemy, openly purporting an identity
between America and the very Word of God incarnate would
surely have drawn his luminous ire. In the Bush era the appeal to

---

4. Ibid., 14. See also his theological analysis of a different political
moment of national self-justification in *The Politics of Spirituality* (Phila-
delphia: Westminster Press, 1984), 52–60.

5. "President Bush's Remarks on September 11, 2002." Citation by
Jim Wallis, "Dangerous Religion: George W. Bush's Theology of Empire"
Sojourners, September–October 2003, 23.

the divine calling of empire was more explicit, more unabashed, more bald-faced than any time in recent memory. A theological framing of the war on terror was made normative on the president's lips. Theology was doctrine and policy. His "sermon" at the National Cathedral was quoted in strategy documents: "But our responsibility to history is already clear: to answer these attacks and rid the world of evil."[6] A foreign policy committed to ridding the world of evil presumes a task which, if worthy of anyone, would belong to God alone. It imagines an American vocation at one with Zion's. It assails the biblical witness.

A yearning might justifiably rise for Stringfellow's discerning eye in the era of Barack Obama. If his rhythm and rhetoric draws more on freedom struggle preachers, if it is circumspect in its acknowledgment of religious pluralism, if it honors the political agency of black and brown Americans, it nonetheless leans upon the sophisticated compromises of Reinhold Niebuhr's imperial theology, commonly called Christian realism. In that guise Obama, at least for his first term, has maintained the Bush policies and more—ongoing wars, torture and imprisonment without charge, extra-judicial assassination by drones (airborne robots), massive capital transfers to, and collaboration with, corporations and banks, deportations of more than a million undocumented residents, and the continuing assault on the environment. (He may believe in global warming, but his policy is practically unaffected).

It is as though an imperial beast has ruled continuously with many different theological heads and horns.

In Stringfellow's view it must be said that imperial theologies such as these are really nothing new. With respect to Christian history they are emblematic of the Constantinian confusion, rooted in the fourth century C.E., when the emperor wrapped Rome, and himself as well, in the biblical mantle and beguiled the church into compromising the Gospel. The Bible was read Romanly, as it were. In consequence the critique of empire,

---

6. Sermon at the National Cathedral, quoted in National Security Strategy, www.whitehouse.gov/nsc/nss3.html.

present in the book from day one, page one, was effectively eviscerated, hermeneutically excised, rendered invisible and inoperative.

The Spiritual Structurality of Empire

It has become a theological commonplace to recognize that the biblical saga is played out not simply against the backdrop of empire, but over against empire itself. Against Ur, Egypt, the Canaanite city-states, Assyria, Babylon, Persia, Greece, or Rome, even against empire taking monarchial form in its own life and rule, the biblical community is called by the prophetic voice to resist, to be unconformed, to come out, to walk away into wilderness.

William Stringfellow was a biblical theologian who names empire for what it is, in the same way that he names the principalities. These tasks are directly related. The one flows from the other.

He first heard tell of the powers at that postwar conference in Europe where the witness of the anti-Nazi resistance was being recounted. Christians otherwise accustomed to thinking of the State as generally benign found themselves in crisis, asking, "What is National Socialism? Where in hell does it come from? How shall we understand its demonic power?" It was as though a beast had risen from the sea to rule.

Then in East Harlem he met the powers empirically face to face in the experience of ghetto residents who spoke of the Man or the cops or the welfare bureaucracy or the utility companies, even the nonprofit agencies, as if they were living predatory creatures allied against the community. Through a biblical lens, the explicitly political language of "the rulers and authorities," or the "principalities and powers," the "thrones and dominions," Stringfellow recognized the powers as images, institutions, and ideologies.

To be brief, he saw them as "creatures" (Col. 1:15), a somewhat mysterious claim, as even he agreed. At the very least, what this means is that they have a life and reality of their own, a spirit and structure, apart from the direction and control of human beings. They have agency in the drama of history. In the manner of the "nations" in Hebrew scripture, they are account-able to God in judgment. They are called to a "vocation" of praising God and serving human life—each in their particulars. But in the fall, under the sway of idolatry, they imagine they are God and enslave human beings (Eph. 6; Col. 2). He called this an inversion of their calling. Instead of serving, they assault and dehumanize. Moreover, in the era of the fall, anxious about their own survival, imagining for themselves a sort of immortality— they place their own institutional and corporate survival above the life of human beings, above the creation they are called to serve—and so they are bound to death. Fearing death, it is death they serve.

Death, with a capital D, is itself, for Stringfellow, a living moral reality. He draws intuitively on St. Paul, for whom death (along with law and sin) is in a matrix of enslaved existence. Stringfellow sees it as the power behind the powers. Death is a kind of synonym for the spirituality of idolatry, domination, and empire.

Not many years after Stringfellow's first publication on the powers, *Free in Obedience* (1964), Dr. Martin Luther King iden-tified the reigning powers of American life in this way: "When machines and computers, profit motives and property rights are considered more important than people, the giant triplets of racism, materialism, and militarism are incapable of being conquered."[7] Here he puts his finger on what biblical scholar Walter Wink has named "the domination system," when pow-ers align and coalesce into a systematic configuration. Not far from what Stringfellow named the power of death. King called for a revolution of values, but went on to say, "Any nation that continues year after year to spend more money on military defense than on programs of social uplift is approaching spiri-tual death."

---

7. From "Beyond Vietnam," speech, April 4, 1967.

Stringfellow went further. He regarded death as a moral power within the nation and thereby as its "social purpose." His own prime example, then current, was the war in Indochina, wherein a field commander had captured the idea in a famous observation that it was necessary "to destroy the village in order to save it." Here was a war manifestly genocidal, where distinction between combatant and civilian was obliterated, where an automated battlefield likewise obviated any distinction between "those who pull the trigger and those who press the button with those who manufacture the means and those who pay the taxes" (*EC*, 73). The usurpation of civilian authority and the absorption of policy into pure technical capability he counted as embellishments foreshadowed in the grotesque example of Hiroshima. In that notorious bombing, unnecessary from a military standpoint, done purely because it had been rendered possible, devastation and destruction were undertaken for their own sake. "Hiroshima means death as social purpose for the nation. Hiroshima, as a moral event, means the spirit of death was victorious in the Second World War" (*EC*, 75).

In *Ethic for Christians*, Stringfellow named the nation-state as the "pre-eminent principality," not only because it literally retains "legitimated" access to the means and power of death—specifically in war and execution—but also for its scale and breadth of authority. Perhaps he only intuited how the power of death would be privatized in the new corporate militarism, but he noticed its expansive role. He was led shortly to wonder if the commercial principalities, the global corporations and the market, were not increasingly becoming the actual and pre-eminent ruling authorities in the world. The Babylon parable of Revelation 18 is heavy on the economic dimension of empire.

Still, if at the time of their writing, these texts served to name and unveil Rome as imperially blasphemous, they serve more currently to recognize the examples in recent history of imperial regimes, including the American empire. For Stringfellow America has the spiritual significance of Babylon. America is Babylon. In that acknowledgment is the beginning of ethical freedom. There begins resistance and fully human living.

Empires fall. We are in such a time of imperial collapse with respect to American empire and the global economy. The strains on the planet, the limits of growth, the breaking bubbles of international finance, the assault on community and local governance, the blowback at home and abroad, the meaningless commodification of everything, the failure of basic institutions which have had the life and resources sucked from them—all signal and bode collapse.

Stringfellow notes that in its arrogance Babylon imagines its divine immortality—"a Queen I sit, mourning I shall never see" (Rev. 18:7). In the face of this arrogance the saints are encouraged in their faithful endurance, their intransigent resistance, though their sufferings and martyrdoms are acknowledged. When Babylon falls, and great is its collapse, the slavers, global merchants, and client kings mourn, but doxologies are sung in heaven. With that observation, *An Ethic,* begins and ends.

The Wrath to Come and Political Devastation

The Wrath of God is a difficult, if not problematic, theological notion. It would seem to impute to God, some would say project onto God, the very violence we have ourselves embraced as human beings. And yet from another angle it represents in effect the consequences of our own violence, folly, and sin come back around. It names in essence the spiritual cycle of violence to which we have allowed ourselves to be bound as captives.

In May of 1964, brushfires of racial violence had erupted in American cities, but the major uprisings and rebellions were yet to come. Stringfellow addressed a Council of Churches gathering in Washington, warning that the Day of Wrath was now at hand.

> As the day of wrath dawns—let it come as no surprise, especially to white people, either Senators or common citizens. After all, what is involved is not merely the frustrations of these past several years of peaceful

protest, nor just the insensibility of the Senate, but the inheritance of the past three centuries of slavery and segregation.[8]

Recognizing a structural cycle of violence, he foretold clearly that on the day of wrath the prospect was not reconciliation, but overwhelming counterviolence, driving the nation irrevocably into a police state which would abort the revolutionary aspirations of freedom.

> In the day of wrath, what could save the nation from such a calamity is the recognition by white people that every hostility or assault by [black folk] against whites and against white society originates in the long and terrible decades of exclusion and rejection for blacks by white men. [Black] violence now is the offspring of white supremacy. The sins of the fathers are indeed visited upon their sons.

Personal note: I witnessed that day of wrath myself. At least from a distance. I graduated from Cooley High School in Detroit in 1967. I was living on the northwest side when the city erupted in flames. I have a vivid memory, I actually picture myself in the middle of Grand River Avenue—one of these radiating spoke streets of Detroit—and looking downtown toward the city in flames. (It was for me a moment, perhaps, like the sight of falling towers is for another generation.) The real estate blockbusters would turn those flames into cash, ramping up the process already apace: "white flight." But my senior year in high school, I'd been reading not only Dr. King, but William Stringfellow. Both marked for me a theological and political awakening. So in that vision of flame, I witnessed the structured cycle of violence and heard there the groan of creation and the cry of the poor. I stood in the middle of Grand River and wept. My heart was pierced and my vocation clarified.

---

8. "Through Dooms of Love," *Fellowship*, July 1965; cited here from *New Theology No. 2*, ed. Martin Marty (New York: Macmillan, 1965).

When Jesus looked upon Jerusalem, he did indeed foresee the destruction of Temple and city. In the movement he brought to town he set before the city a real alternative to its destruction. If you want to know the things that make for peace, do the things that make for justice. He could read the signs of the times. He witnessed the oppression of imperial occupation, foresaw the revolt, the uprising against the structures of violence—and imagined clearly the inevitable counterviolence of imperial repression: the Roman boot coming down. He did so in tears—weeping for the women and children who would be caught in the crush of historical events. In the coming collapse not one stone would be left upon another.

Is it likewise possible to see in the falling Twin Towers a day of wrath come down upon global empire and economy, even while praying for a break in the cycle of violence and weeping for the human lives caught in that collapse?

Or think of Hurricane Katrina and the devastation of New Orleans not many years back. In an early lead, the *New York Times* described it as a catastrophe of biblical proportion. Theological innuendo penetrates the headlines. In point of fact, there are many ways in which Katrina offers us, literally, an apocalyptic glimpse into America. "Apocalyptic," firstly, in its sense of unveiling, revealing, exposing the apparatus and machinations of history. Can it be a parable of living history where the veil of denial is swept away in wind and flood?

A short list of exposures would include the urban architecture of race and poverty. Look in the faces of those abandoned and left behind. (The phrase "left behind" is used quite intentionally—mindful of the popular apocalyptic theology which presumes to know the judgment of God and sanctions the divine abandonment of whole populations.) Consider the levees untended of late by the Corps of Engineers, the choppers requisitioned, and the National Guard personnel shipped out to Iraq. These lay bare the relationship of warmaking to the life and health of American cities. The gutting of emergency services for the common good and their realignment in the war on terror exposes the human consequence of such suicidal priorities. Cities, let it be said, are always an assault on the natural environment, but there are ways to sit more lightly in a bioregion, to honor earth's integrity. Katrina makes plain the human and environmental cost of wetland destruction, coastal sprawl, and runaway development.

Stringfellow observed that the weather was the one arena in which the sovereignty of God is popularly acknowledged, and yet he regarded it the realm of chaos and the fall. Spoken like an Island resident at the whim of the winds. So, compounding ironies, perhaps the most precise theological framing is that which has identified the Wrath of Katrina. Insofar as the frequency and intensity of such storms is related to global climate change, a few degrees of Gulf stream warmth ramping up the severity, is this simply one in a series of unnatural catastrophes? (At this writing New York City and the Jersey coast sit devastated by the winds and floodwaters of Hurricane Sandy.) If American cities, and even more the suburbs, are based foundationally and architecturally upon cheap oil, what does it mean to see earth and sea, ironically, rise up and tear loose oil rigs, shut down refineries, and drive SUV's from the road with flooding and spiked gas prices? Is that a wrath at which heaven may rejoice, even through tears for the victims of its flood? Apocalyptic is always a call to community—not merely how the church can begin to prepare for disasters to come, but how we are summoned to reweave the spiritual fabric of community in our own place.

Stringfellow anticipated "the impending devastation of political authority" in the imminent judgment of the Word of God.

> Judgment—biblically—does mean the destruction of the ruling powers and principalities of this age. I am aware that this is, for professed Christians in America and in many other nations, an unthinkable thought even though it be biblical (1 Cor. 15:24–28; cf. Acts 2:34–36, Rev. 18–20) . . . Christians rejoice, on behalf of all

humanity and, indeed, all creation, at the prospect of the judgment because in that Last Day the destruction of political authority at once signals its consummation in the kingdom of God. (CO, 80–81)

He thought this expectation to be the characteristic stance of biblical people. The loss of that attitude contributed to the "Constantinian confusion," wherein Christians and the church had turned to empire and the powers for "security," thereby lending themselves to bondage. But it is also to say, conversely, that in the lively expectation of powerly dethronement and destruction there arises a certain freedom for human action.

The Stringfellonian Paradox

The "Stringfellonian" of this heading, as elsewhere in the book, is somewhat tongue-in-cheek. He would no doubt look with scorn to see his name turned into any sort of portentious category, let alone a theological method or pigeon hole. Yet it can be a way of asking how he thinks and hopes. In 1963 Bill Stringfellow addressed the first National Conference on Religion and Race in Chicago. Though his remarks were controversial on any number of scores, it was this theological take which provoked the biggest response. He said in part,

From the point of view of either biblical religion, the monstrous American heresy is in thinking that the whole drama of history takes place between God and human beings. The truth, biblically and theologically and empirically is quite otherwise: the drama of this history takes place amongst God and human beings and the principalities and powers, the great institutions and ideologies active in the world. It's the corruption and shallowness of humanism which beguiles Jew or Christian into believing that human beings are masters of institutions or ideology. Or to put it a bit differently, racism is not an evil in human hearts or minds: racism is a principality, a demonic power, a representative image, an embodiment of death over which human beings have little or no control, but which works its awful influence over human life.[9]

Some people found this a bleak assessment. In fact, the Hebrew scholar and prophetic mystic Abraham Heschel, to whom he was a respondent, retorted, "Mr. Stringfellow, if my people had believed as you do, we would still be making bricks for pharaoh." That is how dark a word some were hearing in these remarks. Benjamin Mays, who chaired the conference, wrote in his autobiography that at the time he felt Stringfellow was preaching despair, but he later came to believe that he was right.

This was obviously a very unconventional take on racism. It was racism understood as more than prejudice and more even than an institutional structure. He was contending that racism has a spiritual reality to it. You could dismantle the legal apparatus of American apartheid, that is, repeal Jim Crow and . . . end racism, right? No, it would rise up and reconfigure itself in some more subtle and guileful forms, but every bit as demonic. This is a very potent spiritual reality, with structural (it is always incarnated) dimensions. That is what Stringfellow means in calling it a power. And in that he joins Dr. King in identifying it among those giant triplets ruling American life.

Stringfellow doesn't, however, stop there. Read just little a bit further.

> This is the power with which Jesus Christ was confronted and which at great and sufficient cost he overcame. In other words, the issue here is not equality among human beings but unity among human beings. The issue is not some common spiritual values nor natural law nor middle axioms. The issue is baptism. The issue is the unity of all humankind wrought by God in the life and work of Christ. Baptism is the sacrament of that unity of all humanity in God.

9. "Care Enough to Weep," *Witness,* February 21, 1963, 13.

Here we are offered a concise snapshot of Stringfellow's theological method, his radical sense of paradox. He says: it is worse than you think it is *and* you are freer than you think you are. The powers are raging beyond your control *and* they are already overcome in Christ. The division is an uncrossable spiritual chasm *and* it's been crossed. Death reigns *and* we are freed from its bondage. Each of these things is true, irrevocably and at once.

Notice moreover that by his lights, racism is the very power that Christ confronted. The claim renders racism not simply a social problem, but fundamentally a Gospel matter. This encounter comes to the very heart of the good news. In that sense he anticipates what came to be in South Africa where apartheid was declared a theological heresy. It was understood as something standing outside of the Gospel, verily an affront to it. Stringfellow was already saying the same by vesting the issue in baptism. Yet notice: he says that baptism is the sacrament of the unity, not of all *Christians*, but of all of humanity. This is important. He contends that baptism alters our relationship to all of humanity—ultimately to all of creation. These are no small theological potatoes. Call them "stringfellonian" potatoes.

Because he was so given to the lived freedoms of history and even more to the freedom of the living Word, Bill Stringfellow eschewed any attempt to reduce ethics to principle or narrow method. He refused categorically to entertain hypothetical moral situations. So it would be ironic beyond measure should those tutored by him and yearning for his wisdom and voice somehow reduce him to a hypostasized principle. "What would Stringfellow say?" is a spiritual temptation. The best we can do is read the same Bible, attend to the living Word, look the powers and empire in the eye, find one another in community, and live humanly, joining him in the paradox of radical hope.

An Exemplary Power and the Freedom to Die

One expression of that paradox is the biblical juxtaposition of Babylon with Jerusalem. One is an image of the fallen, the demonic, and the other a figure for the consummation of history, the city as new and renewed creation. This is not a dualism, but countersign. If Stringfellow found Babylon easily and notoriously recognizable, he was frank to admit that the presence of Jerusalem in history was more difficult to identify. He beheld it largely as an event to be glimpsed. It was occasional and improvisational, seen inside prisons or confessing movements, even he thought, in charismatic renewal. Even so, he did not denigrate as such the historic institutional character of the church. If he saw the American churches and denominations as little more than Babylonian shrines, bought, seduced, wedded, and conformed to empire, he still looked for the church as a holy nation freed from bondage to death.

In the manner of Jerusalem as the holy nation—the nation reflecting and embodying what it means to be a nation, one sacramentalizing human life in society—the church has a vocation to be the exemplary principality. Put simply, the church is called to know its vocation to praise God and serve human life. So it may be exemplary in recalling the other principalities to their own vocations, calling them to repentance. Because it knows to Whom it belongs and in Whose hand its life is held, the church is not anxious about its own survival. It is effectively free to die. So it also may be exemplary in confronting the principalities with their finitude and creaturehood. Because it is not in bondage to the other powers, Mammon, say, or racism, patriarchy, homophobia . . . its freedom and vocation are not distorted or diminished. Lord, where is this church? Stringfellow insists it is neither ephemeral nor merely notional. It may be glimpsed in history, even if it comes to life as a momentary transfiguration.

One further note: this freedom to die is prominent in Stringfellow's thought. It is characteristic of baptism where one has already died in Christ, fully and completely. It is a settled matter. During the trial of the Catonsville Nine who were charged with the burning of draft files as a protest against the Indochina war, Stringfellow rose to speak at an evening festival in support of the defendants. By his own account he said:

> Remember, now, that the State has only one power it
> can use against human beings: death. The State can
> persecute you, prosecute you, imprison you, exile you,
> execute you. All of these mean the same thing. The State
> can consign you to death. The grace of Jesus Christ in
> this life is that death fails. There is nothing the State can
> do to you, or to me, which we need fear.   (SB, 133)

What he says of the State is true of empire and all the powers. And
the freedom he names has vast spiritual and ethical implications.

The freedom to die holds no hint of despair. It is not about
cashing in one's chips, but about betting the farm. It is the
prophet's risk of captivity, exile, or martyrdom to be sure. But so
much more. It is the freedom which may undergird any ethical
risk—whether that be joining a struggle (even a losing one), living in a marginal social location, having a career and risking it,
spending down an institutional portfolio for the sake of others,
speaking truth when inconvenient or costly, building and planting when the future seems dim, or just building and planting. It
is the freedom of human living.

Resistance and Resurrection

Another name for this freedom is resurrection. Now some may
find it odd to consider resurrection an aspect of living humanly.
For Stringfellow it was precisely so. He regarded God's decisive
action in the life and story of Jesus as having concrete humanizing pertinence here and now in the everyday life of Christians.
In his view the preoccupation with afterlife or immortality was
a dissipation of the Gospel of Jesus Christ, which is actually concerned with the transcendence of and resistance to the power of
death in the life of this world and this present age.

With respect to death incarnate in Nazism, Stringfellow
had observed that regardless of any apparent effectiveness, but
simply as a means of holding to sanity and conscience, "resistance," in those circumstances, "became the only human way to
live" (EC, 119).

It was, however, in his own life—in connection with the "Berrigan witness," already mentioned—that he came to connect political resistance directly with resurrection. After the assault on his own home by the FBI and the arrest of Daniel Berrigan, he found himself pondering the account in Acts 4 where, occasioned by the public healing of a beggar unable to walk, the disciples were arrested and imprisoned for "proclaiming in Jesus the resurrection from the dead." The incumbent authorities saw their freedom in word and deed as a threat, as a crime against the State.

One time a friend of Anthony and Bill who was probing for what Stringfellow believed about Jesus and the empty tomb, pressed him for what he actually meant by resurrection. Bill's answer: "Phil Berrigan in jail."[10] By this he certainly meant to include the public act of liturgical resistance to the power of death in warmaking and the trial at which he and his brother Daniel, with others, had been convicted. But because he later recounted his visit to the prisoners at Danbury Prison and how he there beheld a witness of the resurrection, it may be guessed that he was thinking especially of Berrigan's demeanor in prison. He told of arranging the visit and how the warden and the other authorities, even the chaplain, had seemed constrained, anxious, dehumanized, unfree in the fulfillment of their functions, unable to undertake the most ordinary decisions without consulting the attorney general. Whereas the prisoners, on the other hand, though certainly inconvenienced by their confinement, seemed truly free and fully human, unconstrained and unencumbered by their location—exemplifying, he thought, the radical freedom of the resurrection.[11]

In *Ethic for Christians*, the association of resistance and resurrection is strong, the former being nearly a synonym for the latter. But he came to wonder aloud, were he to write the book

---

10. As recounted to the author by Scott Kennedy (now of blessed memory), April 8, 1985.

11. William Stringfellow, *Study Guide for an Ethic for Christians and Other Aliens in a Strange Land* (Waco, Tex.: Word, 1977), Programmed Leadership Tape no. 3.

again, whether he would use the word "resistance," since it had in the American experience a more narrow connotation.

Actually, in the present situation of American pluralism where interfaith action is becoming more common, "resistance" might be thought the broader and more useable term. But he found resurrection the more versatile because he wanted it to stress that the No, our resistance to the power of death, entailed simultaneously an affirmation, a Yes to life. By way of illustration he suggested that in the present culture of assault on language and the fundamental capacities of thought and communication by technocracy and commercialization, what he called the profusion and confusions of babel, it was a sensible act of resistance to teach a child or another human being to read. Literacy and its instruction could be the very form of resistance. He even went on to wonder, if he were to continue to write, whether he shouldn't begin to write children's books as a resurrectional form of resistance to babel.[12]

The Holy Spirit and the Gifts

Stringfellow considered listening, as such, an act of resistance to babel.[13] When there is such a profusion of speech, official and commercial, that comprehension and even hearing are stopped, to listen to one another or for the Word is a gift. It is to have, as the Gospels put it, "ears to hear." He never named listening a charismatic gift, but he would count it so.

Many, however, will stumble upon Stringfellow's notion that *glossolalia*, the gift of speaking in tongues, is itself also a refutation of babel, a rebuke even to empire. He heard ecstatic speech as a similar humanizing response to the assault on the verbal capacities of human communication (*EC*, 146–48). It may be helpful to think of other ecstatic forms—musical and cultural ones, jazz, or freestyle hip-hop, among others—as humanizing

---

12. Ibid.
13. Manuscript box, Cornell University Archives, introduction to an unpublished Bible study guide. Published as "Listening against Babel," in *AKW*, 182–83.

forms of resistance, voicing the Spirit's groan in the face of the powers. Without naming them he accounted these too as charismatic gifts.

This may be freely said, because he held that the lists of the gifts enumerated in the letters of Paul were not exhaustive and definitive, but suggestive. In fact, he was convinced that every gift or talent possessed by human beings may be said to become a charismatic gift when they become a new person in Christ Jesus.

When Stringfellow spoke of the "political character" of these gifts he referred to their concern "for the restoration or renewal of human life in society," to their being "the only power to which humans have access against the aggressions of the principalities," to their enhancing the church's "servanthood on behalf of the world," and to equipping "persons to live humanly in the midst of the fall" (*EC*, 144–45). In short, he found in them the fulfillment of what it means to be a human being. The gift of healing might be most obvious in this regard, where the wholeness of human beings in their personhood and community is signified. But the same is true of all the gifts.

Some might say, consider the sweep of Pentecostalism through Latin America and its "apolitical" distraction of conformity and ecstatic quiescence. Stringfellow was quick to name the distortions and perversions of the explicit charismatic gifts which rendered them practically demonic—a source of division or self-justification, not edifying to community. He noted the New Testament experience, tongues being a prime example, in this regard.

> As a shorthand, with all its imprecision, one might think of the demonic as anything whatever that dehumanizes life for human beings, while the charismatic is that which rehumanizes life for human beings within the context of the whole of fallen creation.[14]

---

14. Manuscript box, Cornell University Archives, preface to an unpublished book, "Grieve Not the Holy Spirit," published as "On the Charismatic and the Demonic," in *AKW*, 316–20. In retrospect, Stringfellow

For this, if for no other reason, he deemed discernment to be the preeminent (and also most political) among the charismatic gifts. On the one hand it enables the reading and recognition of "signs" of life or death in the landscape of place and history as well as discerning "spirits," and so enables us to recognize the presence of the Holy Spirit in relation to the powers, to idolatry, and to blasphemy. On the other hand, in community, it enables access to all the other gifts of the Spirit.

A note is overdue here on the Holy Spirit as a name of God. In connection with that it is important first to mention that in the last decades of his life Stringfellow employed "the Word of God" as the name of God in preference to simply "God." Hence his description of the Holy Spirit bears this mark.

> Biblically, the Holy Spirit names the faithfulness of God to God's own creation. Biblically, the Holy Spirit means the militant presence of the Word of God inhering in the life of the whole of creation. Biblically, the Holy Spirit is the Word of God at work both historically and existentially, acting incessantly and pervasively to renew the integrity of life in this world. . . . It was—it is—the biblical saga of the Word of God as Agitator, as the Holy Spirit, that assures me that wheresoever human conscience is alive and active, that is a sign of the saving vitality of the Word of God in history, here and now. (*PS*, 18)

By What Authority? Baptism and Citizenship

Though he openly disparaged the sectarian co-optation which separated "baptism of the Spirit" from being baptized with water, as though it were some isolated thing or experience in itself, William Stringfellow stressed the role of the Holy Spirit

---

thought the charismatic section of *Ethic* to be underwritten, "too succinct and, perchance, too cryptic." This fuller book-length treatment he foresaw as the third in his "ethics trilogy," though it remained unfinished at his death. In the end *Politics of Spirituality* fulfilled that place.

in baptism. He held up the biblical image of Jesus' own baptism in the Jordan with the immediate presence and affirmation of the Holy Spirit. "In ancient practice baptism by water was customarily coupled with entreaties for the action of the Holy Spirit, while baptism of the Spirit was confessed and sacramentally attested by baptism by water."[15] Baptism, and its "political authority," were crucial to Stringfellow's theology. Setting out to write a book on baptism, he began the Introduction citing the challenge to Jesus by the religious rulers:

> And as he was walking in the temple, the chief priests and the scribes and the elders came to him and they said to him, "By what authority are you doing these things, who gave you this authority to do them?" Jesus said to them, "I will ask you a question; answer me and I will tell you by what authority I do these things. Was the baptism of John from heaven or from men? Answer me." And they argued with one another, "If we say, 'From heaven,' he will say, 'Why then did you not believe him?' But shall we say, 'From men?' "—they were afraid of the people, for all held that John was a real prophet. So they answered Jesus, "We do not know." And Jesus said to them, "Neither will I tell you by what authority I do these things." (Mark 11:27–33)

What is so amazing about the repartee of this text is not only that Jesus answers a question with a question, but that in doing so he answers the question, boldly identifying his authority with John's movement, and effectively rooting it in his own wilderness baptism, in the freedom of the Spirit.

The political authority of baptism was significant for Stringfellow in several ways. From his very first book, he advocated that all public ministry was the ministry of the laity, authorized by baptism (see *PPF,* 66–67). It is the calling of lay people to be engaged in the world, constantly involved in its transformation. He was often tagged a "lay theologian," and though he knew it

---

15. "Grieve Not the Holy Spirit," *AKW,* 161.

to be a put-down he embraced the term knowing that his own vocation to be in the world, even to do theology in the world, rested on his baptism. And so he spoke, unphased and unscathed by the erstwhile orders and credentials of others.

There is a freedom here—one he named essential to baptism as "the public announcement to the world that one has been freed in one's own life from the power of death by the grace of God" (*PPF*, 67). No surprise that he was so explicit about baptism as a political action, over against empire and the ruling powers:

> In the Apostolic community, thus, baptism signified the new citizenship in Christ which supersedes the old citizenship under Caesar. With that context, baptism, nowadays no less than in the biblical era, not only solemnizes characteristic tensions between the Church and a regime, but reaches beyond that to confess and uphold the sovereignty of the Word of God now militant in history over against the pretensions of any regime.[16]

Already mentioned is Stringfellow's conviction that baptism is the sacrament of unity—not simply of the church, nor of all Christians, but of all humanity. The relationship of a baptized person to all human beings, and for that matter to all flesh and all creation, is fundamentally transfigured. He noted the meaning of this for the divisions worked by death in white racism, but it might just as readily be explored in relation to war and violence or to environmental breakdown. On this basis he had the audacity to proclaim:

> The baptized, thus, lives in a new, primary, and rudimentary relationship with other human beings signifying the reconciliation of the whole of life vouchsafed in Jesus Christ. The discernment—about any matter whatever—which is given and exercised in that remarkable relationship *is* conscience. In truth, the association of

---

16. "Grieve Not the Holy Spirit," *AKW*, 159.

baptism with conscience, in this sense, is that conscience
is properly deemed a charismatic gift.   (*ST,* 99–100)

Time and the Communion

Following a talk on the politics of Pentecost, a young activist,
thinking to throw Stringfellow a theological softball, once asked,
"How would you identify the marks of Christian discipleship?"
Expecting an answer on the order of resurrection and resistance,
or conscience and obedience, or even the way of the cross, she
was nonplussed to hear, "The first is freedom from bondage to
time." At the very least, this serves notice that for Stringfellow
time itself was an aspect of fallen reality.

> The Fall is not, as the biblical literalists have supposed,
> an event in time, the Fall is the era of time as such—the
> Fall is the time of time, as it were. Human knowledge is
> temporal, fallen, and, as Saint Paul emphasizes, in bond-
> age to death. Time is the realm of death. (*SB,* 122–23)[17]

In his own experience, time and death were yoked in the
regime of medications and meals carefully scheduled to man-
age his total diabetes and his lack of stomach enzymes, both of
which resulted from the surgical removal of his pancreas. That
was a regimen he suffered and kept, but also transcended. It's
fair to say he suffered it in freedom.

When he and Anthony named their home on Block Island
"Eschaton" (the end of time which is also the beginning), they
signaled an intent to make their household a realm of freedom.
It was also partly what he meant in calling their life "monastic."
Guests felt it in a palpable way. Empire accelerates time, be it
the speed up of the assembly line, the double-minded frenzy of
multitasking devices, the hastening anxieties of consumerism,
or even the frenetic activism responding to its relentless and

---

17. Not only biblical literalists place the fall within time and history.
Recent readings of the Genesis 1–11 account, particularly those associated
with anarcho-primitivism, see the narrative as critique of and communal
resistance to the rise of settled agriculture and urban civilization—the fall
into empire which can be identified in a concrete historical epoch.

multifaceted assaults on the poor and the planet. To "step off America," onto the ferry, and then enter their Island home was to shed the anxieties of time-driven existence, to enter a rhythm of prayerful freedom—what he also called "the characteristic attitude of the Communion of Saints."

> I refer, when I use that curious and venerable title, to the entire company of human beings (inclusive of the Church, but transcending time and place and thereby far more ecumenical than the Church has ever been) who have, at any time, prayed and who will, at any time, pray; and whose occupation, for the time being, is intercession for each and every need of the life of this world. As the Communion of Saints anticipates, in its scope and constituency, the full assemblage of created life in the Kingdom of God at the end of time, so prayer emulates the fullness of worship when the Word of God is glorified eternally in the Kingdom. (*SF,* 68)

This was written during the period of his mourning for Anthony's death, and so the invocation of the Communion of Saints and its life is deeply personal, poignantly so. To underscore, however, the transcendence of time, notice the inclusion of all those "who will, at any time, pray." A suggestion: it is not simply that we are called to intercede for those yet to come, but the assurance that yet and already they intercede for us as well.

Advocacy and Pain as Intercession

William Stringfellow was an intercessor.

There is no evidence in his writing that he made much of the Holy Spirit's Greek synonym in the New Testament—the *paraclete,* the Advocate or Counselor. This is, in fact, expressly a legal term for "one who comes along side," who "stands with," and clearly references the Holy Spirit as a defense attorney or resistance counselor, be that in giving utterance when disciples are prosecuted by the political authorities, summoned before governors and kings, or perhaps even when they stand in the end before the judgment of God.

His theological intuitions, however, made the connection nonetheless.

It was in thinking through the law and the legal vocation that he early on worked out his conviction that lay people were to be scattered and present in the world for the sake of the world.[18] Yet he lived to the end with a "relentless tension" between his role as a legal advocate even on behalf of the poor and imprisoned, and "the pastoral calling to which I am disposed charismatically": intercession. Though these could virtually coincide, more often the constraints of the adversarial legal system could openly interfere with the intercessory work of his pastoral calling. He declared, "I continue to be haunted with the ironic impression that I may have to renounce being a lawyer the better to be an advocate" (*SF,* 133).

In *Life Together*, his description of the "monastic" common life of the Finkenwald underground seminary in Germany during the 1930s, Dietrich Bonhoeffer describes intercession as bringing our sisters or brothers before the cross of Christ, before the judgment and mercy of God, and feeling their need, or pain, or sin so deeply that we simply pray their prayer. In their name. On their behalf. For their sake. In their stead. "We feel them as our own and can do nothing else but pray."[19] Stringfellow took this a step further. In considering the monastic tactics of resistance, he counted the work and politics of intercession primary.

> In the tradition of intercession, as I understand it, the one who intercedes for another is confessing that his or her trust in the vitality of the Word of God is so serious

18. See Andrew McThenia, "An Uneasy Relationship with the Law," in *Radical Christian and Exemplary Lawyer,* ed. McThenia (Grand Rapids: William B. Eerdmans, 1995), 167–80. Also Dancer, *An Alien in a Strange Land,* 37–69.

19. Dietrich Bonhoeffer, *Life Together* (New York: Harper & Row, 1954), 86.

> that he or she volunteers, risks, sharing the burden of the one for whom intercession is offered even to the extremity of taking the place of the other person who is the subject of the prayer. Intercession takes its meaning from the politics of redemption. Intercession is a most audacious witness to the world. (*PS*, 84)

An aside: this remarkable claim is the best possible approach to "substitutionary christology," a way to make common sense of it, turning something so easily distorted into a spirituality of substitutionary ethics.

Ironically, and also related to the cross, when it came to his own pain, he eventually turned the prayer on its head. String-fellow first lived with unremitting pain for a number of years in the mid-1960s until his ailment was properly diagnosed, and the radical surgery removed his pancreas. During that period he seldom mentioned or discussed his pain, but "now and then, in excruciation, I would utter the name of Jesus not in common profanity, but as a curse upon the pain, and really, a curse upon the power of death." Even other expletives were "no obscenity, but a most earnest prayerful utterance . . . and it can be put plainly in one word: *Help!* That is the word of Gethsemane's prayer; that is the word of the Lord's Prayer; that is the prayer when Christ repeats the Twenty-second Psalm from the cross" (*SB*, 52, 109).

Here's the twist. Though he cried out in pain as a prayer of help for himself, it was also a cry of human solidarity. Witness the concluding sentences of *The Politics of Spirituality*:

> There are no grounds to be romantic about pain. Pain is a true mystery, so long as this world lasts. Yet it is known that pain is intercessory: one is never alone in pain but is always a surrogate of everyone else who hurts—which is categorically everybody. I consider that this is enough to know if one does trust the Word of God in Judgment. (*PS*, 90)

Vocation: Being Human

It was in the midst of enduring great pain that William Stringfellow was called upon to make the life-risking decision about his pancreatic surgery in 1968. He understood the decision itself to be a vocational event, which is to say a decision that implicated his identity and his humanity. He made it in radical freedom.

> The decision might well affect how long I survived, it certainly would affect the physiology of my survival, but neither of these matters altered the vocational issue, which is to live as a human being while one lives. . . . With this outlook, the decision was made, and quite matter-of-factly, without excitement, lucidly, unanxious about any future, almost casually. I would have surgery. I felt like a human being. I felt free.   (SB, 98)

Each of his autobiographically theological works was precipitated by a crisis and its related decisions: moving to East Harlem and, perhaps even more so, quitting the parish, but remaining in the neighborhood; his illness and the attending surgery; Anthony's death and the reordering of his life on the Island. Each of these radically raised the question of who he was and so how to live freely in the fullness of his humanity.

Once, just weeks before his death, while teaching a course on the powers in New York, he responded forcefully to some suggestion that labeled him politically or theologically. He gathered himself, nearly rising from his chair, to say firmly, "I am called in the Word of God to be William Stringfellow, nothing more and nothing less." That was the vocational issue in full. Ponder this, hear the echo, and notice the further implication:

> In the Gospel, vocation means being a human being, now, and being neither more, nor less than a human being, now. And, thus, is the vocation of other people illuminated and affirmed, and so also is the vocation of the institutional powers and the principalities of this world

exposed and upheld. And, thus, each and every decision, whether it seems great or small, whether obviously or subtly a moral problem, becomes and is a vocational event, secreting, as it were, the very issue of existence.

(SB, 95)

To be fully human, to be freely oneself in decision and presence has ethical import for other human beings, but also for the principalities and powers! Just as the church's vocation to be the exemplary power, the holy nation, summons the other powers to repentance, to recalling who they are uttered in the Word of God to be.

It would seem that just as personal crises and decisions are vocational events, so likewise might institutional and historical crises provoke the same. In the midst of babel, keep the Word. In the face of empire, live humanly.

The Human Being and the Lordship of Christ

Given the biblical spirituality outlined here, one would expect Stringfellow to have taken hold of the redundant Gospel designation of Jesus as "the human being," sometimes translated as "the son of man." Jesus himself employs this perplexing name with roots in apocalyptic. Perhaps it is the only title he actually claimed for himself: the human being.

Stringfellow did not make it central to his own writing and theology, though Walter Wink eventually did in his own *magnum opus* by that very title.[20] He saw in it the basis for the church's earliest christology, from below.

Yet Stringfellow found precisely this same christology in the so-called Lordship of Christ, precisely because he did not count "Lord" (for all its problematics in patriarchy) a divine title, but a human one. For Stringfellow this affirmation of Jesus recognized in him the renewal of human freedom from the powers and the restoration of human authority over them. Call it resurrection.

---

20. Walter Wink, *The Human Being: Jesus and the Enigma of the Son of Man* (Minneapolis: Fortress Press, 2002).

In the lordship of Christ Jesus, the principalities—which, in the inversion of their own vocations, have come to imagine they are gods and enslave human life—are once again summoned to praise God and serve human life. Such are the politics, the ethics, and the spirit of the one who gives form to the new and renewed humanity.

Dear friends, may you rejoice in Stringfellow's words and may you yourselves live so humanly.

1

The Essentials of a
Biblical Theology

Word

LIVING BIBLICALLY

Instead of Death was the only one of Stringfellow's books republished during his lifetime. Originally writing for high school students on topics of loneliness, sex, identity, worship, work, and baptism, he took the occasion of the new edition to add chapters on "Technocracy and the Resistance Witness" and on "Justification, the Consumption Ethic and Vocational Poverty." He also wrote a new introduction, from which the following is excerpted, reflecting changes in his life since the book first appeared.

I spend most of my life now with the Bible, reading or, more precisely, listening. My mundane involvements—practicing law, being attentive to the news of the moment, lecturing around the country, free lance pastoral counseling, writing, activity in church politics, maintaining my medical regime, doing chores around my home on Block Island—have become more and more intertwined with this major preoccupation of mine, so that I can no longer readily separate the one from the others. This merging for me of almost everything into a biblical scheme of living occurs because the data of the Bible and one's existence in common history is characteristically similar. One comes, after a while, to live in a continuing biblical context and so is spared both an artificial compartmentalization of one's person and a false pietism in living.

The biblical adventure continues, I expect, for ever and ever, always familiar and always new, at once complete yet inexhaustible, both provocative and surprising, gratuitous and liberating. Insofar as I am a beneficiary of the biblical witness in the period between writing *Instead of Death* and now, the significant change which I am able to identify concerns the abolition of false dichotomies, as between the personal and the political or as between the private and the public. Thus, *Instead of Death* seeks to cope pastorally with a few issues which confront young people, as well as other persons, in self-conscious individual circumstances. But the theological connection of any of these matters to the ubiquity of the power of death and the redemptive vitality of the Word of God in this world applies equally to political affairs and social crisis and, moreover, does so in a way which renders apparently private concerns political.

Since *Instead of Death* was first written, this connection between the private and the political was verified to me by the illness which placed my life in crisis during the period of 1967 and 1969. A chronicle of that experience is related in *A Second Birthday* so I need not recapitulate the story here. It is enough to say that, through the danger of protracted illness, I realized that death—the death which so persistently threatened me, the death so aggressive in my body, the death signified by unremitting pain, the death which took the appearance of sickness—was familiar to me. I had encountered this same death elsewhere, in fact everywhere. The exposure to death of which I had total recall during the illness had occurred a decade or so earlier while I was working as a lawyer in East Harlem. In that urban context with death institutionalized in authorities, agencies, bureaucracies, and multifarious principalities and powers, slowly I learned something which folk indigenous to the ghetto know: namely, that the power and purpose of death are incarnated in institutions and structures, procedures and regimes—Consolidated

Edison or the Department of Welfare, the Mafia or the police, the Housing Authority or the social work bureaucracy, the hospital system or the banks, liberal philanthropy or the corporate real estate speculation. In the wisdom of the people of the East Harlem neighborhood, such principalities are identified as demonic powers because of the relentless and ruthless dehumanization which they cause.

During my years in East Harlem, I became sufficiently enlightened about institutionalized death so that death was no longer an abstraction confined to the usual funereal connotations. I began then and there to comprehend death theologically as a militant, moral reality. The grandiose terms in which the Bible describes the power of death had begun to have a concrete significance for me. When, subsequently, death visited me in a most private and personalized manner, in the debilitation of prolonged illness and the aggressions of pain, I was able to recognize that this represented the same power—the same death—that I had before beheld in quite another guise, vested in the principalities active on the East Harlem scene. Unrelated as the two situations seemed to be, the one so public the other so private, there was an extraordinary and awful connection between the vitality and intent of death in each situation. The supposed dichotomy between the public and the personal appearance of death is both superficial and deceptive, enhancing the thrall of death over human beings.　　　　　　　　　　　　　　　—*ID*, 2, 3–5

LISTEN TO THE BIBLE:
A PRIMITIVE ACT OF LOVE

Early on, Stringfellow advocated an unencumbered attentiveness to scripture. "Some will think this a naïve approach to the Word of God in the Bible," he wrote. "I suppose it is just that." If one considers a hermeneutical circle: naïve reading—critical distance—new naïveté, Stringfellow did not dismiss or denigrate the critical tools but was effectively stressing the deeper engagement of listening.

I beg you not to be misled by my affirmation of the availability and centrality of the Word of God in the Bible, nor by my
deploration of the diffidence toward the Bible in American Protestant preaching, liturgics, and teaching. As to the latter, I know
that there are, here and there, notable exceptions to the allegations made; that there are such exceptions only sharpens the
indictment. As to the former, let it be said bluntly that my esteem
for the Word of God in the Bible does not mean that I am a biblical literalist or a fundamentalist of any sort.

Paradoxically, the trouble with fundamentalists, as I try to
listen to them, is their shocking failure to regard and use the
Bible conscientiously enough. If they honored the Bible more
highly, they would appreciate that the Word of God will endure
de-mythologizing, that the Word cannot be threatened by anything whatever given to human beings to discover and know
through any science or discipline of the world, or hindered by
textual criticism or hampered by linguistic analysis, or harmed
by vernacular translations. All these are welcome to Christians
as enhancements of the knowledge of the fullness of the Word
of God and of the grandeur of human access to the Word. More
than that, if the fundamentalists actually took the Bible seriously, they would inevitably love the world more readily instead
of fearing the world, because the Word of God is free and active
in this world and Christians can only comprehend the Word out
of their involvement in this world, as the Bible so redundantly
testifies.

I am no biblical scholar; I have neither competence nor
temperament to be one. The ordinary Christian, lay or clergy,
does not need to be a scholar to have recourse to the Bible and,
indeed, to live within the Word of God in the Bible in this world.
What the ordinary Christian is called to do is to open the Bible
and listen to the Word.

Listening is a rare happening among human beings. You cannot listen to the word another is speaking if you are preoccupied
with your appearance or impressing the other, or if you are trying to decide what you are going to say when the other stops

talking, or if you are debating about whether the word being spoken is true or relevant or agreeable. Such matters may have their place, but only after listening to the word as the word is being uttered. Listening, in other words, is a primitive act of love, in which a person gives himself to another's word, making himself accessible and vulnerable to that word.

It is very much like that when a person comes to the Bible. One must first of all listen to the Word which the Bible speaks, putting aside, for the time being, such other issues as whether the Word is credible or congenial or consistent or significant. By all means, if you will, raise these questions, but, first, listen to the Word.   —*CAJ*, 14–15

PARADOX, NOT SYLLOGISM

Stringfellow marked the 1976 imperial liturgy of the U.S. Bicentennial by writing a book on the nature of political authority read with Romans 13 in one hand, and Revelation 13 in the other: Conscience and Obedience *(1977). This selection is from the introduction.*

I harbor no compulsion to neatly harmonize Scripture, as I have elsewhere often remarked. The whole notion that the Bible must be homogenized or rendered consistent is a common academic imposition upon the biblical literature but it ends often in an attempt to ideologize the Bible in a manner which denies the most elementary truth of the biblical witness, namely, that it bespeaks the dynamic and viable participation of the Word of God in the common events of this world. The militant character of the Word of God in history refutes any canon of mere consistency in the biblical witness. To read the Bible is to hear of and behold events in which the Word of God is concerned, attended by the particularity and, to human beings, the ambiguity of actual happenings. Any efforts to read the Bible as a treatise abstractly constructed or conformed usurps the genius of the Bible as testament of the Word of God active in history. If the biblical witness were internally strictly consonant, after the

mode of ideology or philosophy, the mystery of revelation in this
world would be abolished; revelation itself would be categorically precluded.

What is to be expected, instead of simplistic consistency, in
listening to the Bible, allowing for the vagaries and other limita-
tions of human insight, is coherence: a basic integrity of the Word
of God or the fidelity of the personality of God to creation. . . .
This is how I come to the texts from Romans and Revelation.
If the two seem at odds—though variant historical situations
are to be taken seriously, and while the partiality of a person's
perception at a given moment has to be acknowledged—perchance it is because they are at odds. That, to me, becomes pri-
marily significant as a clue to the vitality of the Word of God in
the world. The revelation of the Word of God is, always, more
manifold and more versatile than human comprehension. What
I anticipate in the passages is not consistency so much as coherence. I can live and act as a biblical person without the former,
but without the latter I cannot live.

So in the Bible and, here, in Romans and Revelation, I look
for style, not stereotype, for precedent, not model, for parable,
not proposition, for analogue, not aphorism, for paradox, not
syllogism, for signs, not statutes. The encounter with the biblical witness is empirical, as distinguished from scholastic, and
it is confessional, rather than literalistic; in either case, it, over
and above any other consideration, involves the common reader
in affirming the historicity of the Word of God throughout the
present age, in the biblical era and imminently.   —CO, 178–79

IMPERIAL HERMENEUTICS OR
DE-MYTHOLOGIZING THE NATION

*During a time when de-mythologizing the scriptures was much
in vogue, Stringfellow flipped the script and sought to read the
nation biblically—to use the scriptures to de-mythologize America. He had done this first with* Dissenter in a Great Society, *where
he took on its myths biblically. Here in* An Ethic for Christians

and Other Aliens in a Strange Land, *however, he understands America as aggressively interpreting the Bible for its own sake. Hermeneutics is thus an issue of imperial principalities, as much as imperial principalities are an issue of hermeneutics.*

My concern is to understand America biblically. This book—which is, simultaneously, a theological statement and a political argument—implements that concern.

The effort is to comprehend the nation, to grasp what is happening right now to the nation and to consider the destiny of the nation within the scope and style of the ethics and the ethical metaphors distinctive to the biblical witness in history.

The task is to treat the nation within the tradition of biblical politics—to understand America biblically—*not* the other way around, *not* (to put it in an appropriately awkward way) to construe the Bible Americanly. There has been much too much of the latter in this country's public life and religious ethos. There still is. I expect such indulgences to multiply, to reach larger absurdities, to become more scandalous, to increase blasphemously as America's crisis as a nation distends. To interpret the Bible for the convenience of America, as apropos as that may seem to be to many Americans, represents a radical violence to both the character and content of the biblical message. It fosters a fatal vanity that America is a divinely favored nation and makes of it the credo of a civic religion which is directly threatened by, and, hence, which is anxious and hostile toward the biblical Word. It arrogantly misappropriates political images from the Bible and applies them to America, so that America is conceived of as Zion: as *the* righteous nation, as a people of superior political morality, as a country and society chosen and especially esteemed by God. In archetypical form in this century, material abundance, redundant productivity, technological facility, and military predominance are publicly cited to verify the alleged divine preference and prove the supposed national virtue. It is just this kind of Sadducean sophistry, distorting the biblical truth for American purposes, which, in truth, occasions the moral turmoil which the nation so manifestly suffers today and which, I believe, renders us a people as unhappy as we are hopeless. It is profane, as well as grandiose, to manipulate the Bible in order to apologize for America. To read this tract lucently requires (and, I trust, evokes) freedom from temptations to violate the Bible to justify America as a nation.

This book is necessarily at once theological and political for the good reason that the theology of the Bible concerns politics in its most rudimentary meaning and in its most auspicious connotations. The biblical topic *is* politics. . . .

Despite the habitual malpractice of translating biblical politics as the American story, there is also the odd and contradictory custom among many Americans to denounce the truth that the Bible is political. Frequently, if incongruously, these two convictions are held concurrently by the same person, or by the same sect or church or social faction. American experience as a nation—as well as biblical scholarship—discredits any attempted Americanization of biblical politics and confounds the notion that the Bible is apolitical. What is surprising is that the latter belief persists even though so many of the biblical symbols are explicitly political—*dominion, emancipation, authority, judgment, kingdom, reconciliation* among them—and even though the most familiar biblical events are notoriously political—including the drama of Israel the holy nation, the Kingdom parables in Christ's teaching, the condemnation of Christ as King of the Jews by the imperial authorities, the persecutions of the Apostolic congregations, the controversies between Christians and zealots, the propagation of the Book of Revelation.

Well, I do not amplify the matter here, apart from noticing that the view that the Bible is politically neuter or innocuous—coupled, as it may be, ironically, with an American misuse of biblical politics—maintains wide currency in this nation. And this view sorely inhibits a biblical comprehension of America as a nation.   —*EC* 13–15

MARX AND THE BIBLE

Stringfellow's inclusion of ideologies as fallen idols in the primary list of prevailing principalities led him to eschew any ideological reading of scripture. Liberation theology, which one would expect him to welcome, suffered this idolatry in his view. Again he saw the powers as aggressive in their claim on scripture, looking to conform the Bible to themselves. His view that the Gospel is categorically not ideological is compelling. But he sometimes appears to imagine that theology itself is not such a construction, or that he reads without a theological lens, when his is actually well developed.

My esteem for the biblical witness and my approach to the Bible should be enough to disclose my skepticism about current efforts to construct political theology according to some ideological model. I refer, for one specific example, to attempts to articulate a pseudo-biblical rationale for classical Marxism, which lately become prominent, oddly enough, simultaneously, both in some postindustrial societies of North America and Europe and in still pre-industrialized regions of Asia, Latin America, and Africa. It is persuasive of the ideological bankruptcy of the former that anyone would imagine that Marxism sponsors a social and economic analysis relevant to the conditions of advanced technology and the technocratic state; in the Third World, at least, the prevailing society retains a semblance to those conditions which originally occasioned Marxism, more than a century ago. Given the analytical naïveté of the revived interest in Marxism in a country like the United States, it may be that the phenomenon is mainly rhetorical, with classical Marxism supplying a convenient and ample lexicon with which to denounce the regime. Or, in addition, this belated attention to Marxist ideas may express the profound frustrations of people wrought in the decadence, and obsolescence, of American capitalism. Or, this may also be an aspect of the vogue of nostalgia that accompanies the endemic apprehension of Americans concerning the failure of the system. If that be true, it is quaint and pathetic since nostalgia signifies an inverted eschatology, as such the most fictionalized and forlorn hope of all. Meanwhile, even in sectors of the Third World where Marxism may remain analytically cogent, the attempt to theologize, in biblical terms, ideology is untenable. Even that most venerable identification and advocacy of the biblical witness for the dispossessed and oppressed of this age does not render the biblical people ideologically captivated. The effort to distinguish a biblical apologetic for Marxism is no different from those which have sought to theologize capitalism, colonialism, war, and profligate consumption. Whatever the subject ideology or policy, attempts such as these trivialize the Bible.

In other words, biblical politics *never* implies a particular, elaborated political theology, whether it be one echoing the status quo or one which aspires to overthrow and displace the status quo. The Gospel is not ideology and, categorically, the Gospel cannot be ideologized. Biblical politics always has a posture in tension and opposition to the prevalent system, and to any prospective or incipient status quo, and to the ideologies of either regime or revolution. Biblical politics are alienated from the politics of this age.

Let no one read into these remarks gratuitous comfort for simplistic and unresponsive answers to political issues of enormous complexity, such as all the nations suffer, after the manner, for instance, of those who incant the name of Jesus superstitiously. It is literally pagan, unbiblical, to so recite "Jesus is the answer." The Bible is more definitive, the biblical affirmation is "Jesus is Lord!" The Bible makes a political statement of the reign of Christ preempting all the rulers, and all pretenders to thrones and dominions, subjecting incumbents and revolutionaries, surpassing the doctrine and promises of the ideologies of this world.

Nor is there, here, furnished any pretext whatever for the neglect of the poor or the unliberated, or for abandonment of the biblical advocacy of the oppressed and the imprisoned. On the contrary, the exemplification of redeemed humanity in the

Lordship of Jesus Christ in this age means a resilient and tireless witness to confound, rebuke and undo every regime, and every potential regime, unto that moment when humankind is accounted over the nations and principalities in the last judgment of the Word of God.   —CO 111–12

Jesus

The Bible which Stringfellow carried on his person was a New Testament. Apart from the Psalter, it was from there that his theology largely sprang. And it's fair to say he was enamored of the mind of St. Paul. That is reflected with respect to the powers and the law, to justification and idolatry, discernment and the gifts. He wrote repeatedly of Paul's conversion. However, the person of Jesus as a human being, as Christ, preoccupied him the more—and he took recourse to the person of Jesus and retold his story from many angles.

AS BORN AND COMING AGAIN

The biblical treatment of both advents, the narratives attending Christ's birth and the testimonies about the Second Coming of Christ, is manifestly political. Yet, curiously, people have come to hear the story of the birth as apolitical and even as antipolitical, while, I venture, most listen to news of Christ coming again triumphantly with vague uneasiness or even outright embarrassment. What with the star and the sheep and the stable, it has been possible to acculturate the birth, to render it some sort of pastoral idyll. But the scenic wonders, the astonishing visions, the spectacular imagery associated with the next advent have confounded the ordinary processes of secularization and thus the subject of the Second Coming has been either omitted or skimmed in the more conventional churches or else exploited variously by sectarians, charlatans, fanatics, or huckster evangelists.

Insofar as these allegations are sound, the mystery of both advents has been dissipated, whereas it is an affirmation of the mystery of both events that is most needed in order to be lucid, at all, about either advent.

So I begin by affirming the mystery of these happenings and, furthermore, by noticing that what can be known of the two advents is no more than that evident in their biblical connection. It is the coherence of one advent in the other advent, the first in the second and, simultaneously the second in the first, that is crucial.

Or, in other words, I do not know if, when Jesus was born, there appeared a special star over Bethlehem, any more than I know whether, when Jesus comes as Judge and King, he will be seen mid-air, descending amid the clouds. Nor do I have need to know such things; they by no means control my salvation, much less the world's redemption. Yet, since both advents are mysteries, these styles bespeak those mysteries aptly, or so it seems to me.

There is a secret in the first advent, a hidden message in the coming of Jesus Christ into the world, a cryptic aspect in the unfolding of Christmas. Indeed, the biblical accounts of the birth of the child in Bethlehem, in such quaint circumstances, represents virtually a parody of the advent promise.

A similar discreetness—at times of such degree as to be ironical—marked the entire public life of Jesus Christ, according to the Bible. He taught in parables, finishing his stories enigmatically with the remark—*if you have ears that can hear, then hear* (cf. Matt. 13:1–23). When he healed a person or freed a demoniac, he admonished witnesses to *see that no one hears about this* (as in Mark 7:31–37). When he was accused by the religious and political authorities and confronted by Pontius Pilate, *he refused to answer one word, to the Governor's great astonishment* (Mark 15:5).

The first chapter of the Gospel of St. John tells this mystery in the coming of Jesus Christ: "He was in the world; but the world, though it owed its life to him, did not recognize him. He entered his own realm, and his own would not receive him."

For primitive Christians, so much defamed and so often harassed and sometimes savaged in first-century Rome, the secret of the first advent was thought to be in the consolation of the next advent. The pathos and profound absurdity of the birth of Jesus Christ was understood to be transfigured in the Second Coming of Jesus Christ. The significance of advent could only be realized in the hope of the return of Jesus Christ.

It is the Book of Revelation which most eagerly anticipates the Second Coming, and in Revelation one hears a recurring theme, summed up, for instance, in the 11th chapter at verse 15: "The sovereignty of the world has passed to our Lord and his Christ, and he shall reign for ever and ever!"

The same is repeated, again and again and again in Revelation, in the names and titles ascribed to Christ. He is the *ruler of the kings of the earth*. He is *the sovereign Lord of all*. He is *the King of kings*. He is the *judge* of the nations. He is the One *worthy to receive all power and wealth, wisdom and might, honor and glory and praise*!

All of these are political designations and point to the truth, from the vantage of the next advent, that the first advent's secret is political. And that truth becomes evident in the traditional stories recalled and recited in observance of the first advent.

Thus, the journey of Joseph and the pregnant Mary took place in order that they be enrolled for a special tax which was not simply a source of revenue for the Roman occupying regime but, as all taxes are, also a means of political surveillance of potentially dissident people.

And the profound threat which the coming of Christ poses for mundane rulers is to be seen in Herod's cooption of the Magi to locate the child so that Herod could slay him. When the attempt fails, Herod's anxiety becomes so vehement that he slaughters a whole generation of children in seeking to destroy Christ.

Later, John the Baptist, whose calling as a messenger and herald is especially remembered in the season of advent, suffers terrible interrogation and torture, imprisonment and decapitation because his preparation for the ministry of the Christ who has come is perceived by the rulers as a most awesome warning.

Or, again, the manger scene itself is a political portrait of the whole of creation restored in the dominion of Jesus Christ in which every creature, every tongue and tribe, every rule and authority, every nation and principality is reconciled in homage to the Word of God incarnate.

Amid portents and events such as these, commemorated customarily in the church, the watchword of Christmas—"peace on earth"—is not a sentimental adage but a political utterance and an eschatological proclamation, indeed, a preview and precursor of the Second Coming of Christ the Lord, which exposes the sham and spoils the power of the rulers of the age.

Those first-century Christians, pursued and persecuted, scorned and beleaguered, as they were because of their insight, were right: the secret of the first advent is the consolation of the second advent. The message in both advents *is* political. It celebrates the assurance that in the coming of Jesus Christ the nations and the rulers of the nations are judged in the Word of God, which is, at the same time, to announce that in the Lordship of Christ they are rendered accountable to human life and to that of the whole of creation.   —CO, 76–85

AS TEMPTED

Specific temptations of all sorts—visceral, intellectual, psychical—only mask the singular and ultimate temptation in which the power of death poses as God. In that respect the Faustus legend, told and retold, as it has been in so many ways, is a parable of the truth of human existence in this world, and not just a quaint old fable. The dignity and durability of the Faustus tale is in its portrayal of the ingenious determination with which death beleaguers everyone to escape being haunted by the Word of God by worshipping death instead of God.

That the *only* temptation at all, for any person, at any time, is to succumb to the idolatry of death is disclosed and enacted decisively in the episode of Jesus in the wilderness (Matt. 4:1–11; cf. Mark 1:2–13; Luke 4:1–13). Contrary to many "Sunday School" recitations, the wilderness is not a period in which Jesus withdraws from the hurry and hurly-burly of the cares and affairs of the world in order to escape for awhile, practice asceticism, or mediate about the universe. Jesus Christ in the wilderness, so to speak, is not like Ronald Coleman in Shangri-la serenely pondering the ultimate. Nor is it, as the so-called adoptionists (who are, secretly, very numerous in the churches) would have it, an occasion in which Jesus finally stops procrastinating about His own office and vocation. Jesus—in the wilderness any more than in Gethsemane—doesn't resemble, as it were, Adlai Stevenson agonizing about whether to accept a nomination.

The wilderness experience, first of all, evidences Jesus' remarkable identification with the generic ministry and mission of Israel, recalling the recreating Israel's sojourn in the wilderness in intercession for all humankind.

Moreover, the wilderness interlude sums up the aggressiveness with which death pursues Jesus from His conception and anticipates death's relentlessness towards Him during His entire earthly ministry—in His exercise of authority over the demonic in healing, in His transcendence of time by renouncing the political ambitions that His disciples covet from Him, in His rejection at the hands of His own people, in His confounding of the ecclesiastical and imperial rulers when they seize Him and scourge Him, in His submission to the last vengeance of death on the Cross and in His victory over that humiliation.

It is in such a context—not as some yogi or mystic or magician, not as a novice about the character of temptation—that Jesus is visited and tempted by the power of death in the wilderness.

It is written that Jesus in the wilderness had fasted for some time and was hungry; in the first assault of death upon Him is the challenge to turn stones into bread. The response of Jesus is that human beings live by the utterance of the Word of God, not only bread. (Though, let it be remembered, they do need bread.) The temptation is not so much an exploitation of a vulnerable circumstance—hunger—or even to demonstrate extraordinary powers—as it is the temptation to ridicule the Word of God as the source and substance of life itself and to renounce the Word of God not only in God's own name but for all human beings and for the whole world (Matt. 4:1–4).

By now, it appears, chagrined, the Devil volunteers his own dominion to Jesus Christ—the kingdoms of this world—if only

Jesus will acknowledge death as god. And in reply Jesus banishes the power of death and so heralds the Resurrection (Matt. 4:8–11).

In every instance in the wilderness episode, the confrontation is between the Devil and Jesus; in each it is exposed that the issue lies between the power of death and the Word of God, which means life in the sense of humanity and God reconciled and, hence, the reconciliation of human beings within themselves, among one another, and to all things.

The wilderness encounter does not exhaust death's genius in temptation. Just as the power of death pursues Christ from the instant of His birth—when Herod sought to locate the infant Jesus in order to assassinate Him—so death besieges Christ throughout His ministry unto the Tomb. In truth, it is as if Easter is not some abrupt, startling, out-of-place occurrence, but quite the contrary, simply the consummation and epitomization of the drama of death and resurrection: of the aggressions of death defeated, of the extraordinary power of death but the even more awesome overpowering of death, of the versatile guises of death and of the ubiquity of God exposing each and all of them, of the assaults of death at once turned back and transcended in behalf of human beings.

The marvel of Easter, the glory of this day and event beyond that of any other in all history, is not that it is a unique, disjunctive, miraculous, incredible, or spooky happening, but, rather, that it is definitively historic, wholly credible, typical and predictable, what is or should have been expected exactly, as the fulfillment and fruition of Christ's historical existence and His reiterated victorious confrontations with the power of death. That is why Easter has veracity as the authentic cosmic event.

Consider, for example, the intercession of Christ for humanity in the first utterance of the Lord's Prayer. Matthew 6 precedes the Prayer with a recitation of Jesus' caution against the emptiness of the public display of pietism (Matt. 6:1–9; cf. Luke 18:9–14). In the instruction and example of the Lord's Prayer, prayer has no intrinsic efficacy attaching to its performance, nor does it have to do with human desire; prayer has to do with the actual needs of human beings and the efficacy of prayer attaches to how God addresses those needs. Thus, Jesus admonished, do not be religious, like those who "think that they will be heard for their many words ... for your Father knows what you need before you ask Him" (Matt. 6:7b–8). That is Jesus' own introit to the Lord's Prayer. The summation of the Prayer is "lead us not into temptation, but deliver us from evil," that is "from the evil one," which is the power of death (Matt. 6:13). Evil does not, in the context of the Lord's Prayer, mean moral evil in its conventional definition and usage but refers to that which is evil for everyone and for the whole of creation and that which is in fact secreted in every thought or deed or wish or word called evil: the power of death or, if one renders the proper name, the Devil.

I am aware how medieval it sounds to some contemporaries to speak of the Devil, though it is biblical to do so, and though that which was medieval is not, by that mere token, untrue or inappropriate in the present time. At the same time I am not, in using the term, thinking of some grotesque, supernatural, anthropomorphic being as such. I do not apprehend the Devil after the manner of those who conceive of God as a Santa Claus figure enthroned in the sky. Yet it does not offend my intellect or other sensibilities to invoke the name of the Devil to designate that power—distinguished *only* from God—which is present and militant in this world in all relationships (e.g., work, sex, family, language, success, loneliness, indulgence) and to which all other powers (e.g., race, nation, religion, money, ideology, patriotism, athletics) are subjected. In a word it is the presumption of sovereignty over *all* of life that marks the power of death, and it is, as it were, the notorious vindication of that presumption over against everyone and everything else in this life in this world—apart *only* from God—that makes the employment of the name of the Devil, as unusual or archaic as it may nowadays seem, wholly apt and, so to speak, respectful of such an exceeding great power.

Manifestly, there are other ways in which the Lord's Prayer can be treated responsibly with respect to its origin, biblical situation, and actual usage by Christian people, and, no doubt, as many ways again in which the same Prayer may be manipulated, abused or distorted, but neither of these issues alters or minimizes the intercession of Christ in the Lord's Prayer for a humanity in this world so gravely afflicted by the power of death.

That is verified by the further witness of the valor and consistency of Jesus' own endurance of premonitions, preliminary attacks, and other temptations upon His person, and by the power of death in His prayer for His bewildered disciples at Gethsemane: "I do not pray that thou should take them out of the world, but that thou should keep them from the evil one" (John 17:15). The work of Christ, exemplified in the very prayers in which He is author, and for which He is authority, and as it is embodied in the Cross and the emancipation of Christ from the Tomb, is an intervention by God in this history for each person in their particular suffering of the feigned, but ruthless, sovereignty of death over life.   — *CAJ*, 85–90

AS HEALER

Healing, seemingly, is a most intimate event, distinct and distant from politics. Yet the healing episodes reported in the New Testament are very much implicated in politics. The healings attributed to Jesus become prominent in provoking his condemnation. In the earliest days of the church, healings invoking charismatic authority—along with the preaching of the Resurrection—became pretexts for the arrests of some of the Apostles (Acts 3:1–10: 4:1–4). One speculates whether the repeated admonishment of Jesus to maintain silence about his healing has a political meaning; one recollects that Jesus was subjected to political interrogation because of reports in circulation about his power to heal (Matt. 9:1–8; Luke 5:17–26). The political implications of healing come to focus most lucently in the remarkable incident of the raising of Lazarus, however, since that was not kept

secret (John 11:1–12:19). Far from it, Lazarus accompanied
Jesus in the Palm Sunday procession and some scholars conclude
that this was what exhausted the temporizing of the political
authorities concerning Jesus.

In raising Lazarus, in other words, Jesus reveals what is implicit,
but hidden, in all of the healing episodes, that is, his authority
over death, his conclusive power over death, his triumph over
death and all that death can do and all that death means. To so
surpass death is utterly threatening politically; it shakes and shatters the very foundation of political reality because death is, as has
been said, the *only* moral and practical sanction of the State. Of
course, the political principalities and their vassals would loathe
and fear Jesus—and seek to consign him to death—*because he
healed*, because he raised Lazarus, because he signified the Resurrection from death, because he exemplified life transcending the
moral power of death in this world and this world's strongholds
and kingdoms.   — EC, 148–49

AS NOTORIOUS THREAT

This lack of distinction between the private and the political
realms resolves a secret of the Gospel which bothers and bemuses
many church people (though they seldom articulate their distur-
bance). Most churchfolk in American Christendom, especially
those of white, bourgeois background, have for generations,
in both Sunday School and sanctuary, been furnished with an
impression of Jesus as a person who went briefly about teaching
love and doing good deeds: gentle Jesus, pure Jesus, meek Jesus,
pastoral Jesus, honest Jesus, fragrant Jesus, passive Jesus, peaceful Jesus, healing Jesus, celibate Jesus, clean Jesus, virtuous Jesus,
innocuous Jesus. Oddly enough, this image of Jesus is blatantly
opposed to familiar biblical accounts of the ministry of Jesus.
Those biblical accounts tell of a Jesus who was controversial in
relation to his family and in synagogue appearance, who suffered
poignantly, who suffered complete rejection by enemies and inti-
mates alike, and who was greeted more often with apprehension

than acclaim. This notion of an innocuous Jesus contradicts the notorious and turbulent events now marked as Holy Week in which Jesus is pursued as a political criminal by the authorities, put to trial and condemned, mocked and publicly humiliated, executed in the manner customarily reserved for insurrectionists, and, all the while, beheld by his followers with hysteria and consternation. While the traditional churches have invested so much in the innocuous image of Jesus, they have not been able to suppress the true events of Holy Week. This has placed church people in the predicament of having two conflicting views of Jesus, not knowing whether the two are reconcilable and, if they are not, which one is to be believed. Most people probably never resolve the dilemma.

I recall how uneasy I used to feel when, as a young person in church during Lent and Holy Week, it suddenly seemed that all we had been told about Jesus during the other church seasons was being refuted by the Gospel accounts. There were some obvious questions which would never even be mentioned, much less answered. Why, if Jesus was so private, so kind, so good, was he treated like a public criminal? Why would the State take any notice of him, much less crucify him? I realized that others noticed this discrepancy too. However, many people dealt with it merely by focusing on the image of the innocuous Jesus, overlooking the contradictory and disquieting evidence of Holy Week. Others chose a different way; they ideologized Jesus, rendering him a mere political agitator. I found both of these approaches deeply unsatisfactory; they were narrow and acculturated versions of Jesus, the one pietistic, the other political.

Even if the church failed to deal with this discrepancy, one could still look to the New Testament to ascertain whether there was any basis for these contrasting images of Jesus and to try to comprehend the issues posed by Holy Week. I learned from the Bible that the answer to this problem involves the political significance of Jesus' works, discreet though they may have been, and the political implication of his sayings. Both his actions and sayings are cryptic: Jesus tells a parable ending with the

remark "those who have ears, let them hear" or he heals someone afflicted in mind or body and then cautions this person and
any others who may have witnessed the event not to publicize
it. It is only when the parables or his works become notorious
(the precipitating episode being the raising of Lazarus) that the
authorities move against Jesus. Why do these rulers regard Jesus
with such apprehension? Why is he an offense and a threat to
their regime? The answer that emerges in the biblical accounts
is that, in teaching and healing, Jesus demonstrates an authority
over the power of death. And it is that very same power of death
which supplies the only moral sanction for the State and its ruling principalities.   —*ID*, 3–8

AS CRIMINAL

*Stringfellow preached this sermon at Cornell University in
October 1969. Dan Berrigan, who celebrated the liturgy, was
under appeal for the Catonsville conviction and had not yet
gone underground. The trustees were then in session debating
Dan's continuing status with the university. The sermon makes
only passing mention of Berrigan and events then current, but
the implications were pointed.*

> Then the whole company of them arose, and brought
> him before Pilate. And they began to accuse him, say-
> ing, "We found this man perverting our nation, and for
> bidding us to give tribute to Caesar, and saying that he
> himself is Christ a king."(Luke 23:1–2)

It is unambiguous in each of the Gospel accounts that Jesus
Christ was a criminal.

Of course, it is part of the grandeur of Jesus that many things
may be said of Him. Some of what may be said of Him seems to
contradict other things which may be said of Him. That makes
it tempting for us to overlook or play down attributes and
actions of Jesus which are not congenial to us or convenient for
us. Thus, despite what the Gospels indicate, it is easy for us to

gainsay the criminality of Jesus and to ignore entirely what His status as a criminal may mean for those who profess to affirm and follow Him.

I say that Jesus was, according to the testimonies of the Gospels, a criminal: not a mere nonconformist, not just a protester, more than a militant, not only a dissident, not simply a dissenter, but a criminal. More than that, as the Luke passage emphasizes, from the point of view of the State and of the ecclesiastical authorities as well—from the view of the establishment—Jesus was the most dangerous and reprehensible sort of criminal. He was found as one "perverting [the] nation," and "forbidding . . . tribute" to the State. One translation names Jesus a seditionist. In a congressman's jargon, Jesus was subversive. He was a criminal revolutionary—not one who philosophized about revolution, not a rhetorical revolutionary (such as we hear much nowadays in America), but rather one whose existence threatened the nation in a revolutionary way.

Jesus Christ was, so far as the established authorities and, in the end, so far as the people were concerned, the most loathsome of criminals. And He was so accused, and He was so condemned, and as such He was executed in an aptly ignominious way.

Those Americans who are white, Anglo-Saxon Christians suffer many fantasies about Jesus from the fibs and fairy tales that have been redundantly recited about him in Sunday Schools and from pulpits. Most white churchfolk, for instance, have been brought up to suppose that, in His arrest, trial, and conviction, Jesus was innocent. There is this notion that Jesus was fingered and betrayed by Judas, deserted by His other disciples, and then falsely accused, denied due process of law, and unjustly put to death. Many of us have been taught—wrongly, if the New Testament is credible—to regard Jesus as an ingenuous and hapless victim of a gross miscarriage of justice. But the truth is: He was guilty. Never has a man been apprehended, accused, tried, convicted, sentenced, and executed of whom it may be more certainly avowed: *He was guilty.*

Indeed, as the Luke version attests, far from being a casualty of an abuse of what has come to be called due process of law, there was evidently a serious dispute among the authorities as to where the proper venue lay in the case and as to who had competent jurisdiction over the person of the accused. If anything, it appears that Jesus benefited from more than perfunctory due process. Jesus was in truth treated more conscientiously, as far as due process is concerned—which means, so far as human justice is involved—than, say, Lieutenant Calley or Daniel or Philip Berrigan, or a Green Beret or any Black Panther can expect today in America. For Jesus, the justice of both the Roman State and the nation of Israel was perfected on the Cross.

Now I mention this—Jesus the guilty criminal, remembering that there are other things to notice about Jesus—in order to make two remarks:

One observation has to do with how it is, in this transaction, that Jesus replaces Barabbas. In the Gospels, Barabbas is identified as a convicted murderer and insurrectionist. Barabbas seems to have been sort of professional revolutionary. Perhaps he was such because of ideological commitment—something like an SDS Weatherman—or perhaps he was a mercenary revolutionary—something like a CIA agent. Or maybe Barabbas was a revolutionary idealist—like Judas, before Judas became disillusioned with Jesus. In any case, Jesus takes the place of Barabbas, the revolutionary, and bears the consequences of Barabbas's revolutionary crimes. This is a remarkable intercession which Jesus thereby enters for all human beings—both the futility and the hope of Barabbas's revolution are exposed and fulfilled in Jesus when He is crucified instead of Barabbas. *All* human revolutions—even those like the Revolution of 1776, which you and I may esteem as glorious—are corruptible in the inception in the vanity by which human beings suppose they can achieve their own perfection, and yet all human revolutions—including those which threaten a status quo which you and I enjoy—aspire to that very fulfillment of human life in society which Jesus Christ exemplifies.

Jesus was a revolutionary. Barabbas was a revolutionary. But the two are distinguished one from the other. That distinction is illuminated, I think, if we also remember that, while Jesus took the place of Barabbas, Barabbas was released and, in a sense, he replaced Christ. In days alive with ferment called "revolutionary" in this society and elsewhere, the Christian must be alert, and others must be warned, about the issue of mistaken identity symbolized, in the New Testament, by Barabbas taking the place of Jesus in the world. In the turmoil and excitement of Barabbas's revolution, it is easy to be seduced into supposing that the revolution of Barabbas is actually the revolution of Christ. That temptation is most intensified by the fact that the world can oblige Barabbas's revolution. More concretely, the incumbent political and economic and ideological authorities, in any particular time or place, can accommodate, where they cannot destroy, the factions and ideas that would overthrow them because those revolutionary forces have essentially the same identity and character as do the established powers. That fact does not constitute, in my mind, a persuasive argument against either revolutionary action or revolutionary change; it is just a statement, on one hand, of the most elementary realism about the corruptibility of revolutionary causes and, on the other hand, a theological affirmation about the vitality of death as a moral power in this world affecting all ideologies, all societies, all persons. The Christian must remain aware of how marginal, partial, fragile, transient, and, in the end, literally unrevolutionary the revolutionary cause of Barabbas is. Especially while in the midst of revolution, and even while one risks one's reputation or influence or property or life in suppose of Barabbas's revolution, the Christian must recognize that Barabbas' revolution, as needful as it may be, is not identical with Christ's revolution and is not to be mistaken for Christ's revolution.

The revolution of Christ, as we behold in the exchange of places between Christ and Barabbas, is not a revolution which the world can abide. There is, in other words, an immense, radical, and generic difference between the Christian revolutionaryas

revolutionary and any other revolutionaries. Revolution manifest in Jesus Christ does not have an idealistic or ideological or,
least of all, a mercenary character. It has, rather, an empirical
character: the Christians (not mere churchgoers, but *Christians*)
have had some experience in suffering death in this world—the
death which is a moral power; the death which is at work within
a man, between a man and himself, among all human beings,
between and among human beings and institutions; the death
which is the idol of nations—and the Christians have known the
transcendence of death's assaults, politically as much as personally, so that they live unintimidated by the continuing, ingenious,
and versatile aggressions of death. The mark that distinguishes
a Christian (which, by the way, has nothing to do with either
religion or rectitude) is that he has endured, already, a reconciliation of his own life with the world, so that conflict, injustice,
alienation, brutality, moral confusion, or any other portents of
death are no longer an intimidation, enticement, enslavement,
a threat or defeat for him. The mark of the Christian is, simply,
that he is a matured and freed human being. The direct political implication of this risen character of the Christian is that, as
contrasted with other revolutionaries, of which Barabbas is the
example and symbol, the Christian is an incessant revolutionary. He is always, everywhere, in revolt—not for himself but for
humanity. There is something inherently, invariably, persistently,
perpetually, inexhaustibly, inevitably revolutionary in the suffering of reconciliation—in the experience of one's own personhood as humanity in society—which constitutes the Christian
life in this world. The Christian as revolutionary is constantly
welcoming the gift of human life, for himself and for all men, by
exposing, opposing, and overturning all that betrays, entraps, or
attempts to kill human life. The difference between Christ and
Barabbas as revolutionaries is the difference between life and
death as both the imminent reality and the ultimate value of
revolution.

This issue is dramatized, for us Americans today, poignantly
in the American Revolution which, from the New Testament

perspective, was a revolution of Barabbas and not a revolution of Christ, despite what either Pilgrims or politicians have said. We who are Americans witness in this hour the exhaustion of the American revolutionary ethic. Wherever we turn, that is what is to be seen: in the ironic public policy of internal colonialism symbolized by the victimization of the welfare population, in the usurpation of the federal budget—and thus, the sacrifice of the nation's material and moral necessities—by an autonomous military-scientific-intelligence principality, by the police aggressions against black citizens, by political prosecutions of dissenters, by official schemes to intimidate the media and vitiate the First Amendment, by cynical designs to demean and neutralize the courts. Yet the corruption of the American revolutionary ethic is not a recent or sudden problem. It has been inherent and was, in truth, portended in the very circumstances in which the Declaration of Independence was executed. To symbolize that, white men who subscribed to that cause at the same time countenanced the institutionalization in the new nation of chattel slavery, and many were themselves owners of slaves. That incomprehensible hypocrisy in America's revolutionary origins foretells the contemporary decadence of the revolutionary tradition in the U.S.A.

The second matter I wish to mention, apart from the contrast between the work of death in revolutions like that of Barabbas and the perpetual revolutionary action of the Christian, is the relation of the State, and of established society, to Jesus Christ.

It is instructive, as to the disposition of the conventional churches in this country now, to note that, according to the biblical accounts, the ecclesiastical authorities, for all practical purposes, acted as servants of the State in the confrontation with Jesus. In one version, the chief priests protests: "Caesar is our king, we have no other king but Caesar." In the dispute over jurisdiction between Pilate and Herod, they warn: "If you release Him you will not be Caesar's friend." The ecclesiastics were, practically speaking, surrogates of the State. That is an all-too-familiar situation for chief priests to be found in. That was also the situation in Nazi Germany. It was similar, Kierkegaard says, in Scandinavia about a century ago. It is that way, notoriously, with the Dutch Reformed Church in the Union of South Africa. It has been the role of white Anglo-Saxon denominations in most jurisdictions in this land, both before and since the Civil War. On the issues of race and war—which is to say, on virtually all issues—the white churches and sects can be fairly viewed as the religious arm of the political establishment at the present time, or the same can be viewed the other way around—the incumbent national admiration represents a kind of corny fulfillment of the profoundly secular character of white Protestant denominationalism in America.

When I now speak of the State, therefore, the reference includes the inherited ecclesiastical authorities and institution, just as much as one notices the guilty association of the chief priests and Caesar's interest in the trial of Jesus.

Why is there this terrible hostility between the State and Christ? Why is Jesus so threatening to the nation? Why is He found to be criminal?

The answer to such questions is in the indictment: He says that "He himself is Christ a king."

The kingship of Jesus Christ possesses extraordinary connotations. On the cross, remember, the charge affixed over His head read: "King of the Jews." By the virtue of Israel's election and vocation as the people of God, as the holy nation, as the pioneer of humankind in reconciliation—a calling which is not revoked despite any apostasy of Israel—the King of the Jews is the King of humanity. The kingship of Christ not only exceeds the authority of Caesar but it also surpasses all aspirations for new or wiser or better kings of Barabbas's revolution. The kingship of Christ means Christ as Human—mature Human, fulfilled Human, whole Human, true Human—ruling the whole of time and creation. The kingship of Christ means, as Paul saw it, Christ as Second Adam—as Human Being (again, as it were) exercising dominion in history over all creatures (including all principalities and powers, institutions and ideologies, corporations and nations), over the whole of nature, over all things whatsoever. Christ as king means Human Beings no more enslaved to institutions, no longer a pawn of technologies, no mere servant of the State or of any other authority, no incapacitated victim of a damaged environment. Christ as King means humanity free from bondage to ideologies and institutions, free from revolutionary causes as well, free from idolatry of Caesar, and, not the least of it free from religion which tries to disguise such slaveries as virtuous, free from all these and all similar claims which really only conceal death—only the dehumanization of life—for humanity.

The authorities of Rome and of an apostate Israel perceived quite accurately that Christ as king threatened them poignantly and urgently. Christ as king embodies an unrelenting revolutionary threat to each and every nation and, paradoxically, to all revolutions within any nation as they become incarnations of the power of death feigning to be the definitive moral power in history.

According to the biblical witness, death is not the decisive moral power in history, but it is the *only* moral power the State (or any other principalities) can invoke as a sanction against human beings and against human life as such. That is, also, plainly to be seen now in this nation: death is the moral power upon which the State relies when it removes citizens from society for preventive detention or other political imprisonment, or when it estops free speech, of when it militarizes the police, or when it drives youth into exile, or when it confines millions in black ghettos and consigns millions more to malnutrition and illiteracy, and when it manipulates inflation and credit to preoccupy, demoralize, and thereby conform the middle classes, or when it collusively abets a governor's defiance of the courts, or when it hunts priests as fugitives.

No wonder, in the earlier circumstances, when the State confronted Christ the king—Christ the free human being—that it should find Him a criminal and send Him to the cross.

And no wonder, at this moment, in this country, where the power of death is so militant in the universities, in the corporate structures, in the churches, in the labor movement, in the political institutions, in the Pentagon, in the business of science, in the technological order, in the environment itself, in the realms of ideology, in the State, that, as with Jesus, the Christian, living as a free man, living in transcendence of death's power, living, thus, as an implacable, insatiable, unappeasable, tireless, and resilient revolutionary, should be regarded by all authorities as a criminal.

As in the time of the trial of Jesus Christ, so in this day and place, to truly be a free person is to be a criminal.

—*ST,* 59–68

AS CRUCIFIED
IN THE FREEDOM OF RESURRECTION

Stringfellow wrote this meditation on Jesus in the wake of the death of his partner, Anthony, so it arose from his personal sense of abandonment as well as the transcendence of that existential experience. (Footnote to his introit: Stringfellow was a cheerleader for the football team and editor of the high school paper's sports column, though not to the preemption or exclusion of his theological preoccupations.)

When I was an adolescent, precocious as I then may have been, the mystery of the Incarnation much exercised my mind. At the time in life when (I suppose) I should have been obsessed with football, sex, or pop music, as my peers seemed to be, I was very bothered about the identity of Jesus—preoccupied by issues of who he was and who he is—particularly by the matter of the relationship *in* Jesus Christ of humanity and deity.

I do not know—yet—how to account for this preemptive, and passionate, curiosity that disrupted my youth. I had not been treated in my upbringing, in either family or church, to sectarian stereotypes of Jesus as chum or sentimental intimate. Indeed, I regarded these as vulgar, possibly perverse, and certainly pretentious familiarities, denigrating to Jesus, even though they often induced for the indulgent ecstasies equivalent to a high attained through alcohol or drugs. I had suffered, instead, prosaic indoctrinations that asserted the "humanity of Jesus," while simultaneously alleging the "divinity of Christ." Such instructions had left me with a strong impression that Jesus was an extraordinary schizophrenic. Meanwhile, adoptionist notions that I heard rumored I rejected as probable sophistry since they seemed impotent to dispel the essential incoherence of dogma. In the congregation I received comfort from the introit of the Gospel According to John, which was recited at the end of every Eucharist, because it seemed to affirm the integrity—and indivisibility—of the life of the Word of God in this world, and to do so in appropriate syntax (see John 1:1–14).

Perennially this concern of mine would find focus in the reports in the Gospels of the Crucifixion of Jesus, especially the reference to his cry: "My God, my God, why hast thou forsaken me?" (Mark 15:34; cf. Matt. 27:46). Oh, dreadful words! Ghastly question! Pathetic lament! Ultimate despair! Exquisite agony! This is *Jesus* crying out. *Why would Jesus speak this way? How could* Jesus do so?

Then, one Good Friday while I was still in high school, I heard a preacher, more edifying for the laity than others had been, remark that these words of Jesus from the Cross were the opening verse of Psalm 22:

> My God, my God, why hast thou forsaken me
> and art so far from saving me, from heeding my groans?
> O my God, I cry in the day-time but thou dost not answer,
> in the night I cry but get no respite.   —Psalm 22:1–2

Later that same day I read the Twenty-second Psalm—perhaps a hundred times—but it did not quiet my agitation. I still had all my questions, although I recall that the effort distilled them: Why had not Jesus begun the recital of the Twenty-*third* Psalm, rather than the Twenty-second (like, I thought to myself, more or less everybody else does at the moment of death)?

And yet thou art enthroned in holiness,
thou art he whose praises Israel sings.
In thee our fathers put their trust;
they trusted, and thou didst rescue them.
Unto thee they cried and were delivered;
in thee they trusted and were not put to shame.
—Psalm 22:3–5

It was some time after I had exhausted my adolescence when I began to hear the Twenty-second Psalm as a hymn of eschatological hope, rather than a dirge of ultimate despair. If it is concluded that the outcry of Jesus from the Cross attributes the whole of Psalm 22 to Jesus, then one evidence that hope is the topic, rather than despair, is the radical identification of Jesus with Israel. And this is not simply a matter of inheritance, of Jesus indicating that he shares in Israel's heritage and custom— as had frequently happened in earlier episodes in his life, going back to the time of his circumcision. But in the midst of the Crucifixion, much more is involved; the identification relates to Israel's vocation as the holy nation called in history to recognize the reign of the Word of God in the world and to pioneer the praise and worship of God as Lord of Creation on behalf of all nations, tribes, peoples, and principalities. And, even more than that, the connection between Jesus and Israel signified in the psalm concerns the disposition of Israel's vocation. Thus, condemned by the Roman rulers, defamed by the ecclesiastical authorities, disfavored by the multitudes, betrayed, denied, abandoned by disciples, friends, and family; reviled, rejected, humiliated, utterly beset, crucified: Jesus, crying aloud from the cross, speaks *as* Israel. In that moment, there is nothing, there is no one left who is Israel except Jesus. He is, then, "King of the Jews," as the indictment affixed to the cross states; but he is, at the same time, within himself, the embodiment of the whole people of God, and he alone, then and there, assumes and exemplifies the generic vocation of Israel to trust and celebrate the redemptive work of the Word of God in history. In the drama

of the Crucifixion, Jesus' invoking the Twenty-second Psalm signifies that the Cross is the historic event in which Jesus Christ
becomes Israel.

> But I am a worm, not a man,
> abused by all men, scorned by the people.
> All who see me jeer at me,
> make mouths at me and wag their heads:
> "He threw himself on the Lord for rescue;
> let the Lord deliver him, for he holds him dear!"
>   Psalm 22:6–8

Another way to behold the peculiar and intense identification
of Jesus with Israel's vocation is in terms of the historic fulfillment of that which is written. Jesus was conscientious about
this throughout his public ministry, from the time of his first
appearance in the synagogue—and his reading from Scripture
there (Luke 4:16–30; cf. Matt.13:54–58, Mark 6:1–6). What is
involved in this, so far as I understand, is not some simplistic or
mechanistic process, but faithfulness in the performance of the
witness to which one is called. So, here, the words from the cross
foreshadow the scenario of the psalm, while the psalm portends
the event of the Crucifixion, so that the narrative of the Crucifixion in the Gospel accounts becomes a virtual recital of the
psalm.

> But thou art he who drew me from the womb,
> who laid me at my mother's breast.
> Upon thee was I cast at birth;
> from my mother's womb thou hast been my God.
> Be not far from me.
> for trouble is near, and I have no helper.
> A herd of bulls surrounds me.
> great bulls of Bashan beset me.
> Ravening and roaring lions
> open their mouths wide against me.
> My strength drains away like water

and all my bones are loose.
My heart has turned to wax and melts within me.
My mouth is dry as a potsherd,
and my tongue sticks to my jaw;
I am laid low in the dust of death,
The huntsmen are all about me;
a band of ruffians rings me round,
and they have hacked off my hands and feet.
I tell my tale of misery,
while they look on and gloat.
They share out my garments among them
and cast lots for my clothes.
But do not remain so far away, O Lord;
O my help, hasten to my aid.
Deliver my very self from the sword,
my precious life from the axe.
Save me from the lion's mouth,
my poor body from the horns of the wild ox.
                                           —Psalm 22:9–21

The psalm bespeaks one utterly assailed by the power of death: beset by the pervasiveness, militance, and versatility of death; bereft of any ability to cope with death. The psalm bemoans the agony of death by crucifixion: the psalm bespeaks the helplessness of humanity against the relentlessness of the great array of death. *I am laid low in the dust of death.*

That is the human destiny; more than that, that is the destiny of the whole of Creation, apart from the event of the Word of God in history. And it is that radical confession of helplessness that is at once the preface of faith and the invocation of the grace of the Word of God. Sin is, actually, the idolatry of death. The last temptation (in truth, the *only* one) is to suppose that we can help ourselves by worshiping death, after the manner of the principalities and powers. That final arrogance must be confessed. Jesus confessed that in our behalf when he cried aloud from the cross. When that confession is made, we are freed to die and to know the resurrection from death.

The recital in the Apostles' Creed, *He descended into Hell,* has a similar significance: Hell is the realm of death; Hell is when and where the power of death is complete, unconditional, maximum, undisguised, most awesome and awful, unbridled, most terrible, *perfected.* That Jesus Christ descends into Hell means that as we die (in any sense of the term "die") our expectation in death is encounter with the Word of God, which is, so to speak, already there in the midst of death.

> I will declare thy fame to my brethren;
> I will praise thee in the midst of the assembly.
> Praise him, you who fear the Lord;
> all you sons of Jacob, do him honor;
> stand in awe of him, all sons of Israel.
> For he has not scorned the downtrodden,
> nor shrunk in loathing from his plight
> nor hidden his face from him,
> but gave heed to him when he cried out.
> Thou dost inspire my praise in the full assembly;
> and I will pay my vows before all who fear thee.
> Let the humble eat and be satisfied.
> Let those who seek the Lord praise him
> and be in good heart forever.
> Let all the ends of the earth remember
> and turn again to the Lord;
> let all the families of the nations
> bow down before him.
> For kingly power belongs to the Lord,
> and dominion over the nations is his.
>
> —Psalm 22:22–28

The outcry from the cross is no pathetic lament, but a song for Easter. And the hope it expresses is not vague, illusory, or fantasized, but concrete, definitive, and empirical. The Twenty-second Psalm (hence, Jesus on the cross) manifests that hope in political terms. The influence of the psalm on the Crucifixion accounts underscores the political character of the Crucifixion. The psalm elaborates the politics of the Cross.

Any public execution is, obviously, a political event in a straightforward and literal sense, but the public execution of Jesus Christ has political connotations of immense, complex, and, indeed, cosmic scope. This becomes apparent, for example, when the images of the psalm portray the powerless victim threatened by predatory beasts, a familiar biblical way of denominating political principalities and powers. It is, after all, in the name of Caesar, the overruling principality, that the sovereignty of the Word of God over Creation is disputed and mocked (cf. Luke 23:1–2; Matt. 22:15–22; Mark 12:13–17; Luke 20:19–26; Matthew 27:27–31; Mark 15:16–20; John 19:1–3).

The political reality of the Crucifixion is accentuated in the psalm where it is announced that the cry of the forlorn is heard and heeded (Psalm 22:24b). Notice the circumstances: the scene is the Judgment, with the whole of Creation in assemblage and with all who fear the Lord of history praising Him. Let it be mentioned here that the attribute that chiefly distinguishes Christians is, simply, that they fear the Lord *now*, or already—before the Day of Judgment. That means specifically that they acknowledge that they live and act in the constant reality of being judged by God. Thus, nowadays, when people assemble as congregations in praise and worship of the Lord, this is an anticipation or preview of the Judgment. Where, instead, the regime is glorified, superstition prevails, or religiosity is practiced, then the congregation indulges in scandalous parody of the Judgment.

Notice as well that in the context of the psalm the event of the Judgment is, so to say, the *first* day that the downtrodden are no longer scorned (Ps. 22:24a). For the poor, the diseased, the oppressed, the dispossessed, the captive, the outcast of this world, the Day of Judgment in the Word of God means not only the day of justice, but also the day of justification, when their suffering is exposed as grace.

The politics of the Cross delivers a message to the nations, to all regimes and powers, and even unto the ends of the earth, marked by the cry of Jesus that invokes the psalm: *kingly power belongs to the Lord, and dominion over the nations is his* (Ps. 22:28). *That* is truly what the Incarnation is all about.

> How can those buried in the earth
> do him homage,
> how can those who go down to the grave
> bow before him?
> But I shall live for his sake,
> my posterity shall serve him.
> This shall be told of the Lord to future generations;
> and they shall justify him,
> declaring to a people yet unborn
> that this was his doing.   —Psalm 22:29–31

In the psalm, the last word in the cry of Jesus from the cross is an assurance of the efficacy of the Resurrection. To become and be a beneficiary of the Resurrection of Jesus Christ means to live here and now in a way that upholds and honors the sovereignty of the Word of God in this life in this world, and that trusts the Judgment of the Word of God in history. That means freedom *now* from all conformities to death, freedom *now* from fear of the power of death, freedom *now* from the bondage of idolatry to death, freedom *now* to live in hope while awaiting the Judgment.   —*SF,* 105–13

AS DESCENDED TO HELL

There is no person who does not know loneliness—even Jesus Christ knew it. He did not succumb to loneliness because there is no person who is alone.

On the face of the Gospel narrative is the lonely Christ. Nobody greeted, nobody honored, nobody understood, nobody loved, nobody celebrated his vocation. Nobody loved him for being the one he is. . . .

It was rejection he experienced when his relatives called on him to name them in preference to the crowd. He healed the sick, but both sick and well mistook his power. The same temptations that visited him in the wilderness returned to taunt him in the political triumph of Palm Sunday, and his own disciples were—and many are to this day—astonished and perplexed that he withstood such attractive temptations. Israel, which had boasted in her waiting for his coming, found him subversive when he came. Rome was an accomplice in his condemnation. At Gethsemane, while alone in prayer, his friends slept and his enemies plotted to destroy him. Judas betrayed him, Peter denied him, all the rest fled. A thief ridiculed him on the Cross. People shouted for his death.

Unwelcome, misunderstood, despised, rejected, unloved and misloved, condemned, betrayed, deserted, helpless—he was delivered to death as if he were alone.

Christ descended in to hell; Christ is risen from death.

In the submission of Christ to death, the power of death is dissipated. In the subjection of Christ to death, the dread is taken out of loneliness. Christ suffered loneliness without despair. In the radical loneliness of Christ is the assurance that no one is alone.

In surrender to death, in hell, in the event in which the presence and power of death is most notorious, undisguised, militant, and pervasive, the reality and grace of God are triumphant.

In the event in which you are alone with your own death—when all others and all things are absent and gone—God's initiative affirms your very creation and that you are given your life anew. In the moment and place where God is least expected—in the barrenness and emptiness of death—God is at hand. It is in that event that a person discovers it is death which is alone not he.   —*ID*, 31–34

AS LORD

The biblical witness, as the Gospel according to St. John reminds, does not end in the saga of the fall. The biblical testament is completed in Jesus Christ. Jesus Christ means that though the fall ruins creation, the fall does not dissipate the grace of God. Jesus Christ means that though human beings and, indeed, the whole of creation reject life as the gift of the Word of God, the Word of God is not thereby retracted or refuted or revoked. Christ means that although in fallen creation vocation is distorted and worship is scandalized, the sovereignty of God is neither disrupted nor aborted. Christ means that in the fall, in the midst of the reign of death in time, within the common history of this world, the Word of God nevertheless acts to restore life to the whole of creation. Jesus Christ means that the freedom of God is not curtailed by the fall and not intimidated by the thrall of death, but elects to redeem creation from the power of death. Jesus Christ means the embodiment in human life, now, in this world, of the abundance of the Word of God for salvation from sin and redemption from death for all creation.

Thus it has come to pass that biblical people esteem Jesus Christ as Lord. This is not, as is sometimes erroneously supposed, a title designating the divinity of Christ; it, rather, explicitly explains the humanity of Jesus as the one who epitomizes the restoration of dominion over the rest of creation vested in human life by the sovereignty of the Word of God during the epoch of the fall. Jesus Christ as Lord signifies the renewed vocation of human life in reconciliation with the rest of creation.

Hence, those who live in Christ and who honor Christ as Lord, who are members of the body of the Church of Christ, live in the present age as a "new creation" (2 Cor. 5:17).

It will be, I hope, clear that to reach an affirmation as to the essential character of the church in this way has no basic similarity to the ways of human idealism, the practice of religion, or the entertainment of speculations and visions. The claim of the church that it represents in history restored creation is not contingent at all upon virtue in the church but upon the freedom of the Word of God in this world. It is that, I believe, which is the rudimentary and constant cause of tension and friction— the New Testament sometimes refers to warfare—between the church and the world, particularly between the church and the nation or the State or other ruling principalities and powers.

At the crux of that incessant conflict is the vocational issue and, concretely, the discernment which the church, as the exemplar of renewed creation, practices concerning the vocation of political authority. In that witness, the church confesses, on behalf of every nation or state or regime that political authority has a vocation, as every creature does. The church, as it were, remembers that vocation and honors it duly by confessing that political authority is "ordained" or "appointed" by God. Yet, simultaneously, in the midst of the anarchy which is the fall, in this perishing age, while political authority remains beholden to the power of death, that confession of the vocation of political authority always upholds the preeminence of dominion restored to human life or, in other words, always affirms the Lordship of Jesus Christ. But if the church is faithful to Jesus Christ as Lord, can the church ever support political authority in status quo?

—CO, 31–22

Spirit

ENCOUNTERING THE SPIRIT

This autobiographical account was first written in the preface of an unfinished book on the charismatic and the demonic. It would have been called "Grieve Not the Holy Spirit," and was intended by Stringfellow to complete an ethics trilogy in his work. The account subsequently found its way whole cloth into The Politics of Spirituality, *his final book, which did in effect complete the trilogy. The story takes place at his home church, St. John's Episcopal, Northampton, Massachuetts.*

This whole matter of the elusive significance of so-called spirituality comes into acute focus, for me, in the cursory and profane regard which the name of the Word of God as the Holy Spirit suffers, more often than not, within the churches. I remember, for instance, that I was very impatient to be confirmed in the Episcopal Church. In my rearing as a child in that church I had come to think that confirmation was the occasion when the secrets were told. Confirmation, I supposed, was the event in which all the answers that had been previously withheld from me, because I was a child, would be forthcoming. In particular, I recall, I was eager to be confirmed because I expected in confirmation to learn the secret of the Holy Spirit. At last, I anticipated, my curiosity concerning this mysterious name would be satisfied.

In my experience as a child in the church, when adults named the Holy Spirit in the presence of children it was always an utterly obscure, unspecified, literally spooky allusion.

It did not specifically occur to me as a child to suspect that adults in the church did not in fact know what they were talking about when they used the name of the Holy Spirit. The reference, anyway, was always intimidating. The mere invocation of the name, without any definition, connection, or elaboration, would be effective in aborting any issues raised by a child. "The Holy Spirit" was the great, available, handy estoppel.

Needless to say, confirmation turned out to be a great dis-
appointment to me. I waited through catechism, but no secrets
were confided. If anything, the name of the Holy Spirit was put
to use in confirmation instruction with even deeper vagueness.
On the day of confirmation I learned no secret except the secret
that adults in the church had no secrets, at least so far as the
Holy Spirit is concerned.

It was only later on, after I had begun to read the Bible seriously, on my own initiative, that the cloture about the Holy
Spirit was disrupted and the ridiculous mystification attending
this name of the Word of God began to be dispelled. In contrast
to my childish impressions from experiences in church, I found
the Bible to be definitive and lucid as to the identity, character,
style, and habitat of the Holy Spirit. In the Bible, the Holy Spirit
is no term summoned simply to fill a void, or to enthrall rather
than instruct the laity, or to achieve some verbal sleight-of-hand
because comprehension is lacking. Biblically, the Holy Spirit
names the faithfulness of God to his own creation. Biblically,
the Holy Spirit means the militant presence of the Word of God
inhering in the life of the whole of creation. Biblically, the Holy
Spirit is the Word of God at work both historically and existentially, acting incessantly and pervasively to renew the integrity of
life in this world. By virtue of this redundant affirmation of the
biblical witness, the false notion—nourished in my childhood
in the Episcopal Church—that the Holy Spirit is, somehow,
possessed by and enshrined within the sanctuary of the church
was at last refuted, and I was freed from it. Coincidentally, as
one would expect, the celebration in the sanctuary became, for
me, authentic—a Eucharist for the redemption of the life of the
whole of creation in the Word of God—instead of vain ritual or
hocus-pocus.

It was the biblical insight into the truth of the Holy Spirit
that signaled my own emancipation from religiosity. It was the
biblical news of the Holy Spirit that began, then, to prompt the
expectancy of encounter with the Word of God in any and all
events in the common life of the world and in my own life as a

part of that. It was—it is—the biblical saga of the Word of God as Agitator, as the Holy Spirit, that assures me that wheresoever human conscience is alive and active, *that* is a sign of the saving vitality of the Word of God in history, here and now.

—*PS*, 16–18

PENTECOST, BAPTISM, AND SPIRIT

In the summer of 1982, Stringfellow gave a series of talks at a conference for the American Baptist Convention. Judson Press subsequently asked him to gather and augment those into a book. Occasionally, he would with a wry smile, refer to the project as "explaining baptism to the Baptists." What follows is excerpted from the Introduction to that book, which remained unpublished at the time of his death.

As a matter of history for the disciples and, for all of that, as a matter of theology for contemporary Christians the biblical happening most pertinent to the baptism of the Spirit is, manifestly, Pentecost. The scene, as we learn of it from the Acts of the Apostles, is not private, but quite public; it is not individualistic but notorious, not idiosyncratic, but scandalous; and onlookers are said to behold Pentecost as provocative and controversial; it appears to have been an offense to the ruling authorities. Central in the experience of the power of the Holy Spirit among the disciples, both commonly and severally, is a transcendence of worldly distinction (as race, age, sex, class, occupation, nationality, language, tongue) which anticipates the eschatological consummation of the whole of fallen creation in the Kingdom of God. Simultaneously, in Pentecost, each person receives the renewal of human gifts and capabilities, the restoration, as it were, of one's original personhood, a reconciliation with and within self in utterly intimate detail happening within the environment of each person's reconciliation with the rest of humanity and the whole of created life throughout time. These same aspects of Pentecost—the most intensely personal and the cosmic and ultimate—become, ever after, the marks of authentic and credible conversion of the baptism of the Spirit. When a person nowadays can be said to be baptized of the Spirit it means that the person is, verily, incorporated into the experience of Pentecost.

The sectarian cooption of the baptism of the Spirit has caused some of the churches to construe the two baptisms as alternatives, as if one might *either* be baptized by water *or* be baptized of the Spirit, but venerable liturgical tradition recognizes and recites the association of the two. In ancient practice baptism by water was customarily coupled with entreaties for the action of the Holy Spirit, while baptism of the Spirit was confessed and sacramentally attested by baptism by water. The complementary and edifying interplay of the two baptisms has been characteristic of the faithful churchly life despite the sectarian interpolations which have ridiculed baptism by water as perfunctory or as sentimental or as, somehow, mockery. A lesson to be learned from such ridicule is that the name of God is never invoked in vain—that is, without consequence or effect—even when that name is called upon vainly—that is, for some cause or purpose unworthy of the name.

Therefore, there is no reason to attribute credibility to the sectarian definitions of either baptism. As to the beneficial relationship between baptism by water and that of the Spirit in the biblical context, it is enough to recall the baptism of Jesus by John the Baptist as that was so promptly verified—and transfigured—by the initiative of the Holy Spirit. . . . Those I have called, here, sectarians who make presumptuous claims about baptism of the Spirit do not like the baptism by water or see its significance because that threatens what they habitually assert about a uniquely private character of the relation between God and the person baptized. No one, however, need feel ashamed or deprived in baptism by water. It is, in truth, the confession of the church, in a gathered congregation, that the grace of the Word of God, which has been sufficient to reconcile them, within themselves, with one another and with the whole of creation, is ample for the renewal of the life of the one presented to be baptized.

Such a confession by a congregation is a most audacious political statement expounding the sovereignty of the Word of God, in its imminence as much as its ultimacy, and an open affront to all principalities or persons who feign rule in this world. That in some churchly traditions infants are baptized by water only magnifies the audacity of the congregation's confession and solemnizes its undertaking to nurture the child baptized in resistance to the worldly powers which pretend to rule.

In short, neither baptism by water nor that of the Spirit authorizes or abets conformity to this world. I believe that the two baptisms are, in truth, indivisible. The one cannot be comprehended without reference to the other—it was even so when Jesus was baptized—and if there is not that correlation, that which remains is distorted and ambivalent. Or, to put it another way, in baptism both an act of the church and an action of the Holy Spirit simultaneously are essential ("Authority in Baptism").   —*AKW*, 160–62

Sacrament and
Sacramental Ethics

It is right and fitting that as a lay theologian and, indeed, a theologian of the laity, William Stringfellow should bring sacramental theology so much into his work. In his view, sacraments were for the sake of human life and worldly presence. He discerned them, sought them, named them, defended and commended them. Christian ethics were for him essentially sacramental ethics.

BAPTISM

These are the concluding paragraphs of Instead of Death. *In fact, its very final words comprise his title. Just to note, he had to fight with his publishers to retain that name, as they held no book with "death" in the title would be marketable. He prevailed and it sold more copies than any other of his volumes, eventually becoming the only volume republished in his lifetime.*

A human being who is converted will be baptized. That is, in the midst of the church one will confess the faith; that confession will be confirmed by the church and the members of the church; and that person will be welcomed into the company of the church. But what of the practice of baptism where the one baptized has not yet been converted and does not confess the faith, as is the case in infant baptism?

Such baptism is not an act of the child baptized, but an act of the church on behalf of the child; an act in which the church and the people of the church, both individually and corporately, confess that they trust the Gospel so much that they believe the power of God will save this child from death. The church confesses that the grace of God, which has been sufficient to save the members of the church, is also sufficient for this child. The church and the members of the church then commit themselves to raise, nurture, and love this person in such a way that he or she will come to a full maturity in Christ and later confess the faith.

Too often baptism is profaned in the churches; church people do not realize what a radical action and responsibility is involved in baptizing a child. But the grace of God is not vitiated by the stupidity or frivolity of Christians. Even though Christians sometime invoke the name of God but do not take the matter seriously, God does. The name of God may be invoked vainly, but that name is never invoked in vain. The sufficiency of God's mercy is enough for the child even where the church falters in its responsibility to the child, even when the people of the church fail to love the child maturing in Christ.

Baptism is often profoundly misunderstood. It is widely thought to be the sacrament of the unity of the church. But that is not what baptism is; just as it is not a mere membership or initiation ritual. Baptism is the assurance—accepted, enacted, verified, and represented by Christians—of the unity of *all humanity* in Christ. The baptized are the people in history consecrated to the unity humans receive in the worship of God. The oneness of the church is the example and guarantee of the reconciliation of all creation in the life of God. The church, the baptized society, is asked to be the image of all humanity, the one and intimate community of God.

Baptism is the sacrament of the extraordinary unity among humanity wrought by God in overcoming the power and reign of death; in overcoming all that alienates, segregates, divides, and destroys human beings in their relationships to each other, within their own persons, and in their relationship with the rest of creation.

Thus the vocation of the baptized person is a simple thing: it is to live from day to day, whatever the day brings, in this extraordinary unity, in this reconciliation with all human beings and all things, in this knowledge that death has no more power, in this truth of the resurrection. It does not really matter exactly what a Christian does from day to day. What matters is that whatever one does is done in honor of one's own life, given to one by God and restored to one in Christ, and in honor of the life into which all humans and all things are called. The only thing that really matters is to live in Christ instead of death.

—*ID*, 110–12

OUTLINE FOR A BOOK

The intended Judson Press book, Authority in Baptism: The
Vocation of Jesus and the Ministry of the Laity, *was to have the
following design. Though it provides food for meditation even
as is, one yearns for the chapters that remained unwritten.*

Chapter one: Creation and Baptism
— the ministry of John the Baptist
— the vocation of Jesus Christ
— baptism and dominion in Creation

Chapter two: Fallen Creation and Renewed Creation
— the restoration of Israel
— the sin of blasphemy
— the call to repentance

Chapter three: The Acceptable Time
— what *is* the acceptable year?
— *when* is the acceptable year?
— the political significance of contemporary worship
— eschatology and ethics

EUCHARISTIC LITURGY

Dissenter in a Great Society (1966) *was Stringfellow's account
of poverty and racial crisis in America. It is striking that his concluding argument for the "orthodoxy of radical involvement"
included substantial reflections on both baptism and, here,
Eucharist.*

At no point in the witness of the church to the world is its integrity as a reconciled society more radical and more cogent than
in the liturgy, the precedent and consummation of that service
which the Church of Christ and the members of this body render
to the world. . . . As for the church, all forms of its corporate
life—from the Quakers sitting in silence in a circle, to the exuber-
ance and patience of a Negro congregation, and the majesty and
richness of the venerable Orthodox service—are liturgical. The

only serious question is whether or not a given liturgical practice has integrity in the Gospel. There are both laypeople and clergy who regard liturgy as an essentially religious exercise—separate, disjoined, self-contained, unrelated—confined to the sanctuary and having nothing to do with this world. Some even regard liturgy superstitiously, as something having an intrinsic efficacy, as a means of procuring indulgences, as if God were so absurd— and so ungodly—as to be appeased by the redundant incantations of human beings.

There is, however, nothing so spooky or lucky about the liturgy, and nothing magical or mechanistic about its performance. The liturgy of the Gospel is, on the contrary, a dramatic form of the ethical witness of Christians in this world. In this sense, though there may be much variety in different times and cultures in regard to language, music, action, and movement, the liturgy is always characterized by certain definitive marks:

1. *Scriptural Integrity*—The liturgy of the Gospel is the theatricalization of the biblical saga of God's action in this world, thus relating the ubiquity of the Word of God in history to the consummation of the Word of God in Jesus Christ. A biblically authentic and historically relevant liturgy is always the celebration of the death and Resurrection of the Lord; the most decisive event in all history is remembered and memorialized in a context in which God's every action in this world since creation is recalled and rehearsed, and the hope of the world for the final reconciliation is recited and represented in the liturgical portrait.

The scriptural integrity of the liturgy requires that the laity not be spectators but participants—not as a matter of piety, not merely for their own sake but because they gather, as a congregation, as delegates and, indeed, advocates of the world.

That is why the traditional Protestant "preaching service"— even when the preaching is an exposition of the Word of God, and not some religious diatribe—is an impoverished and inadequate liturgy for the church; by the same token, that is why the Mass recited in the absence of a congregation, or celebrated in a language not familiar to the people, is a compromise of the scriptural integrity of the liturgy.

2. *The Historicity of the Liturgy*—The liturgy of the Gospel is both a transcendent event and a present event. It shatters the categories of time and space and location because it both recalls and dramatizes the estate of Creation in the Word of God, and beseeches and foretells the end of this history. As a transcendent event, the liturgy recollects *all* that has already happened in this world from the beginning of time and prophesies *all* that is to come until the end of time.

But the liturgy is also a contemporary event, involving these particular persons gathered in this specific place in this peculiar way. The reconciliation celebrated in the liturgy is not only a reconciliation remembered from Creation or expected eschatologically but also in actual event the reconciliation here and now of those gathered as a congregation and society within and among themselves, and between each and all of them and the rest of the world.

That is precisely why the confessions and the intercessions of the people of the congregation within the context of the liturgy are so indispensable to its integrity. *This* is the time and *this* is the place and *this* is the way, in a most immediate sense, in which the whole, manifold, existential involvement of the members of Christ's Body in the everyday life of the world—both all that seems good and which human beings are tempted to honor or praise, and all that seems evil and which they are fond of rationalizing or denying—is offered and consecrated for the discretion of Christ Himself, the Redeemer of all.

Thus the liturgy is the normative and conclusive ethical commitment of the Christian people to the world. The liturgy is the epitome of the service which the Christian renders the world. All authentic witness in the name of Christ, exemplifying in the world the virtue of Christ, which Christians undertake in their dispersion in the practical life of the world, is portrayed in the liturgy celebrated in the gathered congregation.

3. *The Sacramental Authenticity of the Liturgy.* It is both this transcendence of time in time and the scriptural integrity of the liturgy of the Gospel which constitute the sacramental essence of the liturgy. The actual, visible, present event retains all its own originality and contemporary significance as a particular reconciled community, and at the same time it is transfigured to embody to the world the cosmic enormity of the reconciling accomplishment of Jesus Christ.

Thus the liturgy as sacrament is inherently different from religious ritualism, in which the propriety of the ritual practice itself is all that matters. (Such may be sufficient for initiation or elevation in the Masons or the Knights of Columbus, but ritualistic piety is radically inappropriate to the Eucharist.) Notice, too, that the liturgy as sacrament appropriates as its ingredient symbols, among others, the ordinary things of the common existence of the world—bread, wine, water, money, cloth, color, music, words, or whatever else is readily at hand. Sacramentally, we have in the liturgy a meal which is basically a real meal and which nourishes those who partake of it as a meal. At the same time, this meal portrays for the rest of the world an image of the Last Supper, of which Christ Himself was Host, and is also a foretaste of the eschatological banquet in which Christ is finally recognized as the Host of all humanity.

The liturgy, therefore, wherever it has substance in the Gospel, is a living, political event. The very example of salvation, it is the festival of life which foretells the fulfillment and maturity of all of life for all of time in *this* time. The liturgy *is* social action because it is the characteristic style of life for human beings in this world.   —*DGS,* 150–54

MARRIAGE AS ORDINARY SACRAMENT

This reflection on the sacramental significance of marriage is mature and sophisticated for the adolescent audience for which he wrote Instead of Death. *To be sure he was openly countering other voices whom they would read or hear. Two points of note.*

These paragraphs light up differently in the present moment when same-sex marriage is emerging in church and culture. They offer wise counsel in that regard and may have actually antici- pated such a change. Lastly, he does not notice the Catholic sac- ramental theology, similarly pertinent, which regards marriage as the only sacrament undertaken by lay people. They do indeed marry one another, even though clergy preside.

The fiction that there is some ideal of marriage for Christians which is better than or essentially different from an ordinary secular marriage is not only fostered by most Sunday School curriculum materials on the subject, but also by the practice of authorizing clergy to act for the State in the execution of the marriage contract. Clergy are licensed by the State to perform the functions of a civil magistrate, in spite of the supposed sepa- ration of church and state in this country. This both lends weight to the confusion about "Christian marriage" and greatly com- promises the discretion of clergy as to whom they shall marry. In the office and function of a civil magistrate, no clergyperson really has the grounds to refuse to marry any two people who present themselves, whether they are Christians or not, as long as they meet the civil requirements for marriage; that is, are of a certain age, have had blood tests, meet any residency require- ments, have a valid license, and pay the fee.

A more theologically responsible practice, I suggest, would be to divest the clergy of the civil office and require that all who will be married present themselves to the civil magistrate to be married. Then, if those who are so married are Christians, they will go to their congregation to offer, within the company of the church, their marriage to be blessed, to seek the intercessions of the whole church for the marriage, and to celebrate their mar- riage in the church as a sacrament. A similar practice is followed in many parts of Europe and Latin America.

To restore such a practice would go a long way toward recov- ering the sacramental integrity of marriage between Christians. For to discard the fiction of "Christian marriage" and to under- stand that marriage is an ordinary, secular, fallen estate in no way denigrates marriage for Christians. On the contrary, in marriage and all else the Christian is fully participant in secular life, but at the same time is constantly engaged in offering the involvement in secular life for the glory of God. In such an offering, that which is ordinary is rendered extraordinary, that which is merely worldly is transfigured, that which is most common becomes a means of worship, and each act or event of everyday life becomes sacramental—a sign and celebration of God's care for every act or event of everyday life in this world. Rather than demean or downgrade marriage to restore such a practice would again give to the marriage of Christians the dignity of that which is secular made holy, of that which is a sign of death become a witness to redemption to all those, married or not, who are not Christian. —*ID*, 42–43

SEX AND RECONCILIATION

This excerpt is from a talk given at Christ Church Cathedral, Hartford, in 1965. It is noteworthy that Stringfellow had made similar connections two years earlier in Instead of Death. *Following the section averring there is no such thing as "Christian Marriage," he goes on to write:*

> *The dishonoring of the body and person of one's self or another may take subtle forms and may be as much present in sexual conduct approved or condoned by society as in that which is disapproved or condemned. Yet the Christian more than recognizes the reality of sin in sex of all sorts. The Christian knows that sex, which is so full of death, may also become a sacrament of the redemption of human life from the power of sin which death is. Such is the mystery of sex and love that what in sex may be dehumanizing, depraved, or merely habitual, may become human, sacramental, and sanctified. For sex to be so great an event, it is essential for one to know who they are as a person, to be secure in their own identity, and indeed, to love oneself."* —*ID*, 53–54

On occasion, there is love between persons of the opposite sexes or of the same sex and, on occasion, sexual intercourse can be and become a sacrament of love. Christians advocate that. Indeed, for Christians all of life is sacramental, that is, the outward sign and symbol of a person's reconciliation within oneself and with all others. For Christians, sex, whether homosexual or heterosexual can be one, among many, sacraments of that reconciliation.

But notice, the ethics of the Christian faith with respect to sex are singular. There are no special ethics for heterosexuals, either in or out of marriage, and then another and separate ethics for homosexuals. For all varieties and forms of sex, for Christians, integrity lies in that which honors the gift of life which God had bestowed on each and every person.

Sexuality is part of that gift, though it is never the fullness of that gift. Sex is a mundane symbol of that gift: a means by which the gift is proclaimed and celebrated and a way in which it is communicated and conveyed among human beings that they are called to love and affirm and help each other in the face of death and, most of all, a way in which a person declares and confirms their own humanity despite the same threat.

In that sense, from a Christian point of view, sex is good.

There is, in other words, no fear in love. In fact, love casts out fear.[21]

EXORCISM AND SACRAMENTAL RENEWAL

There were folks on Block Island who sometimes referred to Stringfellow, almost spookily, as an "exorcist." That is because he was known to employ an ancient liturgical rite both publicly and privately (first to exorcise then President Nixon and later to cast death from his Island home after the passing of Anthony), but also because in his writing he interpreted political events and

---

21. "The Humanity of Sex," 1965, unpublished ms, the William String-fellow Archives, No. 4438, Cornell University Library, Box 8. Stringfellow notes on the page having given this talk prior to the Mattechine Society in New York, the first homosexual organization in the country, for which he served as ally and lawyer.

*action in the light of this biblical practice here connecting it to
the movement for liturgical renewal.*

If, in modern Christendom, exorcism as a gift of the Holy Spirit
has been generally regarded with apprehension and suppressed,
it nevertheless had venerable prominence in the biblical tradition. Not only did Jesus exorcise, but it was part of the Messianic expectation in Old Testament Judaism that the Messiah
would have this power. Furthermore, in the primitive church,
exorcism, being one of the gifts specifically promised by Jesus
for the mission of the church, was widely and effectually practiced, according to the New Testament (Acts 10:38, 13:10).
Indeed, in the ancient church, liturgical forms of exorcism were
commonly in use as a preparation for baptism (1 Pet. 5:8; James
4:7). Vestiges of that early practice survive in baptismal rites to
the present time, though I find little evidence that these are taken
very seriously in instruction for baptism.

Still, exorcism cannot be dismissed as some quaint residue,
if only because of its biblical status. Some psalms are liturgical exorcisms. In the Jewish tradition of exorcism, as has been
mentioned earlier, there is the story of Moses exorcising the
pharaoh. It seems to me that this citation alone is sufficient to
show the contemporary relevance of the gift and the necessity
for its practice. And, in fact, exorcism is far more widely implicated in witness today than is usually acknowledged directly,
the Lord's Prayer itself being a form of exorcism. Whether many
who redundantly and ceremoniously recite the Lord's Prayer are
cognizant of it or not, the fact remains that the invocation of the
name of God, followed at the end of the prayer by the plea to
"deliver us from evil" or from "the evil one," constitutes an act
of exorcism (Matt: 6:9–13).

All that has been affirmed about the political connotations of
healing must be reaffirmed, of course, about this specific kind
of healing. The political significance of exorcism is rendered
even more emphatic by the content of the Lord's Prayer and by
the political circumstances of the impending condemnation of

Christ which attended his commendation of this prayer to his disciples.

Politically informed exorcisms, which I believe to be as exemplary as that involving the pharaoh, do still occur, if occasionally. This, indeed, was the witness of the Catonsville Nine when they burned draft records in May of 1968. As those attentive to their trial or those who have read or seen the play about the trial can apprehend, the action at Catonsville was a sacramental protest against the Vietnamese war—a liturgy of exorcism, exactly. It exposed the death idolatry of a nation which napalms children by symbolically submitting the nation to the very power upon which it has relied, by napalming official pieces of paper. It is relevant to understanding the significance of the Catonsville action that the Berrigan brothers and others of the defendants had been involved over a long time, particularly since the extraordinary papacy of John XXIII, in the renewal of the sacramental witness in the liturgical life of Christians. They had become alert to the social and political implications of the Mass as a celebration and dramatization of the reconciliation and renewal of Creation or as a portrayal and communication of the Jerusalem reality of the Church of Christ loving and serving the world. The Catonsville action is, thus, a direct outreach of the renewal of the sacramental activity of the sanctuary, a liturgy transposed from altar or kitchen table to a sidewalk outside a Selective Service Board office, a fusion of the sacramental and the ethical standing with the characteristic biblical witness.   —*EC*, 149–15

SACRAMENTAL RECOURSE
TO SCRIPTURE

Stringfellow's personal introduction to the faith-rooted anti-Nazi resistance movements came as a senior in college when he attended the World Conference of Christian Youth in Oslo, Norway—a nation which had itself been occupied. There he encountered the Norwegian Bishop Belgrave, but also Madeline Barot and Jacques Ellul from the French resistance, and Hans Lilje and Martin Niemoller from Germany. Over time what struck him most deeply was the confluence, or rhythm, of Bible study and resistance.

Lately, as might be expected, while totalitarian tendencies have achieved so much momentum and become more obvious and more ominous in America, I have found myself recalling most vividly the conversations I attended with these Resistance leaders in which I listened to them recount their anti-Nazi experiences. . . . The recollection which now visits me from listening to those Resistance leaders concerns Bible study. While not a practice of the entire Resistance, it strongly engaged the whole confessing movement implicated in that Resistance. Most appropriately, it often included Jewish as well as Christian participants. I recall being slightly bemused at the time of which I am speaking by the strenuous emphasis placed upon Bible study. No doubt that bewilderment reflected my own biblical deprivation, a lack in my American churchly upbringing which I have since struggled gladly to overcome.

In this dimension of the Resistance, the Bible became alive as a means of nurture and communication; *recourse to the Bible was in itself a primary, practical, and essential tactic of resistance.* Bible study furnished the precedent for the free, mature, ecumenical, humanizing style of life which became characteristic of those of the confessing movement. This was an exemplary way—a sacrament, really—which expounded the existential scene of the Resistance. That is, it demonstrated the necessities of acting in transcendence of time within time, of living humanly in the midst of death, of seeing and foreseeing both the apocalyptic and the eschatological in contemporary events. In Bible study within the anti-Nazi Resistance there was an edification of the new, or renewed, life to which human beings are incessantly called by God—or, if you wish it put differently, by the event of their own humanity in this world—and there was, thus, a witness which is veritably incorporated into the original biblical witness.   —*EC*, 117–18, 120

MAMMON SACRAMENTED

In 1954 Jacques Ellul published a little book titled Money and
Power,[22] *in which he argued that because money is the realm of
the sacred in modern culture, enshrining the logic of exchange,
to give it away liturgically in the offering not only violated its
sacred logic but thereby desacralized it, freeing humans from its
powerly bondage. Because Ellul's book was not translated into
English until just before Stringfellow's death, it could not have
directly influenced his writing of what follows. It remains an
instance of their inspired parallelism. Here Stringfellow makes
exactly the same point in the language of idolatry and sacrament.*

Idolatry, whatever its object, represents the enshrinement of
any other person or thing in the very place of God. Idolatry
embraces some person or thing, instead of God, as the source
and rationalization of the moral significance of this life in the
world for, at least, the idolater, though not, necessarily, for anybody else at all. Thus human beings, as idolaters, have from time
to time worshiped stones and snakes and suns and fire and thun-
der, their own dreams and hallucinations, images of themselves
and of their progenitors; they have had all the Caesars, ancient
and modern, as idols; others have fancied sex as a god; for many,
race is an idol; some worship science, some idolize superstition.
Within that pantheon, money is a most conspicuous idol.

The idolatry of money means that the moral worth of a person is judged in terms of the amount of money possessed or
controlled. The acquisition and accumulation of money in itself
is considered evidence of virtue. It does not so much matter how
money is acquired—by work or invention, through inheritance
or marriage, by luck or theft—the main thing is to get some. The
corollary of this doctrine, of course, is that those without money
are morally inferior—weak, or indolent, or otherwise less worthy as human beings. Where money is an idol, to be poor is a sin.

---

22. Jacques Ellul, *L'Homme et l'argent* (Lausanne: Presses Bibliques
Universitaires, 1954). English translation, *Money and Power* (Downers
Grove, Ill.: Inter-varsity Press, 1984).

This is an obscene idea of justification, directly in contradiction with the Bible. In the Gospel none are saved by any works of their own, least of all by the mere acquisition of money. In fact, the New Testament is redundant in citing the possession of riches as an impediment to salvation when money is regarded idolatrously. At the same time, the notion of justification by acquisition of money is empirically absurd, for it oversimplifies the relationship of the prosperous and the poor and overlooks the dependence of the rich upon the poor for their wealth. In this world human beings live at each other's expense, and the affluence of the few is proximately related to, and supported by, the poverty of the many.

This interdependence of rich and poor is something Americans are tempted to overlook, since so many Americans are in fact prosperous, but it is true today as it was in earlier times: the vast multitudes of people on the face of the earth are consigned to poverty for their whole lives, without any serious prospect whatever of changing their conditions. Their hardships in great measure make possible the comfort of those who are not poor; their poverty maintains the luxury of others; their deprivation purchases the abundance most Americans take for granted.

That leaves prosperous Americans with frightful questions to ask and confront, even in customs or circumstances which are regarded as trivial or straightforward or settled. Where, for instance, do the profits that enable great corporations to make large contributions to universities and churches and charity come from? Do they come from the servitude of Latin American peasants working plantations on seventy-two-hour weekly shifts for gross annual incomes of less than a hundred dollars? Do they depend upon the availability of black child labor in South Africa and Rhodesia? Are such private beneficences in fact the real earnings of some of the poor of the world?

To affirm that we live in this world at each other's expense is a confession of the truth of the Fall rather than an assertion of economic doctrine or a precise empirical statement. It is not that there is in every transaction a direct one-for-one cause-and-effect relationship, either individually or institutionally, between the lot of the poor and the circumstances of those who are not poor. It is not that the wealthy are wicked or that the fact of malice is implicit in affluence. It is, rather, theologically speaking, that all human and institutional relationships are profoundly distorted and so entangled that no person or principality in this world is innocent of involvement in the existence of all other persons and all institutions. . . .

It is the freedom from idolatry of money that Christ offers the rich young man in the parable. Remember, it is not that money is inherently evil, or that the possession of money as such is sin. The issue for the Christian (and ultimately, for everyone) is whether a person trusts money more than God and comes to rely on money rather than on grace for the assurance of moral significance, both as an individual and in relationship with the whole of humanity.

As a Christian I am aware—with more intimate knowledge and, therefore, with even greater anguish than those outside the church—that the churches in American society nowadays are so much in the position of that rich young man in the parable that they are rarely in a position to preach to prosperous Americans, much less to the needy. Even where the churches are not engaged in deliberate idolatry of money, the overwhelming share of the resources in money and other property inherited by and given to the trust of the churches ends up being utilized just for the upkeep of the ecclesiastical establishment. Appeals are still being made that to give money to the churches is equivalent to giving money to God. Of course anyone who cares to, or who is free to do so, can see through such a claim: it is just a modern—albeit less candid, yet more vulgar—sale of indulgences, an abuse against which there is a venerable history of protest beginning with Jesus Himself when He evicted the money-changers from the temple.

Freedom from idolatry of money, for a Christian, means that money becomes useful only as a sacrament—as a sign of the restoration of life wrought in this world by Christ. The sacramental use of money has little to do with supporting the church after the manner of contributing to conventional charities, and even less with the self-styled stewardship that solicits funds mainly for the maintenance of ecclesiastical salaries and the housekeeping of churchly properties. The church and the church's mission do not represent another charity to be subsidized as a necessary or convenient benevolence, or as a moral obligation, or in order to reassure the prosperous that they are either generous or righteous. Appeals for church support as charity or for maintenance commonly end up abetting the idolatry of money.

Such idolatry is regularly dramatized in the offertory, where it is regarded as "the collection" and as an intermission in the worship of the people of the congregation. Actually, the offertory is integral to the sacramental existence of the church, a way of representing the oblation of the totality of life to God. No more fitting symbol of the involvement of Christians in the everyday life of the world could be imagined, in American society at least, than money, for nearly every relationship in personal and public life is characterized by the obtaining or spending or exchange of money. If then, in worship, human beings offer themselves and all of their decisions, actions, and words to God, it is well that they use money as the witness to that offering. Money is, thus, used sacramentally within the church and not contributed as to some charity or given because the church, as such, has any need of money.

The sacramental use of money in the formal and gathered worship of the church is authenticated—as are all other churchly sacramental practices—in the sacramental use of money in the common life of the world. . . . The charity of Christians, in other words, in the use of money sacramentally—in both the liturgy and in the world—has no serious similarity to conventional charity but is always a specific dramatization of the members of the Body of Christ losing their life in order that the world be given life. For members of the church, therefore, it always implies a particular confession that their money is not their own because their lives are not their own but, by the example of God's own love, belong to the world.

That one's own life belongs to the world, that one's money and possessions, talents and time, influence and wealth, all belong to the whole world is, I trust, why the saints are habitués of poverty and ministers to the outcasts, friends of the humiliated and, commonly, unpopular themselves. Contrary to many legends, the saints are not spooky figures, morally superior, abstentious, pietistic. They are seldom even remembered, much less haloed. In truth, all human beings are called to be saints, but that just means called to be fully human, to be perfect—that is, whole, mature, fulfilled. The saints are simply those men and women who relish the event of life as a gift and who realize that the only way to honor such a gift is to give it away.   —DGS, 40–47

STREET SACRAMENTALS

The street is perhaps an unorthodox place to counsel clients, but whatever the inconveniences of such a practice, there were advantages as well. For one thing the overhead was very low. Moreover, I admit enjoying the freedom of wearing chinos and sneakers while practicing law. I remember one afternoon going to the northern part of East Harlem to visit an old woman who was having difficulties with the welfare authorities. The matter took several hours to settle, and by the time I was returning to East 100th Street, it had turned rather cold. I had gone out in the afternoon, when it was warmer, dressed only in a shirt, chinos, and sneakers, but now that the weather had changed, I was shivering from the cold. About two blocks from my tenement, a boy I knew, who had been loafing on the corner, called out that he wanted to ask me something. As we talked he saw that I was freezing to death and so he took off his jacket and gave it to me to wear. The boy is an addict and I happened to know that the clothes on his back were virtually the only ones he had—he had pawned everything else. Sometimes, when his clothes were being laundered, he would have to stay in the house because he had nothing else to wear, unless he could borrow something from someone. But he saw that I was cold and gave me his jacket. That is what is known as a sacrament.

Practicing law in Harlem has some similarities to small town practice. The differences between the inner city and the outer city induce and enforce an intense localism and immobility. Many of my neighbors, especially women and younger children, seldom left the block. The localism, the attachment to one block, is sanctioned by apprehension about places that are unknown or unfamiliar, but it is also sanctioned by a sense of being unwelcome anywhere but on the block where one lives. I found, for example, that grocery prices were higher generally in the little stores in my immediate neighborhood, and so I used to go five blocks south—across the border and outside of East Harlem—to buy food at a supermarket. Several times I asked women on the block why they did not do the same and thereby save a little money, but the answer was usually that the place where I shopped was "a white man's store," though an additional factor is the relatively easy credit extended by the stores on the block.

The cases which arise in a law practice such as this were usually acutely personal: family squabbles, truancy, desertions, addiction, abandoned children, gang fights, evictions, securing repairs or heat or light from a slum landlord, intervening with the welfare investigators, legitimizing children, stopping repossession of furniture, complaining about police abuse of persons arrested. Legal counseling in such cases is as much a vehicle of pastoral care as it is of the practice of law.

To practice law in Harlem requires more than a professional identification with these kinds of cases. It involves more than knowledgeability about the neighborhood, and something different from just sympathy for the people of the ghetto. Humanitarian idealism is pretentious in Harlem and turns out to be irrelevant. It is, rather, more important to experience the vulnerability of daily life. It is necessary to enter into and live within the ambiguity, and risk the attrition of human existence. In a way, it is even more simple than that: It is just essential to become and to be poor.

I do not say this in a moral sense, but exactly the contrary; I do say it in a theological sense and, therefore, in the most concrete and most practical sense (for unlike philosophic morality, theology deals with the care of God for all in the common life of the world as it actually is now, while morality deals with some ideal life out of this world). As a practical matter, then, it is essential to share life just as it is in a place like Harlem. It is the only way there is to honor the Incarnation.   —MPE, 42–44

A SACRAMENTAL ETHIC

Though the subheading above is Stringfellow's own, neither the words "sacrament" nor "sacramental" appear in this section. This may suggest the way a sacramental ethic "pours itself out" as an incarnational, or as he says at the conclusion, a vocational ethic. Moreover, because it describes an explicitly biblical ethic, Stringfellow may be effectively stressing the traditional connection of Word and sacrament.

On obvious, ominous, urgent fronts, society in America is right now desperately beleaguered by war and the entrenched commerce of war, by ecological corruption and the population problem, by profound racism and urban chaos, by technology and unemployability, by inflation and taxation. And all of these issues are compounded by unaccountability, secrecy, and practiced deception in government, by manifold threats to established authority and intimidating official abuse of the rule of law, by vested intransigence to significant change and primary recourse to violence by agents of conformity and advocates of repression as well as some few professed revolutionaries. If a person looks to Revelation—especially its Babylon passages—as a political as much as theological tract at the time and in the circumstances in which it was uttered, is that of any help now, in this American situation? If, as urged here, the biblical Babylon represents the essential estate of all nations and powers, verified empirically in the moral condition of any nation at any time in history, and if the biblical Jerusalem refers to Christ's Church in her vocation as the holy nation, standing apart from but ministering to the secular powers, how is that edifying to a Christian (or anyone else) who is today an American citizen? How must that concern him in decisions and conduct affecting allegiance to the nation, the claims of civil obedience, assent to prevalent social purposes, response to the pressures for conformity, participation in the response of the pressures for conformity, participation in the rituals of national vanity, rendering honor to the incumbent political authority, the prospects for reform or other change, the efficacy of protest, the tactics of resistance? Again, how does the biblical juxtaposition of Babylon and Jerusalem set a precedent for and inform the lifestyle and witness of the Church of Christ in America now? What do the ethics of biblical politics have to do concretely with the politics of principalities and powers in America now?

To all such queries, biblical politics *categorically* furnishes no answers.

The ethics of biblical politics offers no basis for divining specific, unambiguous, narrow, or ordained solutions for any social issue. Biblical theology does not deduce "the will of God" for political involvement or social action. The Bible—if it is esteemed for its own genius—does not yield "right" or "good" or "true" or "ultimate" answers. The Bible does not do that in seemingly private or personal matters; even less can it be said to do so in politics or institutional life.

This is not to say that biblical people, living on the contemporary scene in America or anywhere else, are thus consigned to holy ambivalence, well-intentioned indecision, or benign negligence in social crisis or public controversy. This does not counsel, comfort, or condone apathy, default, withdrawal, or any type or quietism (which, appearances to the contrary, are forms of political commitment, not options of abstention from politics). This does declare that the biblical witness affords no simplistic moral theology, no pietistic version of social ethics. Folks who yearn

for the supposed reassurance of that kind of ethics can resort to
the nation's civil religion or one of its legion equivalents; they
will find no support or encouragement in the Bible.

The importance of any scheme of ethics boasting answers of
ultimate connotation or asserting the will of God is that time
and history are not truly respected as the context of decision-
making. Instead they are treated in an abstract, fragmented,
selective, or otherwise arbitrary version hung together at most
under some illusory rubric of "progress," or "effectiveness," or
"success." From a biblical vantage point as much as from an
empirical outlook, this means a drastic incapacity to cope with
history as the saga in which death as a moral power claims sovereignty over human beings and nations and all creatures. It
means a failure to recognize time as the epoch of death's worldly
reign, a misapprehension of the ubiquity or fallenness throughout the whole of Creation and, in turn, a blindness to imminent
and recurrent redemptive signs in the everyday life of this world.

Meanwhile, biblically speaking, the singular, straightforward
issue of ethics—and in the elementary topic of politics—*is how
to live humanly during the Fall.* Any viable ethics—which is to
say, any ethics worthy of human attention and practice, any
ethics which manifests and verifies hope—are both individual
and social. It must deal with human decision and action in relation to the other creatures, notably the principalities and powers
in the very midst of the conflict, distortion, alienation, disorientation, chaos, decadence of the Fall. . . .

Let me state the same concern somewhat differently, in the
context of biblical politics. Here the ethical question juxtaposes
the witness of the holy nation—Jerusalem—to the other principalities, institutions, and other nations—as to which Babylon is
a parable. It asks: *How can the Church of Jesus Christ celebrate
human life in society now?*

I hope this manner of expressing the basic concern of social
ethics, as posed biblically in contrast with various nonbibli-
cal or pagan constructions, sufficiently emphasizes the vocational aspect of ethical decision and political action. The ethical

wisdom of human beings cannot, and need not, imitate or pre-empt or displace the will of God, but is magnificently, unabash-edly, and merely human. The ethical discernment of humans cannot anticipate and must not usurp the judgment of God, but is an existential event, an exercise of conscience—transient and fragile. To make such an affirmation and confession involves a radical reverence for the vocation of God and an equally radical acceptance of the vocation to be human. Moreover, it is the dignity of this ethical posture which frees human beings, in their decisions and tactics, to summon the powers and principalities, and similar creatures, to their vocation—the enhancement of human life in society (Gen. 1:20–31; cf. Mark 10:42–43).

—*EC,* 53–55, 57

Church

Once at a conference on Stringfellow in Oxford, a young theologian, Anabaptist no less, accused Stringfellow of lacking a developed ecclesiology. In fact, his theology of the church is not only developed but rich and versatile. The following samples give witness to that richness.

AS CONFESSIONAL PRACTICE:
RESIGNATION

Though it was duplicated on the Parish's Ditto machine, mailed out widely, and eventually adapted to a long passage in My People Is the Enemy, *William Stringfellow's letter of resignation from the East Harlem Protestant Parish has not previously been published. It is long. He was thirty years old at the time, and this may be thought of as one of his earliest ecclesial statements. Because EHPP was the flagship of the renewed urban ministry movement, it could as well be framed as a response to movement as church. It is certainly a call to the corporate practice of biblical theology. The epistle is a fully confessional statement drawing on the Corinthian correspondence and employing texts from both Paul's so-called severe letter and the "letter of reconciliation." Note that here the new Jerusalem image functions to name an idolatry of presumption. Another member of the Parish, George Todd, regarded the letter as Stringfellow's attempt to honor the Group Ministry's discipline of communal accountability.*

Date   April 2, 1958
Re: Resignation
To: The Group Ministry
             East Harlem Protestant Parish
From: William Stringfellow

I hand you my resignation from the group ministry effective April 30, 1958.

I will still live in East Harlem, engage here in law practice, continue to participate in politics in the neighborhood.

The reasons for my resignation elaborate my vocation as a Christian. Really they are a single reason stated variously. As with any member of the church, my own authority as a Christian rests in my loyalty to Jesus Christ: in that is comprehended my responsibility to other Christians and my care for others. I resign now because I understand that this loyalty conflicts with participation in the group ministry as it is still conceived and constituted and as it actually operates from day to day. In such a matter and for the discussion of it, I depend heavily upon the Corinthian Letters, not to make unseemly identifications, but rather to be edified by Paul.

> *I beg of you that when I am present I may not have to show boldness with such confidence as I count on showing against some who suspect us as acting in worldly fashion.* (2 Cor. 10:2)

It will be easy for some of you not to listen—I make it easy for you to do so—but to say instead: "He is too bold and impertinent." Yet the boldness that I have to address you is the same upon which I call every day to witness to Jesus Christ. It is the boldness of Christians which constitutes their evangelism. It is the boldness of obedience to the Lord. It is the boldness of faithful testimony. It is the boldness always required to expose the world to the Gospel, but it is the boldness required also in the church where the church suffers in unfaithfulness. This is to say, it is the boldness of confession of faith, as distinguished from the audacity of preemption of judgment. Judgment for everyone belongs to Jesus Christ, as Christians confess, and, in fact, the boldness of their confession is the very opposite of preemptory judgment. Too bold? I am only bold enough to confess the faith among you, and thereby to call upon you to do the same.

Now some will murmur: "He is not very humble either." If God were not the living God, if God were an abstraction, I would have humility before your different versions. But God is not an abstraction, God is the living God—known to all in Jesus Christ and through Christ is known to all in everything which

God has made—and I am humble to God. Again, if God were
an idol, I would face the imagination which spawned the idol,
I would be humble before that person, though not before the
idol. But God is not anyone's imagination—not Aristotle's nor
Aaron's nor Adam's—but the One in whom and through whom
and for whom all things were created, all things are sustained,
all things are being reconciled, and I fear God. *For although
there may be so-called gods in heaven or on earth—as indeed
there are many "gods" and many "lords"—yet for us there is
one God, the Father, from whom all things and for whom we
exist, and one Lord, Jesus Christ, through whom are all things
and through whom we exist* (1 Cor. 3:5–6). It is not humility
which easily tolerates disregard for God that is to be desired
within the group ministry, it is fear of the Lord.

Even as, I suppose, some will persist: "He is an Episcopalian,
not one of us." But this is utterly unresponsive. Such an evasion points to the estrangement of the group ministry from the
historical church and to the hostility in the group ministry to
the church outside East Harlem. If it were not so, there would
be more experience in the church among members of the group
ministry than there is. If it were not so, there would be a greater
sense of identification among members of the group ministry
with the church through history than there is. If it were not so,
the group ministry, or many members of it, would know more of
the church and remember more of the church and have a keener
responsibility to the church outside the Parish. Nothing is more
debilitating to the emergence of the church in East Harlem than
the ignorance within the group ministry about the reality of the
church elsewhere.

I am an Episcopalian and that points, not in every case but in
my own case, to both experience in the church outside East Harlem and knowledge of the historic church. It points to a sense of
belonging to the church, wherever I happen to be in the world.
It enables a concrete identification not only with Canterbury, so
to speak, but also Colossae. Really it informs me as an heir to
Abraham. I know the constant peril of corruption in the church

but I know that only because I know the reality of the church as a living worshipping congregation. I cannot for the sake of the group ministry forget or deny that knowledge, nor fail, while in any way among you, to uphold it. Indeed it is precisely for your sake that I uphold it and that not only in discourse but in the event of remaining a communicant in the congregation of Holy Trinity Parish, nearby, instead of joining, as some of you have thought I should, a congregation of the East Harlem Protestant Parish.

> *Blessed be the God and Father of our Lord Jesus Christ, the Father of mercies and God of all comfort, who comforts us in all our affliction, so that we may be able to comfort those in any affliction, with the comfort with which we ourselves are comforted by God.* (2 Cor. 1:3–4)

To become a Christian is to have confronted the power of death and to know that the power of God is greater. To become a Christian is to die in Christ: it is really *to die*—to experience in every facet of individuality and in comprehension of every event of personal history the reality of death. A Christian has been exposed already to the total extinction which one day everyone experiences. But it is to die *in Christ*—the event of becoming a Christian is the utter exposure to death and the utter exposure to the triumph of God over death in Jesus Christ. There is nothing theoretical about the Gospel or about the conversion of anyone. It is on the contrary absolutely concrete: Christians— because they have been in the hands of the living God—know from what they have been saved, by whom they have been saved, for what they have been saved. They have died in Christ, now live in Christ: now are freed to participate in the intercession of Christ for the world—now are freed to share the burden of anyone to make known how Christ bears all burdens of everyone—now they are able to comfort those in any affliction with the comfort with which they themselves are comforted by God.

There are no abstract limits to my freedom as a Christian in involvement in the world. *For while we live we are always being*

*given up to death for Jesus' sake, so that the life of Jesus may
be manifest in our mortal flesh* (2 Cor. 4:11). There are limits of
course in time and skill, in personal history and constitution, in
talent and health, in strength and weakness, and I make decisions in my vocation accounting for these. The decision to resign
is such a decision. Insofar as I am able to engage in politics, let
it be the politics of the East Harlem neighborhood. The attrition
of membership in the group ministry greatly inhibits this. It is
not only that in my judgment the group ministry convenes itself
an improvident number of times in the course of even a week,
but that constant attention is required to relationships with individual members of the group ministry. I resign, in short, to be
free to engage in the neighborhood politics rather than continue
to be engaged in group ministry politics.

Moreover, I have long since reported my uneasiness with the
economic discipline of the group ministry. It is not that it is particularly ingenerous; on the contrary it is too generous to be
called a discipline, but the chief issue, at least for myself as a
layman, is that it is a contrived arrangement. The work that I do
as a lawyer is not related to whether or not I eat. The kind or
number of cases I handle does not bear upon my income. In a
community so much afflicted by poverty, I think that to continue
in this arrangement amounts to my abstention from the world—
amounts to a reluctance to share the most primitive risks of life
in the world. So, I resign for that, so that my work is related to
my livelihood, as it is for most human beings.

> *We refuse to practice cunning or to tamper with God's
> word, but by the open statement of the truth we would
> commend ourselves to every man's conscience in the
> sight of God.* (2 Cor. 4:2)

I am persuaded by the mercy of God to be more zealous in
Bible study, to have more diligent access to the Bible, to rely upon
the Bible in my daily life and work. I resign out of my regard for
the Bible, out of my humility before the Bible, out of my need
for the Bible. The group ministry, or some in it, are appallingly

diffident toward the Bible. Where there should be expectancy and vigilance, there is slothfulness and slumber. Those who are most self-serious in, say, the analysis of culture, are more often the dilettantes in Bible study. Those professing condolence for people show mostly indolence for the Bible.

Even when there is a less superficial attention accorded Bible study, the nature of the fundamental disunity of the group ministry is exposed. It is exposed then that some affirm human wisdom and regard not the Bible as God's Word. Heads are filled with notions of truth and ideas of good and interesting hypotheses and strong sentiments and deep feelings and current events—and these are actually asserted to test the Word of God. Do you not know what peril this is? Do you not know that all these things, for all of us, are rather tested by God's Word? *Has not God made foolish the wisdom of the world?* (1 Cor. 1:20).

I count the diffidence apparent in Bible study as the reason for the misapprehension among some in the group ministry about theology. (It would be a therapy if some would read John Bunyan on these matters, especially in *The Pilgrim's Progress* the dialogues of Ignorance and Christian in the Cassell 1903 edition pages 132–34, 153–59). It is supposed that theology is the theory of Christian faith to be executed in action in the world. But theology is not out of this world; it is rather the knowledge of God given to human beings in this world, it is the integration of faith and existence in history, it is the appropriation of the whole experience of human life to faith; it is confession, not speculation; it is existential not ethereal ; it is personal, not propositional, at the same time it is corporate—the knowledge; it is, in short, Scriptural, not non-Scriptural. There is no such thing as being a Christian without having theology. Christians will vary in their articulation, but there is no Christian faith where there is no knowledge of God.

In so saying, of course, I distinguish theology as the confession every Christian makes from theology as a discipline of scholarship in the church. Christians in any congregation need the support and illumination of responsible theological scholarship—but they can be constituted as congregation without it; they can plainly not come into life as a congregation without theology which is confession of faith.

It is not apparent that in the group ministry this has been understood. If it were so, everything would be different! The laity would long since have been admitted to their proper responsibility in the government of the Parish congregations—they would have had effectual voices in calling their ministers—they would have become far more self-supporting. Again, preaching of the Word in the congregation would have been less erratic, more edifying. The liturgy would not be so often extemporaneous and intuitive. There would be more pastoral nurture, and then not only by seminarians nor only in time of emergency. There would be a constant zeal for evangelization among the ministry and the laity. There would be fewer devotees of individual ministers.

I know full well that in none of these last named matters the situation in the Parish or in any of its congregations is unambiguous, either all one way or all the other. What I question is whether indeed they are taken seriously in the group ministry, and for that I used not even to cite my own observations among you, but rather the repeated complaint of one who has been among you far longer than I. Moreover, it is repeatedly said and over and over again the fact that many of you regard the group ministry in a way which usurps the prerogatives of the congregations, in a way which really claims that the ministry is the community of faithful in East Harlem which has outreaches in the congregations and in various other services. It was said, for example, when testimony was made before the Joint Legislative Committee on Narcotic Study that the East Harlem Protestant Parish "is a group ministry of 12 men and women working at the neighborhood level to help people face and work on their own problems." This is more than an imperialistic view of missions, it is in its first part a presumption that the group ministry is a congregation. That presumption explains as well the practice of the group ministry engaging in a group life in policy making, in action in the neighborhood, in religious exercise, in worship independent of the lives of the various congregations. The paradox of the group ministry, as it actually operates here, is that it is the chief and constant threat to the emergence of living congregations among the people of the neighborhood, while at the same time the emergence of some congregations here is the most substantial threat to the group ministry.

Look again at what was said to the Legislative Committee—"to help people face and work on their problems." What social worker would not say the same? What politician does not run on such a claim? What psychiatrist or social engineer or housing project manager or judge or publican does not profess as much? The central Word of the Gospel is more than that, no, it is different from that: it is that the extremity of God's love for human beings is such that God has taken the whole burden of human life, that is, really, the whole burden of the unfaithfulness of humanity to God. This is a Word, my friends, that overturns all problems and all solutions to all problems. This is a relentless Word from which none escape. This is a comprehensive Word in which all good works are confounded. The mercy of God and the judgment of God are the same event so that none of us may accept the grace of God in vain.

> *And, apart from other things, there is the daily pressure upon me of my anxiety for all the churches. Who is weak, and I am not weak? Who is made to fall, and I am not indignant?* (2 Cor. 11:28–29)

Christians are related to each other in a way unique from all other relationships among human beings. Christians are held together in Christ. Christians are constituted as the Body of Christ and this is more than a nice image; it is the substance of their constitution as the church in the world. Christians share an incomparable proximity unknown to others. Now the authority of each Christian in loyalty to Christ is an authority over fellow Christians. It is not a nebulous, nor intangible, nor sentimental authority. It is not wistful. Rather it is an authority concretely expressed in the confirmation of faith by faith.

My own testimony, if it is faithful, is confirmed in the faithfulness of all other Christians and that not only of contemporary Christians but also of all who have been before us in the present age. At the same time that the faith of a Christian finds its confirmation in the faith of the whole church, it finds its examination there. The faithful witness of each Christian tests the faithfulness of all Christians; the faithful confession of all Christians examines the faith of each Christian. This is only to say, of course, that God has integrity, that God deals not erratically with anyone, but faithfully through the ages, so that the testimony of all about God is in every instance in concord. Where there is not that concord there is instead faithfulness and apostasy. Now, therefore, for every Christian there is the constant and felt anxiety for all others who profess and call themselves Christians; there is the anxiety for the whole church; there is the anxiety for all the churches. It is the anxiety for the concord and unity of the church in the world; it is the anxiety for the wholeness and catholicity of the church in the world; it is the anxiety for the purity and fidelity of the church in the world; it is as well an anxiety that is attentive to the vocational disposition of every Christian.

Since God indeed has integrity, the issue is, so to say, the integrity of the church in response to God. And of what does the integrity of the church consist? It is the manifestation in the world of God's accomplishment of reconciliation. And this means in its plainest terms that the integrity of the church is the substance of the concern of Christians for the world. This is literally and radically the case: my own care for the world, my own involvement in East Harlem is comprehended not, so to speak, in the terms of the problems of the East Harlem neighborhood in themselves, but in anxiety for the integrity of the church. Being even more concrete about it, my concern for an addict is not simply informed by his addiction, but is far more informed by the estrangement in East Harlem between Protestants and Roman Catholics. This is, to put it another way, the difference between the Church in the world and the police department;

it should be the difference between the Parish and the Union Settlement; it is the difference between the work of faith and good works.

Within the group ministry I am not persuaded that these very matters are acknowledged, otherwise the group ministry would not be so complacent not only about its internal disunity but about the brokenness of the church everywhere. Otherwise there would be upon the group ministry the daily pressure of anxiety for all the churches. Otherwise the group ministry would find its unity and concord in Christ rather than in the East Harlem culture or in the rejection of "middle class" culture outside East Harlem. Otherwise the locus of unity would be, not the group ministry, but the congregations. Otherwise there would be no beguilement with "nondenominationalism" which regards not the substance of the unity which is given by Christ to His own Body. Otherwise no pompous superstitions would be entertained in the group ministry that the group ministry itself is a "new Jerusalem." The emergence of the church in East Harlem with integrity and a lively conscience about the unity of the whole church, which is also the real concern for the world, could be by the grace of God a real instrument of reformation in the whole church. But first there must be here more than a cultus unity. First the group ministry must understand and bear the burden of anxiety for all churches.

> *You are not restricted by us, but you are restricted by your own affections.* (2 Cor. 6:12)

The substance of faith is reliance upon the sufficiency of God's grace in all things. That is a very great freedom: it makes us free to give up everything to Jesus Christ, to give up all our affections. It means simply that conversion is total, without recourse, without qualification, without reservation, without holding any matter back, without trying to strike a bargain with God. Human beings may come to God without the restriction of any of their affections because God has come to them in a consummate way in Jesus Christ. In Jesus Christ, God comes to human beings without reservation, God comes to everyone whatever sort or condition, and in the event of Jesus Christ all are enabled to come without restriction to God. The sign of dwelling in that freedom in the group ministry will be when all of its members are willing even to give up the group ministry. It is not that it may have ever to actually be given up, though surely in some of its aspects it must be radically altered, in my own judgment. But it is necessary that there be a full freedom to give it up. It is necessary that the only affection of members of the group ministry be for Jesus Christ; it is necessary that members of the group ministry be slaves to Christ and not to the group ministry in fact, not to the group ministry idea, not to themselves as the group ministry.

Is this sedition? If it is, make the most of it! For to be free in Christ is seditious for the world and for all things in the church which are conformed to the world. I am gladly guilty of that. That same sedition upholds the church; that same sedition is loyalty to Christ; of God; it exposes temporizing, where there should be testimony; it assails discord, because we are given concord in Christ; it denies the exclusions from the group ministry, because Christ welcomes all who are faithful; it puts the task of church before the success of group ministry.

I will most gladly spend and be spent for your souls.
(2 Cor. 12:15)

Yet let it be understood among you, and that emphatically, that I resign for your sake, both for the sake of those within the group ministry whom I can confirm and for the sake of those within it whom I cannot do so. I resign to enhance my availability to East Harlem and to the Christians of East Harlem. I resign to be more disposable for the church in East Harlem. That is, I resign to point to the disunity in the group ministry, which is a disunity also manifest among the Parish congregations, and thereby to attest a unity given in Jesus Christ which transcends even the group ministry. I resign not to boast in my own behalf, but as a boast in Jesus Christ. I resign not in anger, but in love, and that specifically for each member of the group ministry, for that love is not fond sentiments—it is not so much psychological as theological—but is either the love which celebrates conversion, which is the love evident among Christians, or else is love which bears evangelism, which is the love of Christians for others.

I resign, thus, not in malice, but in zeal, not for envy, but for edification; not harshly, but hopefully; not with guile, but with realism; not to make gossip, but to be persuasive; not to be stilled, but to be heard the more; not to provoke strife, but to call for real accord; not in self-reliance, but in reliance upon the presence and power of God; not to conserve myself, but to be more fully expended. *Have you been thinking all along that we have been defending ourselves before you? It is in the sight of God that we have been speaking in Christ, and all for your upbuilding, beloved* (2 Cor. 12:19).

> *And what I do I will continue to do, in order to undermine the claim of those who would like to claim that in their boasted mission they work on the same terms as we do.* (2 Cor. 11:12)

AS BODY OF CHRIST

In Jesus Christ there is no chasm between God and the world. Jesus Christ means that God cares extremely, decisively, inclusively, immediately for the ordinary, transient, proud, wonderful, besetting, frivolous, hectic, lusty things of human life. The reconciliation of God and the world in Jesus Christ means that in Christ there is a radical and integral relationship of all human beings and of all things. *In Christ all things are held together* (Col. 1:17b).

The church as the Body of Christ in the world has, shares, manifests, and represents the same radical integrity. All who are in Christ—all members of Christ's Body in the world—know and live in the same integrity in their personal relationships with every other creature in their own, specific personal histories. Existentially and empirically, the reconciliation of the world with God in Jesus Christ establishes a person in unity with both

God and the whole world. The singular life of the Christian is a sacrament—a recall, a representation, an enactment, a communication—of that given actual unity, whether in the gathering of the congregation now and then or whether in the scattering of the members within the daily affairs of the world. To put it mildly, then, it is careless and misleading to speak of the action of God in the world in Christ in terms of "making the Gospel relevant" to the secular. The Body of Christ lives in the world in the unity between God and the world wrought in Christ and, in a sense, the Body of Christ lives in the world *as* the unity of God and the world in Christ.

The Body of Christ lives in the world on behalf of the world, in intercession for the world. In the most esoteric and, even to many clergy and church people, apparently remote and irrelevant image of that life, when a congregation gathers in sacramental worship, the members of the Body are offering the world to God, not for God's sake, not for their own sake, but for the sake of the world, and the members then and there celebrate God's presence in the world, and on behalf of the world, even though the world does not yet discern God's presence. . . .

For lay folk in the church this means that there is no forbidden work. There is no corner of human existence, however degraded or neglected, into which they may not venture; no person, however beleaguered or possessed, whom they may not befriend and represent; no cause, however vain or stupid, in which they may not witness; no risk, however costly or imprudent, which they may not undertake. This intimacy with the world as it is, this particular freedom, this awful innocence toward the world which Christians are given, makes them look like suckers. They look like that to others because they are engaged in the wholesale expenditure of life. They look like that because they are without caution or prudence in preserving their own lives. They look like that because they are not threatened by the power of death either over their own lives or over the rest of the world. They look like that because they are free to give their lives—to die—imminently, today, for the sake of anyone or anything at all, thereby celebrating the One who died for all though none be worthy, not even one (cf. 1 Cor. 12:19).

Christians are not distinguished by their political views, or moral decisions, or habitual conduct, or personal piety, or, least of all, by their churchly activities. Christians are distinguished by their radical esteem for the Incarnation—to use the traditional jargon—by their reverence for the life of God in the whole of creation, even and, in a sense, especially, Creation in the travail of sin.

The characteristic place to find Christians is among their enemies.

The first place to look for Christ is in Hell.

For those ordained by the church for the priesthood, this means that their office and ministry are located at the interstices of the Body of Christ and of the congregations which represent that Body visibly and notoriously in the world. The ministry of the priesthood is a ministry to the members of the Body in their relations to each other, relations consequent to their incredibly diversified ministry within the world. The ministry of the priesthood is one directed to the most sophisticated life of the church, the church, that is, gathered as a congregation in worship, assembled for the exposition and exhibition of the Word of God. This is the ministry addressed to the care and nurture of the members of the Body of Christ for the sake of their several, various, and common uses in the world. This is the ministry serving those people who come out of the world now and then to worship God together and encompass and include in their intercession to God the cares of the world as they know it and are involved in it. This is the ministry of confession in which the task and witness of each member of the Body is heard and related to that of all other members of the Body who are now or who have ever been or, indeed, who are yet to be. This is the ministry which cares for and conserves the tradition of the Church—that is, the continuity and integrity of the Christian mission ever since Pentecost. This is the ministry devoted to the health and holiness of the Body of Christ in the world.   —*PPF,* 40–41, 42–44

AS COMMUNITY

I recognize that one way to construe my affirmations of the communities of East Harlem and Block Island, and of their similar virtues, is as *church*. The life of these communities—as I have known them—resembles the society that the church is called to be in the world. At the least, this is true of East Harlem and true of Block Island at some times. The same rubric explains my seriousness about the circus; the circus often seems to me to bear more characteristics of the church than the professed church can claim. Indeed, much the same can be affirmed concerning *any* society. Every society aspires, no matter how tawdry or ambiguous it is, to be the church. This is just another version, put backwards, of the confession that the church is called to be the exemplary principality in the midst of fallen Creation.

A few years ago, some parents asked me to give confirmation instruction to their children, in the absence of an Episcopal priest on the Island. I agreed, with the bishop's authorization, to do so. I almost immediately lamented that decision when I examined the materials currently being published by the established churches, like the Episcopal Church, for these purposes. The stuff was theologically untrustworthy. The day of the first class I informed the children that we would not be using any curriculum, but in its place we would do some Bible study in the Book of the Acts of the Apostles, because it reports the precedent of the church historically, and because the purpose in the class was to find out what it meant to be a consenting and witnessing member of the church. We would also review the catechism, as it is set forth in the *Book of Common Prayer*, to see if we could make any sense of it. (Oddly, I once had a somewhat similar occasion to become involved in Bible study with some East Harlem adolescents; that experience is related in detail in *Count It All Joy*.) Toward the conclusion of the class, which had ten sessions during which we managed to read the first four chapters of Acts, I asked each of the students—they were all either eleven or twelve years of age—whether or not there was any reason for the church to be on Block Island, in view of what the class had discovered the church to be from reading in Acts. They were unanimous, some rather strenuous, in the opinion that, because the community as a whole acted so much like the church, there was no special cause to have a separate institution on the Island that professed the name *church* (and certainly not four churches). Now Providence, and other places on the mainland, of which they had knowledge almost exclusively via television, was different, they volunteered: Providence really needs the presence of the church.

Later I shared their insights with Anthony. He readily agreed with them, both about Block Island and Providence. I did, too.

Nevertheless, in due course, they were each confirmed in the Episcopal Church. Some have remained on the Island and become involved in the curious little congregation, or para-congregation, that professes to be the Episcopal Church on Block Island. When it was organized, it took the name St. Ann's-by-the-Sea and in due course a small church building, featuring a Sanctuary, was constructed. The congregation is said to have flourished modestly for many years until the Great Hurricane of 1938, which was devastating for Block Island. In that storm, St. Ann's Church literally blew away. Ever since, Island wags have referred to it as St. Ann's-*in*-the-Sea. The congregation remained moribund in the aftermath of this hurricane, which, after all, was officially designated "an act of God."

Then, about a dozen years ago, St. Ann's began to revive. Initially, people—including recent immigrants to the Island like Anthony and myself—gathered as a house church, reciting the daily offices, or, occasionally, antecommunion, doing some Bible study, and discussing the news of the Island and of the world. Once in a while a priest would visit and there would be Holy Communion. Free of the usual parish encumbrances of organization and property, the house church gradually attracted more and more people, and in the summer weeks, it seemed appropriate

to begin to have weekly services with a visiting priest at the site
of the ruins of the building that had been demolished by act of
God in 1938.

That may have been a fatal decision. Since then, the congregation has been canonically recognized as a mission of the
Diocese of Rhode Island, the traditional polity for missions
has been instituted, and, predictably, the sentiment for rebuild-
ing has steadily increased. We do not do Bible study any more;
we do not seriously consider the mission of the church in the
world, including Block Island; we seldom ask any ecumenical
questions. We are into raising money, which we will likely spend
to embellish the social life of Episcopalians and their kindred in
the summer colony. Has anyone ever heard this story about the
church before?

Anthony and I and some few others became dissenters from
the prevailing attitude in St. Ann's-in-the-Sea, with its ecumenical indifference and preoccupation with property and pretense.
We have understood all this to signal the process of radical secularization that the Episcopal Church—in common with the other
"established" churches in America—suffers. There has been a
basic surrender to the culture in which the preservation of the
ecclesiastical institution and fabric *for its own sake* has acquired
a priority that trivializes the Gospel of Jesus Christ and scandal-
izes the Apostolic precedent of the church.   —*SF*, 100–103

AS EVENT

*In the Book of Revelation, Babylon is the image of empire and
Rome is openly juxtaposed with Jerusalem. In* Ethic *Stringfellow
read the former as an image or parable of Rome and empire. He
read the latter as a parable for the church as the exemplary society or "holy nation," living in the midst of the nations and the
other principalities. For him the parable enabled recognition of
the Jerusalem reality as church in our present history.*

But if one bespeaks Jerusalem, as the new or renewed society of
mature humanity, where is this Jerusalem? The answer cannot be

in some spiritualized, spooky, sentimental conception of church. The biblical precedents in the Old Testament witness and in Pentecost are not of some nebulous, ethereal, idealistic, otherworldly, or disembodied church but of a visible, historic community and institution. They signal a new nation incarnating and sacramentalizing human life in society freed from bondage to the power of death. Where, nowadays, in America, is there such a Jerusalem reality in the church?

It requires more bravado than I can muster to respond to this question by identifying *any* of the churches or sects or denominations or ecclesiastical principalities of the American status quo with the Jerusalem aspect of the Church of Christ. In their practical existence, the familiar, inherited churchly institutions here bear little resemblance—even residually—to the church as holy nation. In fact, some American religions falsely impute the biblical vocation of the holy nation to America, in place of the Church of Christ. If Jerusalem and Babylon are each regarded as parables, it is the Babylon image which is most apt for the conventional American churches—along with many other comparable powers within the precincts of Babylon, like the Pentagon (to name a rival bureaucracy), or the Mafia (to mention a rival in wealth), or the Teamsters Union (as an ethical rival). . . .

I do not hereby dismiss categorically the whole of American Christendom. I do not suppose, either, that none of the churches on the American scene have memory of the biblical witness, because some do, notably the immigrant (as contrasted with the indigenous) churches. I do not conclude that no Christians can be found on churchly premises, including those which most blatantly are Babylonian shrines. I am saying that if you look for the Jerusalem reality of church among the established ecclesiastical and churchly bodies, what you will find is chaos. Yet in the very same places, as well as elsewhere, can also be identified and affirmed some congregations and paracongregations, some happenings, some celebrations, some communities, some human beings who do suffer and enjoy the Jerusalem vocation in the midst of the chaos. The bizarre estate of the American churches does not mean, after all, that the Holy Spirit, so militant at Pentecost, has never visited America. Whether secreted within the established churches or detached from them, there lives in America a confessing movement—dynamic and erratic, spontaneous and radical, audacious and immature, committed if not altogether coherent, ecumenically open and often experimental, visible here and there and now and then, but unsettled institutionally, most of all—enacting a fearful hope for human life in society.

A specific instance of the emerging confessing movement in American can be found in the jails and prisons. In many of these, communities of mutual help and social concern have come into being and among some prisoners, an intercessory witness, which is virtually monastic in character. What is taking place within prisons is deeply rooted in and informed by Bible study. The same is true of aspects of the confessing movement evident among young Christians such as the "Post-Americans." The charismatic renewal, immature though it yet may be, must also be comprehended within the reality of a confessing movement, along with some of the house churches or similar gatherings.

I have some hesitation, I must admit candidly, in using any name or term—like "confessing movement"—to refer to manifestations of the Jerusalem vocation of the church. Naming any happening as church tends to diminish the spontaneity and momentary character of the reality of the Jerusalem event in history. Or, to put the same concern differently, while Babylon represents the principality in bondage to death in time—and time is actually a form of that bondage—Jerusalem means the emancipation of human life in society from the rule of death and breaks through time, transcends time, anticipates within time the abolition of time. Thus the integrity or authenticity of the Jerusalem event in common history is always beheld as if it were a singular or momentary or unique happening. To be more concrete about it, if a congregation somewhere comes to life as Jerusalem at some hour, that carries no necessary implications for either the past or the future of that congregation. The

Jerusalem occurrence is sufficient unto itself. There is—then and there—a transfiguration in which the momentous and the great is recognized as trivial, the end of history is revealed as the fulfillment of life here and now, and the whole of creation is beheld as sanctified.   —*EC*, 58, 59–61

AS MOVEMENT I

When William Stringfellow elaborated a list of principalities, he included both churches and movements. That is sobering. The following reflections, the first from the mid-sixties and the second from the early seventies, provide different takes, in distinctive moments, on the relationship of church and movement.

But let Christians remember that integration is not the equivalent of reconciliation. Segregation is a synonym, theologically, for one of the works of death, but integration is not the same thing as freedom from death, even though it may be a process through which some will be emancipated from those apparitions of death which masquerade in racism.

And make no mistake about it. Unwilling as I am to furnish any pretexts for rationalization to anyone who refuses civil rights for all citizens, there are frightening indications of the meddling of death in the civil rights movement, just as it (the more precise pronoun, in Christian orthodoxy, is *he*) does in every other thing.

Death is tempting some to support integration as a convenience to their own justification, as a demonstration of moral rightness and self-righteousness, as a means to purchasing the ease and silence of their own consciences. Death, in other words, is occupied in the civil rights movement luring some to behold integration as an idol, and though it be a more benign idol, subjectively speaking, than segregation or slavery, the most that can be expected by advocates of civil rights—and the worst that can happen, the segregationists can be assured—is that public integration will salvage the nation from the moral suicide of racism. The world will thereby be edified about the American idea of society, but the world will not be saved by so puny a human accomplishment.

There is also the danger both for society and the churches that the involvement of some Christians in the racial crisis will result in the revival of a simplistic social Gospel similar to that which entrapped so many Christians during the social reconstruction in the aftermath of the Depression, in which it was so widely assumed that the issue was the mere existence of evil in its transient and relative sense rather than the real presence of death in this world—even in America.

Meanwhile, let neither the self-conscious nor the de facto white supremists—that is, most white citizens—have any unwarranted pride in the foibles and ambiguities of those within the civil rights movement. Let none of them suppose that death has been preoccupied in tempting integrationists only. They are only too willing to believe that acceptance of what is being forced upon them is an indication of their generosity. An evasion such as this is simply another temptation in the repertoire of death. Death is now encouraging many clergy and laity from the churches to regard the civil rights movement as a parachurch, as a secular movement which has more similarity, reality, and integrity as *church* than the more familiar, conventional, and prosperous bureaucracy called church in the American white Establishment. Unfortunately, those who have this view imitate in their supposed real church the same thing against which they protest in the churches of bourgeois society—a cheap and quick conformity to the world. Those who now regard the civil rights movement as a parachurch suffer from the same kind of delusion as those, for example, who equate laissez-faire capitalism with the Gospel, or who think of Gandhi as a "better Christian" than most professing Christians (whereas he was just a more mature human being than most professing Christians), or who think that God prefers any worldly standard over any other.

The actual church, the Church of Christ, which lives in this history—not to be confused with any status quo in secular existence, including the contemporary denominations and sects which claim the name in their incorporations—exists as a society in this world where human beings already suffer their reconciliation, where they already discern each ingenious assault of death and are yet set free because God's grace is so extravagant and relevant. The church, as such, lives wherever human beings recognize that the only real enemy is death and not something so trivial as their own evil, all the while remembering that their own malice is not thereby erased or discounted. The church is wherever there are no longer any separations in any dimension of creation, whether within one's self, or with others, or with any things, or between and among any of them.

The Church of Christ is, quite literally, the Body of Christ, engaging in His witness in this world. Thus the church is given to the world and established in the world by God, not to offer some religious apologetic for any secular ideas or hopes, however appealing some of them may be. Instead, the church lives now as the new society in the midst of the old, as the reconciled community when in the midst of the old, as the reconciled community when all else is broken and distorted, as the new creation during the era of the Fall, as the example and vindication of life transcending the power of death. The Church of Christ is the prophet and pioneer, actually the herald and foretaste of God's own accomplishment in Christ, confronting every assault and disguise of death, and exposing and overcoming them all within this history, in order to restore men to life here and now.

Hence the vocation of the Church of Christ in the world, in political conflict and social strife, is inherently eschatological. The church is the embassy of the eschaton in the world. The church is the image of what the world is in its essential being. The church is the trustee of the society which the world, not subjected to the power of death, is to be on that last day when the world is fulfilled in all things in God.

To the world as it is, then, the Church of Christ is always, as it were, saying yes and no simultaneously. They are, in fact, the same word, for they each say that the end of the world is its maturing in Christ. It is that maturity of human life in society which the church as the reconciled community foreshadows in this world.

Thus, also, the church is constantly engaged, in and through her actual existence as the new society, in beseeching the end of the world; therefore, the church is always authorized to complain, for the sake of this world, about everything in this world. By the mercy of God, the inherent, invariable, unavoidable, intentional, unrelenting posture of the church in the world is one of radical protest and profound dissent towards the prevailing status quo of secular society, whatever that may be at any given time, however much men boast that theirs is a great society.

—*DGS*, 139–43

AS MOVEMENT II

One of the ironies of our present situation is that everyone—those who are against us as much as those who are for us—assumes that we did something for Daniel Berrigan. We did, gladly, give our hospitality to him, of course, as we have on many other occasions. Still, in this visit, the more significant fact is that Dan did something for us.

Those who followed his interviews and articles and other messages during the months he remained at liberty as a fugitive know that Father Berrigan put increasing emphasis upon the necessity of extemporizing new modes of living as community in America even as the inherited social order—including the churchly institutions—is being exposed as anti-human and becomes manifestly desperate.

Berrigan's witness, though fixed upon Vietnam as the gruesome epitome of death, as a moral power, ruling the nation and literally demoralizing its citizens, transcends the war. While being hunted as if he were a criminal, Berrigan has been expounding, exemplifying, nurturing life: Berrigan has been showing us, and all of us, a more excellent way, as it has previously been named, in which life is constantly being emancipated from death, in which human beings are not awed or cowered by the State, in which there is a hope for a society worthy of human life.

We have no doubt that Dan perseveres in this same task from within the federal penitentiary at Danbury. Indeed, we intuit that his fugitive status during the past four months and his fate now as a captive, if not essential to such a ministry today in America, at the least is a seal of its authenticity and of its authority.

And of its appeal. Daniel Berrigan has not been engaged in a solitary or eccentric witness, but one with which *so* many other persons have identified—from the virtually anonymous ranks of those who have, like Dan and like his brother Philip, suffered prosecution and imprisonments for political reasons, to those who have been driven by conscience into exile from their birthright, to still more, like ourselves—that, in truth, an astonishing ecumenical community has been called into being. It is, we suppose, too much to expect official comprehension of this reality by the authorities of the State, or by others imbued with a conspiratorial mentality, or, for that matter, by any pharisees, or by very many of the hierarchs. Nevertheless, there it is—Father Berrigan has been, and remains, in our midst improvising the church.

All of this is related, obviously, to the specific jeopardy which Berrigan has borne as a defendant, as a convicted felon, as a fugitive, and which he now bears, in solidarity with so many others, as a prisoner. Yet the jeopardy does not attach to him alone, as he knows, and he has not been and is not alone in bearing it. His particular jeopardy symbolizes and represents—it, practically speaking, sacramentalizes—a common jeopardy threatening all citizens who do not conform, who will not lapse into silence, who refuse to acquiesce to the totalitarianization of the nation, and who, thus, decline to resign as human beings.

"A community of resistance" it has been called. Father Berrigan baptized it "a community of risk." Some speak of it as an emergent "confessing movement," in that way invoking a previous experience of Christians and others in the days of the Nazi totalitarianism. We are ready to testify that there is, in America, now, a community of resurrection, sharing a common jeopardy—death—in order to live in a common hope as human beings.   —*ST*, 112–13

AS PRINCIPALITY

Sometimes the church dishonors the freedom which God has given it by supposing that the public freedom which the nation accords the institutional existence of the church is essential to the proclamation of the Gospel and its service and witness in the world. Sometimes the church yields or gravely imperils its integrity as the church by becoming the handmaiden of the ruling principalities of race, class, or commerce. At other times the church becomes so preoccupied with the maintenance and preservation of its own institutional life that it too becomes a principality. Within American Protestantism, where the church is radically divided into sects and denominations, this last situation is most acute and apparent.

When churches are principalities they bear the marks essential and familiar to all other principalities of an institutional and ideological character. The moral principle which governs their internal life, like that which governs a corporation or university, is the survival of the institution. To this primary consideration, all else must be sacrificed or compromised.

Churches and church bodies may be principalities in a variety of forms. A single congregation or parish may be a principality. Or a great denominational headquarters may be one. The tradition of a given church, in much the same way as in society, may rule as a principality. The image of a church leader or ecclesiastical authority may be a principality. Committees, commissions, and councils that burgeon into vast bureaucracies may be principalities. In all these situations the churchly principality invites the world to serve its own preservation and prosperity, seeks and needs the service of men for its own survival, and, indeed, demands that men regard it as an idol.

The demonic character of a churchly principality cannot be hidden by the simple retention of some of the condiments of the Christian faith. Thus, much of what is now discussed and practiced in the American churches as the witness of the church does not really pertain to the witness of the church to the life and action of God in the world, but rather to the witness of the church to itself as churchly institution. And while there may be a legitimate witness to the church as Christ's Body, service to the institution is not synonymous with it and certainly not synonymous with witness to the Word of God.

In some times and places, the churchly institutions make extravagant demands of homage and service both upon human beings and other principalities. For example, in some societies, including some regions of this country where a particular sect or denomination has achieved such political and economic power that it dominates the government, the State may be required to defend its property, safety, and even its doctrines. Apart from such local exceptions, however, the churchly principalities do not have that much dignity vis-à-vis other principalities, although they still exist and can be identified in American life.

Such churchly principalities stifle and suppress Christians who resist putting the institutional self-interest before their freedom in the Gospel. One might cite dozens of specific cases of this. I mention only one here to illustrate the problem, because I know at first hand the extraordinary measures that were taken to conceal what happened. The incident involved a clergyman who had worked for some years, mainly in the Deep South of which he was a native, in the racial crisis. This Christian minister recognized that more was involved theologically and confessionally in the racial crisis than recitations of humanistic ethics and assurances of good intentions, or programs of study about "race relations" and the annual observances of Race Relations Sunday. He therefore used his access to white Southerners to preach the Gospel, to go among his native people as an evangelist and apologist. He understood that as a person has his own life renewed in the life of Christ he is set free to love himself and *all* human beings. He knew that the reconciliation wrought by Christ encompasses the only real reconciliation there can be among those of different races. As he saw it, the racial crisis had more to do with the meaning of Christ for human life than all of these programs and pronouncements and conferences and committees. He thought that race also had something to do with the renewal of the church.

But it came to pass that he was summoned by his superiors and colleagues within the churchly institution and told that he had become a great embarrassment to the institution because some people were beginning to think that the institution had no "positive program" in "race relations"; and, besides, the institution could not afford to have someone on its staff who was just going here and there preaching the Gospel. There had to be a "positive program"; in other words, the priority in the preacher's work had to be that which would gain recognition for the institution, enhance its prestige, and prove that it was doing something. Homage to the churchly principality had to come before esteem for the Gospel.

One of the serious issues for laity when confronted with the claims of such a churchly principality for homage and service is that the laity who do enter into such service are dissipated in it and are thereby diverted from their witness to and against the principalities of commerce and politics to which they are exposed in their daily life and work. They are dissipated not because the struggle against a churchly principality is any different as witness than that against any other principality, but because they will find no courage for the struggle if all that they know or are involved in, in the name of the church, is some churchly principality.

It is worth repeating that to discern that there are churchly principalities such as these mentioned does not in itself reflect upon the sincerity or motives of any person related to such institutions. Rather, it is to recognize that this is, after all, a fallen world, and church institutions are not exempt from the fall, though there be another sense in which the church is free from the bondage to death which characterizes the fall. It is important to note also that on the part of many who are privy to the churchly principalities there is a certain naïveté about their personal capability to change and reform the institution. Indeed, the void in Protestant moral theology in accounting for and treating the principalities and powers is nowhere better illustrated than in situations where the notion continues to prevail among church bureaucrats that they control the institution; whereas, in truth, the principality claims them as slaves.

This does not mean that Christians should be loath to work in churchly institutions, but it does mean that those who do should be aware of the reality which confronts them and should not be romantic about it because the principality bears the name "church." Above all, they should be prepared to stomach the conflict which will surely accompany their use of the freedom from idolatry of even churchly principalities which Christ has secured.   —*FO*, 95–99

AS HOLY NATION

Let it be said that when I name the church, I do not have in mind some idealized church, or some disembodied or uninstitutionalized church, or just an aggregate of individuals. I mean the church in history, the church constituted and precedented in history at Pentecost, the church which is an organic reality: visible as a community, institutionalized as a society. I refer to the church as a new household or to the church as congregation. Most concretely, I name the church as the holy nation.

The church which is the holy nation is not metaphorical, but it is the church called into being at Pentecost: the church which is the new Israel of God in the world; the church which is both progeny of the biblical tradition of Zion and pioneer of the Kingdom of God; the church which is the exemplary nation juxtaposed to all the other nations; the church which as a principality and institution transcends the bondage to death in the midst of fallen creation; the church which presents and represents in its corporate life creation restored in celebration of the

Word of God; the church in which the vocation of worship and advocacy signifies the renewed vocation of every creature; the church which anticipates the imminent and prompt redemption of all of life.

The church's calling as the holy nation has been profoundly distorted since Pentecost, and, manifestly, especially so under the aegis of the Constantinian détente with the rulers and regimes of the present age. Insofar as there was in the fourth century definite incentive to enter that comity in order to alleviate persecution, the purpose remains unaccomplished. If Christians have been spared the savagery of beasts or if the more notorious vulgarities of emperor worship have been abated, other forms of persecution have succeeded and the hostility of demonic principalities and powers toward the church has not diminished. By the twentieth century, the enmity of the power of death toward the church had come to be enacted in the grandiose idolatry of the destiny of British colonial imperialism, or in the brutal devastation of the church following upon the Soviet Revolution, or in the ruthless Nazi usurpation of the church in the name of "Germanizing" or "purifying" Christianity so as to have this accomplice in the pursuit and in the incineration of the Jews.

Meanwhile, in America, the pluralism of religions and the multiplicity of denominations have abetted the inception of civil religion, which has assorted versions, but the major thrust of which imputes a unique moral status to the nation, a divine endorsement for America, which, in its most radical composition, disappropriates the vocation of church as the holy nation.

Thus the church becomes confined, for the most part, to the sanctuary, and is assigned to either political silence or to banal acquiescence. Political authority in America has sanctioned this accommodation principally by the economic rewards it bestows upon the church. The tax privilege, for example, to which the church has acceded, has been a practically conclusive inhibition to the church's political intervention save where it consists of

applause for the nation's cause. Furthermore, the tax preference or political subsidy the church has so long received has
enabled, perhaps more than anything else, the accrual of enormous, if unseemly, wealth. In the American comity, the church
has gained so huge a propertied interest that its existence has
become overwhelmingly committed to the management of property and the maintenance of the ecclesiastical fabric which that
property affords. It is a sign certainly of the demonic in institutional life where the survival of the principality is the dominant morality. That mark is evident in very many professed
churches in America. I cannot imagine any other way, at this
point, to free the church to recover its vocation as the exemplary principality or holy nation, than by notorious acts of
disavowal of this traffic with political authority. The church in
America needs to divest property, not hoard it any longer and,
as part of that I urge renunciation of the tax privilege so that
the church could be freed to practice tax resistance. If that portends direct collision with political authority and involves such
risks as official confiscation of church properties—which it
does—then my only response is that it promises a way of con-
solidating losses.

The suppression of the comprehension of the church as the
holy nation or as the priest among the nations, whether in America or elsewhere, cause, I think, the importance of the dispersion of the church to be minimized or even overlooked. Yet it is
impossible to contemplate the nationhood of the church without retaining the sense of the eschatological imminence that has
been previously discussed. The imminence is conveyed where
the church lives in dispersion throughout the world, confronting
every nation and tribe, tongue and culture as an embassy of the
Kingdom. Such dispersion is, on one hand, incompatible with
the Constantinian ethos, but, on the other, it verifies the truly
ecumenical reality of the church in this world.

More than that, the dispersion inherent in the church's identity as the priest of nations and forerunner of the Kingdom is, I
believe, temporal as much as spatial. The church is dispersed in

space and thus indulges no dependency upon particular nations or regimes of nations but by its presence disrupts every nation and every regime. The church also remains dispersed in time, forebearing to become vested in a specific institutional mode indefinitely, or as if in perpetuity, but the event of the church constantly, repeatedly fractures time. That is to say, the church as institution or nation is, first of all, an event of the moment, gathered here or there, but that does not predetermine whether or how the church will appear again. The church is episodic in history; the church lives in imminence so that the church has no permanent locale or organization which predicates its authenticity as the church. This may seem a hectic doctrine of the church to the Constantinian mentality. It is. But it is so because it suggests the necessity of breaking away from Constantinian indoctrination in order to affirm the poise of the church awaiting the second advent of Jesus Christ.   —CO,102–5

AS CONFESSIONAL PRACTICE:
A NEW BARMEN?

In May of 1934, a gathering of German Christians in Barmen, Germany, signed and promulgated a confession of faith, which effectively separated itself from the German Evangelical Church and founded the "Confessing Church" or "confessing movement," which became an ecclesial locus of resistance to Nazism. Though Hitler's name was not mentioned, the embrace of following Jesus Christ as Lord and no other set the course. Dietrich Bonhoeffer was among the signers, and he eventually became head of the church's underground seminary at Finkenwalde. In the early 1970s in the United States there was an active discussion as to whether the time was right for something similar. Stringfellow was himself considering the prospects of an underground seminary and here he weighs the issues for a public confessional document.

The consideration of a question such as *do we need a new Barmen Declaration?* or *do Americans now need a Barmen Declaration?*

at once discloses how history is comprehended. The very way the issue is framed furnishes temptation to suppose that history repeats itself in an eventful manner, so that the current American political circumstances are beheld as constituting a recurrence of those in Germany forty years ago and are, in turn, thought to warrant a response analogous to that of the Barmen Confession.

To succumb to this temptation stereotypes history. It reduces history to redundancy. It represents a modified predestinarianism that deprives creatures—both persons and principalities—of responsibility for decisions and actions at the same time that it narrows and ridicules the militant judgment of God in history. As a conception of history it is categorically unbiblical and, furthermore, it is dull.

For all of that, the present American crisis is sufficiently bewildering to entice many citizens to treat history in just such a simplistic, imitative manner. In this vein, Nixon is compared with Hitler; Amerika is named fascist; Watergate is equated with the Reichstag fire.

I reject this view of history as false, misleading, escapist. I esteem history as ambiguous, versatile, dynamic.

I do not imply that there are no appropriate comparisons to be ventured or no significant similarities to be noticed. But I find that history "repeats" itself as parable rather than analogue, and that the edifying similarities are topical rather than eventful, having to do with perennial issues embodied in changing circumstances from time to time instead of with any factual duplication transposed from one time to another.

As a practical matter, this means that for some American church people today to recall Barmen and to inquire as to its relevance requires attention as much to situational differences and analytical distinctions as to any apparent similarities.

Or—to put this concern in other words—we must not address the question of the need for a new Barmen in a way that relieves us of making the decisions we must make. It would be a grandiose paradox to recall the Barmen Confession in a way that abets default on our part in America now. Under this rubric I offer these remarks concerning both the political situation and the church situation in the United States today in reference to the precedent of the Barmen Confession.

One important distinction between Germany in 1934 and America now is that Germany then was arising as a nation from the calamity of defeat in World War I. She was a nation regaining her vanity after the most profound humiliation of her history. She was on the ascendancy (again); indeed, Germany in 1934 was a nation on the verge of blitzkrieg, conquest, plunder. And her hope, fantastic as it may now seem, outreached the glory of triumph in war over enemies who had once subjugated her millennial pretensions of world domination.

The contrast with contemporary America is startling. America is now rapidly losing world preeminence. The nation is in decline in virtually every sense in which such matters are commonly calculated—morally, monetarily, culturally, ideationally, militarily, productively, environmentally. Her power—her superpower—proves preposterous and ineffectual and is more mocked than feared elsewhere in the world. Her vanity is confounded; the popular myths about her destiny are ridiculed and doubted; her citizens are sullen, bemused, despairing, vulnerable.

In 1934 Germans were becoming excited and enthralled with the Nazi ambition for their country, and they were being mobilized in that cause. Americans have lately become demoralized, distracted, apprehensive as to *any* cause—especially that of the nation—except, perhaps the purchase or pursuit of individual safety and survival in the most mundane connotations of those terms.

More concretely, in comparing the Nazi totalitarianism and the totalitarianism that threatens America, there is in the latter official propaganda and heavy deception, but there is not the pervasive ideological ambience that marked the German scene in the thirties. Americans have never been regarded as ideologically sophisticated anyway, but now technology has practically displaced the political function of ideology.

In contrast to the Nazi reality, political authority in America has little need to launch indoctrination or practice much ideological manipulation because the available means, furnished by technology, of transmitting information have transfixing capabilities to paralyze human comprehension. Even the truth can be dispatched in the American technocracy with such acceleration and redundancy that it estops human beings from hearing or understanding it. Or, as another instance, how can the right of privacy be safeguarded and honored in a society where technology has made surveillance, both private and public, cheap and accessible to virtually any institution or person? Does not the technical capability for ubiquitous surveillance of citizens in itself render a constitutional right of privacy quaint?

Related to the displacement of ideology by technology has been the transplantation in America of the long entrenched commercial ethic into politics. Not only surveillance but secrecy, manipulation, fabrication, fraud, espionage—all familiar in business practice for generations—have now become politically commonplace. Rationalizing such tactics is a reverence for property as the rudimentary value in society, taking precedence over human life and justifying any expedient abuse of human beings.

It is the transfer into politics of this ethic—that property bears intrinsic worth and that human beings have moral significance only insofar as it may be imputed to them because of their relationship to property—that occasions remarks like that of John Mitchell, erstwhile attorney general of the United States, that in the Watergate scandal he was innocent of offense since he had not stolen any property. In much the same way Richard Nixon—apparently oblivious to constitutional misdemeanors that involved specific aggressions against persons and that, in principle, mean contempt for all persons living under the American government—has assured citizens that he is not a crook but has earned whatever property he possesses.

In short, the political implementation of the property ethic in a late technocratic society spawns totalitarianism in America in the seventies, as distinguished from the joinder of ideology and national vanity that characterized Germany in the thirties. The assault upon human sanity and conscience would seem no less in the American circumstances than in those in Germany, however, and where some sense of human outrage does survive, some similarities between America today and Germany then begin to emerge.

There are relatively few dissenters and resisters, for one thing, and where they speak and act they suffer defamation and persecution. In recent years in the United States, it is not only political prosecutions, trials, and imprisonments that document this fact but the less visible economic coercions, such as those exerted against students and faculty following the Kent State infanticide, which chiefly accomplished the quietism the campuses have suffered ever since.

There is a kind of psychological dividend for the regime, whether Nazi or American, in this state of affairs. For every person politically prosecuted or conformed by coercion, there are numberless others, geometrically accrued, who are sufficiently intimidated by the fate of the more conspicuous victims to acquiesce. This is, precisely speaking, the secret of such success as totalitarianism anywhere, at anytime, attains.

Not to be, any longer, overlooked is the issue of the pathology of political leaders. In retrospect much significance has been attributed to it in the Nazi emergence in Germany, but it is more the problem to consider this aspect contemporaneously. If Christians—if no one else—were now earnest about the pathology of Richard Nixon as president, I venture, without pretensions toward psychobiography, that they would be attentive to matters peculiarly within the pastoral care and competence of the Christian witness. That is to say, they would be concerned with how guilt becomes arrogant motivation, with how delusive power victimizes a person, with the futility of flagellation, with the reality of truth and the redemptive power that adheres in telling the truth, with healing, with exorcism, with confession, with forgiveness and, indeed, with God's own judgment of persons and nations.

For Germans and Americans, at the center of the profound social changes they both have suffered or suffer is the matter of law and authority. If this issue takes many forms, it nevertheless can be succinctly stated: It is the problem of authority usurping the law, of authority merging with the law, of authority displacing the law, of authority becoming a law unto itself, of unaccountable authority, of the very premise of government becoming the exercise of authority per se, of authority abolishing law and of coercion substituting for order, and of all persons made vulnerable to political aggression.

In this connection Nazism is sometimes represented as a revolution for the German nation. Whether, analytically, that be the case or not, America has been enduring a counterrevolution for the past quarter-century that the Nixon administration has epitomized but did not instigate. It is a counterrevolution with respect to the social ethic of the American Revolution, in which the governing institutions have been usurped or set aside by the power of extraconstitutional agencies (like the CIA, the White House plumbers, the Pentagon, the secret police operations, the industrial-technocratic complex) that have come to function as a secret, second government beyond the reach of public control. It is this that renders the contemporary American political situation chaotic. If there be a sense in which it can be said that Hitler saved Germany from anarchy, it must also be said that Nixon feigns to rule where anarchy has become predominant political reality.

The churchmen who gathered at Barmen made their confession of the Gospel as an exposure of and rebuke to the "doctrinal monstrosities" of Nazism's so-called positive Christianity.

In America we have nothing so definitive or so self-conscious as "positive Christianity" was in Germany in 1934. The American civil religion has grown and has become diffuse and vague. It represents a loose and jumbled collection of memories and myths and other notions permeating the national ethos, and it lacks the coherence and formality that the Nazi version of "positive Christianity" had. Yet this does not imply that the civil religion here is less pernicious or any less hostile to the Gospel. One monstrous doctrine, for example, of American civil religion is the false and uncritical identification of the American churches with incumbent political authority and, beyond that, with the national vanity claiming a unique or divinely named destiny for America.

Associated with this grossly unbiblical view is the redundant assertion of America's moral superiority, as among the nations, commonly said to be verified by war and weapons capabilities, productivity, and consumerism. And this moral pretension, in turn, requires an endless supply of scapegoats and other victims to explain away whatever goes wrong or otherwise detracts from the supposed national preeminence. Thus we are implicated in constant denials of corporate responsibility in society, as in casting upon Lt. Calley the burden of common guilt for the genocide of the Indochina war.

If there are American Christians inclined to utter a new Barmen Declaration, a place to begin is with "doctrinal monstrosities" such as these, which remain virtually unchallenged among the American churches.

Another issue at Barmen sharply contrasts with American circumstances. The Nazis not only had sponsored a widespread propagation of their positive Christianity but had also engaged in blunt ecclesiastical interference, directly subverting the government of the German churches. The effort was organized under a Reichbishop whom the Nazis foisted upon the churches, and by the time of the synod at Barmen more than eight hundred pastors had been ousted from their pulpits by the regime's church administration.

Here there is no similar ecclesiastical meddling—perchance because the churches in America are more innocuous—nor does there need to be. Instead, there is an elaborate American comity by which political domination of the churches is sanctioned by the status of church property holdings. Thus, tax exemption for the churches inhibits a critical political witness by the churches. Thus, a presidential assurance of aid to church-related schools can insure the silence of the ecclesiastical hierarchy on certain public issues. In short, the dependence of the American churches upon property renders the churches so utterly vulnerable to political manipulation as to obviate a more direct ecclesiastical interference.

For all of this, if it is concluded that something like a Barmen Confession is appropriate now in America—and, it must be said, confession of faith is *always* apropos—there remains a question of how such a confession could happen. Who is there to confess? At Barmen the churches at least had a unity and cohesion sufficient to convene a synod that could speak out. The inherited churches here exist in such disarray, such disunity, such incoherence as to supply the inference that they have, as yet, no capability of confession.

Another Barmen Declaration may be timely, but we cannot overlook the fact that the very idea of such a confession is un-American—disruptive of that basic comity thought necessary to the nation's religious and ecclesiastical pluralism. Nor can we gainsay the depth with which it is embedded in the American mentality that anything like a confession of faith is a matter of resolute privacy (which is the reason the content confessed typically affirms "Jesus saves" but not "Jesus Christ is Lord"). On the other hand, a doubt lingers as to whether the so-called social activists from the nation's churches are able to distinguish between some mere political manifesto and a historic confession of the Gospel.

Perhaps the answer to the question about any new Barmen Declaration is to be found in another way altogether. Perhaps the question is answered in what actually happened to those who signed the Barmen Confession. Every one of them was executed, exiled, or imprisoned.

When American church people are ready for such consequences, we will be enabled to confess the faith. Ironically, if we are not able to confess we will certainly suffer the same consequences—ignominiously.[23]

---

23. *Christianity and Crisis*, December 24, 1973, 274–76; see *AKW*, 266–72)

2

In an Age of
Empire and Death

BABYLON AS PARABLE

The failure of conscience in American society among its reputed
leaders, the deep-seated contempt for human life among the
managers of society, the moral deprivation of so-called middle
Americans resembles, as has been observed, the estate described
biblically as "hardness of the heart." This same condition, afflict-
ing both individuals and institutions (including nations) is otherwise designated in the Bible as a form of demonic possession
(Luke 8:9–15; cf. Matt. 16:21–28; Mark 8:14–31, 9:19–25).

If that seems a quaint allusion, more or less meaningless in
modern times, keep in mind that *demonic* refers to death comprehended as a moral reality. Hence, for a person to be "possessed of a demon" means concretely that he is a captive of the
power of death in one or another of the manifestations which
death assumes in history. Physical or mental illnesses are fre-
quent and familiar examples, but the moral impairment of a person (as where the conscience has been retarded or intimidated)
is an instance of demonic possession, too. In a somewhat similar
way, a nation, or any other principality, may be such a dehumanizing influence with respect to human life in society, may be of
such antihuman purpose and policy, may pursue such a course
which so demeans human life and so profits death that it must

be said, analytically as well as metaphorically, that that nation or other principality is in truth governed by the power of death.

The spectacular example, in the earlier part of the twentieth century, of a nation and society and its majority classes and its leaders existing in precisely this condition is, of course, Nazi Germany.

The biblical story of such a realm is the saga of Babylon.

The extraordinary instance in the present time of the same situation in the United States of America.

That is not to say, please remember, that Nazi Germany and emergent contemporary American totalitarianism are identical. There are, unhappily, significant and literally ominous comparisons that are warranted between the two. But there are distinctions of importance too that argue against too hasty or oversimple equation of one with the other. (For one thing, the ideological element so conspicuous of Nazi totalitarianism is, to an appreciable extent, displaced by technological methodism in the gathering American totalitarianism.)

What I do say is that Babylon represents the essential version of the demonic in triumph in a nation. Babylon is thus a parable for Nazi Germany. And Babylon is thus a parable for America. In *that* way, there is an inherent and idiopathic connection between the Nazi estate in the thirties and what is now happening in America.

I do not, by the way, overlook a sense in which the biblical witness in the Babylon material in Revelation may be regarded as an apocalyptic parable having cosmic as well as historic relevance. On the contrary, within the sphere of apocalyptic insight, the Babylon epic bespeaks the moral character of *every* nation and of every other principality which is or which was or which may be. At the moment, however, I am deliberately putting this emphasis in the background, lest anyone embrace it as an excuse to play down or gainsay the specific relevance of Babylon for the contemporary American experience.

The risk in so treating the Babylon adventure is that some will conclude that these times in America are apocalyptic and then hasten on to confuse an American apocalypse with *the Apocalypse*. Well, these are apocalyptic days for America, I believe, but an American apocalypse is not likely to be the terminal event of history. To indulge this confusion is, I think, an inverse and perverse form of the same vanity in which the "American dream" or the popular mythology concerning a unique destiny of the American nation has come to so many, many Americans to mean grandiose visions of paradise found.

Americans of all sorts, of every faction and each generation, have by now suffered enough consequences—which only glorify death—of ridiculous national vanity and of the truly incredible theological naïveté and moral incapacity from which it issues.

My concern is for the exorcism of that vain spirit. My plea is for freedom from this awful naïveté and for healing from this moral flaw. My hope, therefore, as a human being, begins in the truth that America *is* Babylon.   —*EC*, 32–34

TECHNOCRATIC TOTALITARIANISM

Since the Second World War, when technology superseded industrialization as the dominant institutional and ideological power in society, America has been suffering a counter-revolution of extraordinary scope and consequence. One of its most conspicuous features is the proliferation of *extra-constitutional* agencies and authorities which, taking into account their complex social, economic, and political impact, become the effectual regime of the nation, displacing the rule of the inherited governmental institutions and usurping the rule of law as such.

This is a counter-revolution in the classical sense of the term. That is, the effort is the undoing of the political and social ethic of the American Revolution or, at least, of that aspect of the societal ethic of the revolution which embodied a policy which values human life. The ethical origins of the nation can be seen as ambiguous because they contain so much that renders property, as a social ethic, more basic than the concern for human life. It may be argued that technology and the technocracy that it supports are an implementation, in extremely elaborate and sophisticated terms, of the primitive property ethic which was so prominent in the settling and founding of the nation. Whatever the truth about such a proposition, the reality in this past quarter century or so has been the emergence of such a militant technology that the historic tension between the property ethic and the priority of human life has been practically surpassed. The political development of technology has produced a form of government which virtually abolished that familiar tension by its destruction of human rights, its coercion of human life, its domination of human beings; in short, by its undoing of that part of the constitutional fabric which values human life in society. Technology has installed a counter-revolutionary regime—a technocratic totalitarianism—which has set aside, if not literally overturned, the inherited constitutional institutions thereby creating a vested ruling authority outside the law and beyond accountability to people.

I do not want to be indefinite about my meaning: I am referring to the remarkable principalities that have proliferated since the Second World War such as the Pentagon, the CIA, the FBI, and the whole array of secret police and security agencies, as well as the private principalities—the multinational corporations, the conglomerates, and the utilities—which are politically associated with the military, intelligence, and police powers. I am talking about the famous military-industrial-scientific complex which, in its operation as a clandestine second government, is outside the realm of law or accountability to those who are governed or the American Constitution, which has neutralized, obviated, or captivated the publicly designated government.

Hence, I question the accuracy of those who have been saying, in the wake of war and Watergate, that the American political crisis is focused in the "imperial presidency" and that a semblance of democracy might be restored by presidential power. The expansion of presidential power has been largely theatrical and superficial, nourishing the impression that the president governs. In reality, the president's part in policy-making—as is documented by the way in which the budget is determined—has sharply diminished, while the policy initiatives of the Pentagon bureaucracy, the so-called intelligence community, and some of the great corporate powers have fantastically increased. If Vietnam proved nothing else, it proved that the nation is not governed by the constitutional system, that public policy is not wrought in the White House, much less the Congress, and that the president and the presidency as an institution are more in the position of victim or captive of an *ad hoc* ruling technocracy than a political control.

American technocratic totalitarianism is, from the point of view of a constitutional system, inherently lawless. The morality which dominates the functioning of this array of principalities conjoined in the military-industrial-scientific complex is the survival of the principalities. Everything and everyone else is sacrificed to that overwhelming goal. The principalities of technocracy are predatory. If there is some human benefit that arises out of their political ascendancy, it is either incidental or illusory, a means by which people are further enthralled and demeaned. The stereotypical claim—sponsored in one version by the military establishment, in another by the police power— is that human freedom cannot be politically honored because "security" would be jeopardized. In context, "security" can refer to "the national security"—a concept which may have had some validity during the Second World War but, as used today by the military establishment, has deteriorated into a vague, ritualistic term used to intimidate citizens opposed to adventurism, waste, and aggrandizement of the Pentagon's political and economic power. Or, in relation to the escalation of the internal police power, "security" commonly means the protection of official or corporate property, the convenience of technical procedure or routine, or the conditioning of people to exist in fear ("for their own safety") whether or not any empirical basis for fright is warranted. Amidst the multifarious variations of the excuse for "security," the central consequence is the same: the exercise of human rights is removed because it is an impediment to the operation of lawless authority. The same "security" issue was used to justify both the illegality of the war in Indochina and the unconstitutional surveillance and harassment of the thousands of citizens who sought to expose the genocide there.

It is significant that the burden of the anti-war protests, notably that part informed by the conscience of Christians, was both theologically traditional and politically conservative. The official defamations which portrayed the Christian opposition to the war—exemplified by the Berrigan brothers—as a movement of extreme radicalism or perverse rebellion were categorically false. These Christian protesters understood that the war was both criminal and unconstitutional and that it was being waged through illegitimate political authority which Christian people are called in the New Testament to resist. In political terms, the effort was to expose and oppose a lawless counter-revolutionary regime so that the constitutional system might be restored in America—an authentic conservative cause, indeed.

In the light of that, of course, the Christian anti-war protests would have to be considered failures, since the end of combat for Americans has not affected the way in which the nation is ruled. The same lawless authority which administered the war policy with such savagery in Indochina and such deceit in America remains incumbent in the great principalities of the "second government"—the military-industrial-scientific complex—along with every other feature of the totalitarianism of advanced technocracy. The biblical mandate—in the Letter to the Romans no less emphatically than in the Book of Revelation—to resist illegitimate regimes remains as impelling and unequivocal since the end of the war in Southeast Asia as it was at any moment during the open hostilities in Vietnam or the covert warfare in Cambodia and Laos. At the same time, the political effort to put a halt to this counter-revolution wrought by advanced technology and to restore political authority, lawful and accountable to human life through the constitutional system, has become more relevant and compelling than ever because of the endemic temptation to assume that the crisis is over.   —*ID*, 89–93

DEATH AS SOCIAL PURPOSE

Now I am aware that some persons are inhibited from apprehending death as so powerful, so ubiquitous, so important
a moral reality. Within American culture, there is a strenuous
reluctance to admit death even at funerals. To the extent that
death is customarily gainsaid within American society, it is not
surprising that many people have difficulty in conceiving and
speaking of death as a militant moral power as compared to the
manner in which human beings usually think and talk of God.
Indeed, it is an aspect of death's remarkable moral appeal, for
both persons and principalities, that comprehension of death is
so much beclouded. The efficaciousness of death as the preemptive idol in this world is occasioned, in part, by the deceptions
and delusion which induce human beings, and nations, to under-
estimate death or misconstrue death, ignore death, or, even, pretend that death does not exist.

This customary American denial of death as a visceral fact
and the common oversight of death in its social implications
have lately been modified by a growing fascination with the topic
of death. It has surfaced in the so-called counterculture and, at
the same time, in several American subcultures, noticeably those
of elderly citizens, of ghettoized blacks, of prison inmates, and
of servicemen and Vietnam veterans. In these subcultures, the
banishment or abandonment of human beings to loneliness,
isolation, ostracism, impoverishment, unemployability, separation—all of which are social forms of death—has become so
dehumanizing that the victims suffer few illusions about their
consignment to death or to these moral equivalents of death by
disaffected offspring of the white bourgeoisie, the extraordinary
proliferation of occult and pseudo-occult arts, or the escapades
of the drug scene which parody the conventional death rituals
of inherited culture, furnish evidence of specific awareness of the
moral sway of death in the nation.

Still, concerning death, there is much confusion and there are
many timidities; there is little lucidity and there is not too much

coherence, so that the issue must be posed straightforwardly, *what does it mean to recognize death as a moral power?*

Let it be acknowledged that death is a mystery quite inexhaustible, as to which there will forever be more to notice, more to learn, more to say. Yet death is not utterly mysterious, and if, in speaking of death, there seem to me many innuendos, or if ambiguity is heightened, or if the name of death carries multiple allusions or diverse connotations, human beings are not bereft of insight or rendered inarticulate about death. The truth is that human beings are concerned with nothing else but death, though that be seldom realized. Thus in this book, when the name of death is used, I intend that it bear *every* definition and nuance, *every* association and suggestions *every* implication and intuition that *anyone* has *ever* attributed to death, and I intend that the name of death, here, bear all meanings simultaneously and cumulatively.

To be more concrete, death in the sense of biological termination and death as defined in the efforts of the undertakers are both encompassed within the significance of death deemed a moral reality. These ordinary or vulgar designations or descriptions of death by no measure sufficiently explicate death's moral status, however. The name of death refers to clinical death and to biological extinction and includes the event of the undertaker, but, much more than that, the moral reality of death involves death comprehended sociologically and anthropologically, psychologically and psychically, economically and politically, societally and institutionally. Death as a moral power means death as social purpose.

. . . A grotesque example. In domestic society, during the war, death has been so pervasive that few persons have failed to sense death's vitality in America, in the compounding neglect of elementary human needs in shelter and education and work and health and in so much more. In the relentless assaults upon truth and reason and comprehension and conscience, through omnipresent and seemingly omniscient surveillance, by presumption of legal authority, by the charades of secrecy and deception, by the atmosphere created by official babel, by the virtual abolition of credibility as a premise and discipline of government: citizens are left anxious and bewildered and numbed—dehumanized, or morally in a condition of death.

These are some of the ways in which death enshrined as social purpose in the nation can be described in terms of a specific episode in the national experience—the war in Southeast Asia. But do not conclude therefore that this war has happened in a void or is somehow isolated from the rest of the American story. The power of death militant in America is neither unique to this nation (it is common to all nations) nor novel in this war (it is a historic feature of the nation from its origins). Morally, the "search and destroy" missions in Vietnam villages have their context in the genocide practiced since the seventeenth century against American Indians. More immediately, the Indochina war in its most peculiar aspects was foreshadowed at Hiroshima. Hiroshima is the appropriate event and symbol (though others might be chosen) because when Hiroshima happened, that war—the Second World War—strategically and technically had already been won. Hiroshima, thus, represents a decisive triumph of self-serving technological capability joined with military professionalism, a nation's doing something essentially because it can be done. Hiroshima is the momentous, though not the first, instance of policy-making so dominated by technological facility as to be absorbed into the technical process. Hiroshima symbolizes devastation, destruction, obliteration for its own sake. Hiroshima means death as purpose for the nation.

Hiroshima, as moral event, means that the spirit of death was victorious in the Second World War. All that has happened lately in Indochina effectuates, and embellishes, Hiroshima.

—EC, 68–70, 74–75

CHRIST AND THE POWERS OF DEATH

Stringfellow sometimes writes in a series of questions. Those included in this section are from many which he put to Karl

Barth in their conversations at the University of Chicago during the great theologian's American visit in 1962. Stringfellow's book Free in Obedience, *from which the following material on the powers is drawn, may be considered his direct response to their exchange, furthering the conversation.*

> Now in subjecting all things to human beings, God left nothing outside of their control. As it is, we do not yet see everything in subjection to them, but we do see Jesus, who for a little while was made lower than the angels, now crowned with glory and honor because of the suffering of death, so that by the grace of God he might taste death for everyone. (Heb. 2:8b–9, NRSV)

Christ defeats the temptations of worldly power with which death confronts him on Palm Sunday; and in the days immediately following he is delivered to death by one of his disciples, condemned to death by the ruling authorities of the nations of Israel and Rome, and abandoned to death by the rest of his disciples.

Christ is neither delivered nor abandoned by his disciples into the hands of just some evil, envious, or frightened men: he is given over, and he surrenders, to Israel and Rome. And in the encounter of Christ with these powers there is exposed the relationship between Christ and all principalities and powers. The ecclesiastical and civil rulers who accuse, try, condemn, and execute Christ act not essentially for themselves as individuals, but as representatives—indeed, as servants—of the principalities. It is, of course, in the name of these powers that Christ is put on trial. He is accused of subverting and undermining the nation, of threatening the nation's existence, survival, and destiny.

That *this* is the accusation should, by the way, dispose of the legend, so popular in modern treatments of the trial of Christ both in Good Friday sermons and popular secular versions of the event, that Christ is innocent of any offense and tried and condemned because of some corruption or failure or miscarriage of justice. Of the charge against him, Christ is guilty beyond any doubt.

In any case, the significant aspect of the trial is that it is not just an encounter between Christ and some men who were his enemies. The most decisive clash in all history is this one between Christ and the principalities and powers of this world, represented by and symbolized in Israel and Rome.

The understanding of principalities and powers is lost nowadays in the churches, though, I observe, not so much so outside the churches. About a year ago, for example, I was invited to lecture at the Business School of Harvard University; earlier on the same day, I also met informally with some students at the Divinity School. Since graduates of the Business School live their professional lives and work so obviously within the spheres of dominance of great corporate and commercial principalities, I decided to speak there about the meaning of the principalities. Though the Business School students were not especially theologically sophisticated, and certainly none had been theologically trained, they displayed an awareness, intelligence, and insight with respect to what principalities are and what are the issues between principalities and human beings. Yet, when the same matters had been discussed earlier with the divinity students, I found that most of them felt that such terms as "principalities and powers," "ruling authorities," "demons," "world rulers of the present darkness," "angelic powers," and the like—terms so frequently used in the Bible—were archaic imagery having no reference to contemporary realities.

It appears, in other words, to be widely believed in the churches in the United States that the history of redemption is encompassed merely in the saga of relationships between God and human beings. What there is of contemporary Protestant moral theology typically ignores any attempt to account for, identify, explicate, and relate the self to the principalities, although empirically the principalities seem to have an aggressive, in fact possessive, ascendancy in American life. Because the biblical references to principalities and angelic powers are so prominent, and because the powers themselves enjoy such dominance in everyday life, their meaning and significance cannot be left unexamined.

What are principalities and powers? What is their significance in the creation and in the fall? What is their relationship to human sin? How are these powers related to the presence and power of death in history? What is the meaning of the confrontation between Christ and the principalities? Does a Christian have any freedom from their dominion? There can be no serious, realistic, or biblical comprehension of the witness of the church in the world unless such questions as these are raised and pondered.

What Are Principalities?

There is nothing particularly mysterious, superstitious, or imaginary about principalities, despite the contemporary failure to discuss them theologically. The realities to which the biblical terms "principalities and powers" refer are quite familiar to modern society, though they may be called by different names. What the Bible calls "principalities and powers" are called in contemporary language "ideologies," "institutions," and "images."

A principality, whatever its particular form and variety, is a living reality, distinguishable from human and other organic life. It is not made or instituted by human beings, but, as with humans and all creation, made by God for God's own pleasure.

In the biblical understanding of creation, the principalities or angelic powers, together with all other forms of life, are given by God into human dominion and are means through which human beings rejoice in the gift of life by acknowledging and honoring God, who gives life to all and to the whole of creation. The dominion of humanity over the rest of creation, including the angelic powers, means the engagement of human beings in the worship of God as the true, realized, and fulfilled human life and, at the same time and as part of the same event, the commitment by them of all things within their dominion to the very

same worship of God, to the very same actualization of true life
for all things. All persons, all angels, and all things in creation
have origination, integrity, and wholeness of life in the worship
of God.

Principalities as Institutions

The institutional principalities also make claims upon human
beings for idolatrous commitment in that the moral principle
which governs any institution—a great corporation, a government agency, an ecclesiastical organization, a union, utility, or
university—is its own survival. Everything else must finally be
sacrificed to the cause of preserving the institution, and it is
demanded of everyone who lives within its sphere of influence—
officers, executives, employees, members, customers, and students—that they commit themselves to the service of that end,
the survival of the institution.

This relentless demand of the institutional power is often presented in benign forms to a person under the guise that the bondage to the institution benefits the person in some way, but that
does not make the demand any less dehumanizing. I recall, for
example, the situation of a law school classmate of mine. When
he was graduated he accepted a position with one of the great
Wall Street law firms, an institutional power in its own right,
though engaged in serving some of the great corporate principalities. During the summer, before he began work at the firm, he
married. He did not consult or inform his superiors in the firm
about his marriage prior to the event. Later, when he reported
for work and the firm learned that he was now married, he was
told that he should have consulted the employer before marry-
ing, but, since he was married, it would be advisable for him and
his wife to refrain from having any children for at least two or
three years. Furthermore, for the sake of his advancement in the
firm, he should and would want to devote all of his time both in
the office and in his ostensibly personal life to the service of the
firm, and children might interfere with this. In the end, the claim

for service which an institution makes upon human beings is an invitation to surrender their lives in order that the institution be preserved and prosper. It is an invitation to bondage. . . .

It should be recognized that in describing the principalities and powers in terms of the realities which are nowadays called images, institutions, or ideologies no attempt is intended to sharply distinguish the varieties of principalities. Frequently, one will have characteristics of the others. Though according to these descriptions the principality bearing Hitler's name would be called an image, this was, as has been pointed out, a principality which had the attributes of ideological and institutional principalities. For example, every nation is a principality, but it would be ridiculous to identify a nation as just an institutional power, although it is that clearly when one considers it in the sense of the governmental structures in a society. At the same time, the nation is associated with ideological powers and partakes of the nature of them—the American nation with the ideological elements of democracy and capitalism, the Soviet nation with the ideological forces called communism, some of the new nations of Africa and Asia with the ideologies of nationalism, and so on. Sometimes, too, the principality of the nation is, as it were, personified in the image of a ruler. Thus in France, de Gaulle *is*, as he himself seems fond of mentioning, France. And that is not only embodied in the constitutional institutions of the French nation, but in the image of de Gaulle himself.

The Meaning of the Demonic

Like all people and all things, the angelic powers and principalities are fallen and are become demonic powers. "Demonic" does not mean evil; the word refers rather to death, to fallenness. An angelic power in its fallen estate is called a demonic power, because it is a principality existing in the present age in a state of alienation from God, cut off from the life originating in God's life, separated from its own true life and, thus, being in a state of death. In the fall, every human being, every principality, every thing exists in a condition of estrangement from its own life, as well as from the lives of all other human beings, powers, and things. In the fall, the whole of creation is consigned to death.

The separation from life, the bondage to death, the alienation from God which the fall designates is not simply to be accounted for by human sin. The fall is not just the estate in which humans reject God and exalt themselves, as if they were like God. The term does not merely mean the pretensions of human pride. It is all that and something more. The fall is also the awareness of human beings of their estrangement from God, themselves, each other, and all things, and their pathetic search for God or some substitute for God within and outside themselves and each other in the principalities and in the rest of creation. So human beings, in their fallenness, are found sometimes idolizing themselves, sometimes idolizing snakes, bugs, other creatures, or natural phenomena, or sometimes idolizing nation, ideology, race, or one of the other principalities.

The search is pathetic because it is futile. The principalities are themselves consigned to death just as much as the people who worship them. Thus, the idolatry of the demonic powers by humans turns out always to be a worship of death.

To put it another way, that dominion which human beings receive from God over the rest of creation (including their dominion over the principalities) is lost to them in the fall and, as it were, reversed, so that now the principalities exercise dominion over human beings and claim in their own names and for themselves idolatrous worship from human beings. People do not create the principalities nor do they control them; on the contrary, people exist in this world in bondage to the principalities. No one escapes enduring the claims for allegiance and service of the principalities. For a person to live in the state of fallenness is to endure these very claims.

Whatever other distinctions may be made among the various principalities, remember that they are themselves fallen and demonic; the substance of the claim for idolatry which all principalities assert against human life is the same. Concretely, each principality boasts that people will find the meaning and fulfillment of human life in service to the principality and to that which abets its survival; a profound concern for self-survival is the governing morality of every principality. This comes first. To this all other interests must be sacrificed; from this all else, including an individual's life and work, takes its significance; by this is a person judged.

The principalities claim, in other words, sovereignty over human life and history. Therefore, they not only compete and conflict with one another for the possession and domination of the lives of human beings, but they also deny and denounce the sovereignty of God. But do not let the arrogance of the idols conceal this fact: when a principality claims moral pre-eminence in history or over a person's life, it represents an aspiration for salvation from death and a hope that service to the idol will give existence a meaning somehow transcending death.

—*FO*, 49–59, 62–64, 70–73

DEMONIC TACTICS AND THE PREVALENCE OF BABEL

The most comprehensive and definitive account of the principalities is to be found in An Ethic for Christians and Other Aliens in a Strange Land. *Following one chapter outlining the biblical and empirical traits of the powers, Stringfellow offers another suggesting their tactics. What follows is a compression of the latter. A reading of both in their entirety is actually to be commended. Among other things the present summation omits certain details related to the historical moment of the mid-1970s, though any number of contextual hints remain.*

I do not attempt, here, any exhaustive account of the ploys and stratagems of the powers that be. But I do cite some of those most familiar, as a matter of illustration and, moreover, in order to underscore the significance of the verbal element in the tactics which the principalities mount against human beings. That the verbal factor is so prominent among multifarious stratagems is related directly to the fact that it is the human mind which is being contested and that it is human conscience which is being threatened by the demonic. Indeed, I regard the verbal as definitive in all the ploys of the principalities.

The Denial of Truth

A rudimentary claim with which the principalities confront and subvert persons is that truth in the sense of eventful and factual matter does not exist. In the place of truth and appropriating the name of truth are data engineered and manufactured, programmed and propagated by the principality. The truth is usurped and displaced by a self-serving version of events or facts, with whatever selectivity, distortion, falsehood, manipulation, exaggeration, evasion, concoction necessary to maintain the image or enhance the survival or multiply the coercive capacities of the principality. Instead of truth as that may be disclosed empirically, the principality furnishes a story fabricated and prefabricated to suit institutional or ideological or similar vested interests (Rev. 18:23, 20:3, 10). This ploy is commonplace commercially in American merchandising and advertising, and has been for a long time. It has lately been transported into politics and sophisticated for political purposes on a scale and with a persistence that is profoundly ominous for human beings.

What is most significant . . . is, I think, not the doctoring of the truth per se, but the premise of the principalities that truth is nonexistent, that truth is a fiction, that there can be no thorough or fair or comprehensive or detached discovery and chronicle of events, and that any handling of facts is ideologically or institutionally or otherwise tainted . . . Ominous, indeed! This presumption of the principalities that truth does not exist or cannot with some human diligence be uncovered and conscientiously communicated outreaches the subversion of the discipline of journalism. It abolishes any work of scholarship; it renders education—both teaching and learning—partisan and farcical and, in the end, condemns and banishes all uses of human intelligence.

Doublespeak and Overtalk

The preemption of truth with prefabricated, fictionalized versions of facts and events and the usurpation of truth by propaganda and official lies are stratagems of the demonic powers much facilitated by other language contortions or abuses which the principalities and authorities foster. These include heavy euphemism and coded phrases, the inversion of definitions, jargon, hyperbole, misnomer, slogan, argot, shibboleth, cliché. The powers enthrall, delude, and enslave human beings by estopping comprehension with "doublespeak," as Orwell named it.

Orwell's prototype of the phenomenon of doublespeak declares "war is peace." That very example of doublespeak has become by way of the war in Indochina the literal watchword in America, more that a decade before Orwell's doomsday date of 1984. The plethora of doublespeak contrived and uttered because of this war has been fantastic and evidently inexhaustible. Doublespeak has been solemnly pronounced to deceive citizens, not to mention the Congress, about every escalation, every corruption, every wasted appropriation, every casualty report, every abdication of command responsibility and every insubordination, every atrocity of the war. For example, the cliché "winding down the war" has concealed the most deadly acceleration of firepower and destructive capability in the entire history of warfare on this planet.

If the war has furnished innumerable specific instances of the doublespeak ploy, so has American racism. In the sixties, it will be recalled, "violence in the streets" became the slogan for suppression of peaceful black protest. More recently, the so-called busing issue refers to barring black migration to white suburbs and to a presidential pledge of apartheid.

Sometimes doublespeak is overtalk, in which the media themselves so accentuate volume, speed, and redundance that communication is incapacitated (even where the data transmitted may not be false or deceptive). The auditor's mind is so insulted, inundated, or transfixed by verbal and visual technology that it is crippled or immobilized. Thus Americans had been for so long saturated on newscasts by "Vietnam"—"Vietnam"— "Vietnam"—"war"—"war"—"war"—day after day after day that these words, relayed this way, became signals to the head to turn off.

Secrecy and Boasts of Expertise

An aspect of the delusive aura enveloping the demonic powers is the resort to secrecy. Secrecy in politics is dehumanizing per se; political secrecy begets a ruthless paternalism between regime and citizens which disallows human participation in government and renders human beings hapless against manipulation by trick or propaganda or other babel. (The Pentagon Papers document this so far as governmental principalities are concerned; some of the Nader reports on the automobile industry reflect the same issue as do corporate powers.)

Nowadays, Americans are told that secrecy is an indispensable principle of government. Frequently, that claim is embellished by pleas of expertise, that is, the assertion by a principality— like the Pentagon or the CIA or the Kissinger operation—that certain affairs are too sensitive or too complicated for human beings to know about or act upon. In ferocious application this really becomes a boast that bureaucratic routine or computer programming or institutional machinations are superhuman and obviate human abilities to be informed, to think, to decide and to act, thus relegating the person to a role of spectator or acolyte, submissive and subservient to the requirements of the principality. One common and homely example is known to anyone who has ever tried to register a complaint or otherwise secure his rights in relation to principalities like the telephone company or the power company or a credit card outfit only to find himself in correspondence with a machine, the convenience of which takes priority.

Surveillance and Harassment

Ancillary to secrecy in politics and commerce and in other realms is surveillance and the abolition of human privacy. The prevalence of industrial and commercial espionage; the monitoring of shoppers and elevator passengers and similar, now commonplace, so-called security precautions affecting ordinary business; the everyday atmosphere of apprehension in which people have come to live in America—all have worked to enlarge greatly the tolerance of citizens toward political surveillance and the loss of privacy. The kind of open society contemplated by the First Amendment seems impossible—and, what is more ominous, seems undesirable—to very many Americans. So there is little outrage when Senate hearings expose illegal military oversight of civilians or when the unprecedented political espionage at the Watergate is exposed or when education (if that is what it can then still be called) is conducted in so many schools in the presence of the police or other "security" forces.

It is not necessary to dwell upon such contemporary citations, however, because surveillance is a very old ploy of the principalities and not at all an innovation of electronics. One recalls that the purpose of the famous journey to Bethlehem of Joseph and the pregnant Mary was to be enrolled for a special tax applicable only to the Jews. It was not only a means by which the Roman occupiers collected revenue but was also a harassment of potential dissidents and a minute political scrutiny of a captive and oppressed people.

Exaggeration and Deception

In certain situations principalities act or overact so as to engender a belief that their conduct is warranted though no empirical justification exists. It is the audacity of the deceit, the grossness of the falsehood, the sheer excessiveness of the stratagem, the massiveness of the exaggeration which works to gain public credence or acquiescence.

In American merchandising this wantonness has foisted a
huge quantity and a startling array of phony, worthless, dangerous goods and services upon purchasers. What may be more
significant, such commercial deception has been so common, so
widespread, and practiced for such a long time that when the
same techniques are politically appropriated human resistance
has already been made pliable.

This was a weapon of Nazi anti-Semitism. It was the snare
of McCarthyism. This was the devious ploy summoned to
defeat Congressman Jerry Voorhees and, later, Helen Gahagan
Douglas. Thence the Department of Justice inherited it and has
utilized it more often than one cares to recount but, most men-
acingly so far, to obtain public passivity to the unconstitutional
mass arrests in Washington on May Day, 1971.

Cursing and Conjuring

The demonic powers curse human beings who resist them. I
mean the term curse quite literally, as a condemnation to death,
as a damnation.

In earlier times, American Indians were cursed as savages in
order to rationalize genocide. Somewhat similarly, chattel slavery involved cursing blacks as humanly inferior. In more recent
American experience, the most effectual instance of cursing,
probably, has been the official defamation of the Black Panthers
through indictments which conjure images of them as blood-
thirsty black revolutionaries. If, by now, most of these prosecutions have failed and the charges have proved to be false or
frivolous or fantastic, the curse nonetheless survives.

From available reports, the principalities and powers of the
Soviet Union employ cursing and conjuring more radically
and even more recklessly than has yet happened in the United
States. Their procedure involves officially diagnosing certain dissenters as insane and then confining and treating them
accordingly. . . .

Diversion and Demoralization

It must be borne in mind that any effort to designate and describe or illustrate characteristic ploys of the principalities is artificial to the extent that it necessarily abstracts a particular stratagem from the havoc and frenzy within which all the powers exist and act. None of these technics or tactics can be sharply defined; they all overlap, and, moreover, they most commonly can be cited in simultaneous use. The matter is, of course, further compounded by the intense rivalries and apparent collaborations as much as by how many of the powers besiege humans all at once. This is most pertinent to those ploys which have a distracting or diversionary aspect. That is illustrated by the political importance in contemporary American society of commercial sports. Sports engage the attention, time, and energies of multitudes of human beings, diverting them from politics as such and furnishing vicarious activity in substitution for their participation in political struggle. More than that, in circumstances where there is little citizen involvement in the realpolitik of a nation, the persecution and punishment of nonconforming persons becomes itself a form of public spectacle. For the governing authorities, and for citizens who acquiesce to a spectator role, the recent American political prosecutions like those of Angela Davis or Daniel Ellsberg or Philip Berrigan serve the same purpose as the arena events involving lions and Christians in ancient Rome.

This same distracting factor is prominent, obviously, wherever scapegoats are sacrificed for the survival of principalities, whether the scapegoat be an individual (as Stokely Carmichael was for awhile in the sixties, for instance) or a class of persons (as welfare recipients have now become).

The Violence of Babel

There are numberless other diversions convenient to the demonic powers, some of which may be thought of as dividends which accrue when other ploys are at work. The relentlessness of multifarious babel in America, for example, has wrought a fatigue both visceral and intellectual in millions upon millions of Americans. By now truly demoralized, they suffer no conscience and they risk no action. Their human interest in living is narrowed to meager subsisting; their hope for life is no more than avoiding involvement with other humans and a desire that no one will bother them. They have lost any expectations for society; they have no stamina left for confronting the principalities; they are reduced to docility, lassitude, torpor, profound apathy, and default. The demoralization of human beings in this fashion greatly conveniences the totalitarianism of the demonic powers since the need to resort to persecutions or imprisonments is obviated, as the people are already morally captive.

All of these snares and devices of the principalities represent the reality of babel, and babel is that species of violence most militant in the present American circumstances.

Babel means the inversion of language, verbal inflation, libel, rumor, euphemism and coded phrases, rhetorical wantonness, redundancy, hyperbole, such profusion in speech and sound that comprehension is impaired, nonsense, sophistry, jargon, noise, incoherence, a chaos of voices and tongues, falsehood, blasphemy. And, in all of this, babel means violence.

Babylon is the city of babel. The language and liturgies of emperor worship in Imperial Rome were babel. The Nazis practiced babel against the Jews. Babel spawns racism. In 1984, babel is the way advanced technocracy dehumanizes persons. By the 1970s in America, successive regimes had been so captivated by babel that babel had become the means of ruling the nation, the principal form of coercion employed by the governing authorities against human beings.

—*EC*, variously excerpted from 97–107

A CHEERFUL NOTE ON
THE FEAST OF STEPHEN

I consider by the way my books, especially these two just cited [*An Ethic for Christians*, and *Conscience and Obedience*], to be

intrinsically cheerful—glad in the Gospel, informed by hope. . . .
I am, thus, dismayed when I hear reports that some suppose
me pessimistic—a doomsayer of some sort. I attribute this misapprehension of what I write (and do) to the concentration in my
work upon the nature, scope and potency of the demonic in the
common existence of this world affecting the principalities and
powers as well as persons. Albeit a biblical theme, it is not one
which has generally received the attention it merits in the American milieu, either secular or religious. I realize that news of the
power of death may be hard to hear; yet talk of the resurrection
from death is gratuitous or facetious unless or until the fullness
of the reality of the power of death is risked. The goodness of the
good news is relative to the veracity of the bad news. This is why
I often warn people not to be religious—not to be deceived that
any species of pietism has any efficacy whatever against death's
power. And why I remain wary that any version of success which
professed Christians pursue is equivocal, vain, and supercilious.
Or why I plead that religious enthusiasm, whether self-generated
or otherwise induced, not be mistaken for joy.

I believe we are beneficiaries of a hope, which transcends
death now, wrought in the vitality of the Word of God in this
life in this world. The joy of living in that hope is manifest in
patience, steadfastness, resilience, or in the sense of being justified by the sufficiency of the grace of the Word of God.

The Day of Saint Stephen, 1977[24]

---

24. Preface to a book unpublished, "Grieve Not the Holy Spirit," *AKW*,
319–20.

Live Humanly

LIVING IN THE MIDST

In the midst of babel, speak the truth.

Two major blunders based upon false perceptions or delusions have repeatedly been indulged by Christians, as well as other citizens, who have sought to resist official violence and to refute babel. One is the presumption of rationality in the nation's leaders. That presumption is often coupled with the superstition that incumbency in high office, notably in the White House, somehow enhances the faculties of sanity and conscience, whereas the evidence is that occupancy of the presidency, or similar heights, is a pathetically dehumanizing ordeal, harmful to both sanity and conscience. This has become acutely obvious in the past decade during which the idolatry of death as the nation's moral purpose has been so grotesquely magnified in the Indochina war.

It is more accurate, more truthful, to perceive the president as a victim and captive of the principalities and powers. (*The Pentagon Papers* document and detail the process by which presidents and other officials are victimized by demonic powers.) In fact, the captive status of the person occupying the office has by now reached such proportions that the presidency has become a pseudo-monarchy functioning as an elaborate facade for an incipient technocratic totalitarianism. That sham points to the second tactical error: imputing malice to the nation's reputed leaders. If Mr. Nixon or General Westmoreland or John Mitchell, or any of their predecessors or any of their successors, can be said to be wicked men, that is of much less moral significance, or political relevance, than the enthrallment of men such as these with the power of death and their entrapment and enslavement by the powers and principalities in relation to which they nominally have office. The critical question is not whether these "leaders" bear malice, but whether they are captivated and possessed by the violence of babel.

And if they are, if that is what can be discerned, what then? If this nation, and its reputed leaders, be sorely beset so specifically by the demonic, what befits the Christian witness?

In the face of death, live humanly. In the middle of chaos, celebrate the Word. Amidst babel, I repeat, speak the truth. Confront the noise and verbiage and falsehood of death with the truth and potency and efficacy of the Word of God. Know the Word, teach the Word, nurture the Word, preach the Word, define the Word, incarnate the Word, do the Word, live the Word. And more than that, in the Word of God, expose death and all death's works and wiles, rebuke lies, cast out demons, exorcise, cleanse the possessed, raise those who are dead in mind and conscience.

—*EC,* 42–43

FREEDOM IN PLACE—GHETTO

The stairway smelled of piss.

The smells inside the tenement—number 18, 342 East 100th Street, Manhattan—were somewhat more ambiguous. They were a suffocating mixture of rotting food, rancid mattresses, dead rodents, dirt, and the stale odors of human life.

This was to be home. It had been home before: for a family of eight—five kids, three adults. Some of their belongings had been left behind. Some of their life had, too.

The place, altogether, was about 25 × 12 feet, with a wall separating the kitchen section from the rest. In the kitchen was a bathtub, a tiny, rusty sink, a refrigerator that didn't work, and an ancient gas range. In one corner was a toilet with a bowl without a seat. Water dripped perpetually from the box above the bowl.

The other room was filled with beds: two double-decker military cots, and a big ugly convertible sofa. There wasn't room for anything else. The walls and ceilings were mostly holes and patches and peeling paint, sheltering legions of cockroaches.

This was to be my home.

I wondered, for a moment, why.

Then I remembered that this is the sort of place in which most people live, in most of the world, for most of the time. This or something worse.

Then I was home.

It was to Harlem that I came from the Harvard Law School.

I came to Harlem to live, to work there as a lawyer, to take some part in the politics of the neighborhood, to be a layman in the church there.

It is now seven years later.

In what I relate about Harlem, I do not wish to indulge in horror stories, though that would be easy enough to do. Even less do I wish to be analytical—to recite the statistics of poverty or to speculate about the coincidence of poverty with racial segregation or to probe the causes of poverty and racism in America or to venture speculations about how any of the issues of poverty and racism may be somehow resolved. I am by no means sure that in this world such issues can be resolved.

Be cautioned that in what follows I am only a witness, testifying, as accurately as I am able, to what I myself have seen and heard during the time I lived and worked in Harlem.

I am an Anglo-Saxon white man, not a Negro nor a Puerto Rican, and I do not pretend in any sense to speak for the Negroes or the Puerto Ricans of Harlem. They don't need white men to speak for them—they speak for themselves with ample clarity and admirable passion.

I try here only to relate what I see happening in Harlem and what I hear Harlem saying nowadays.

Only that—and a word or two about a terrible premonition I suffer about what lies ahead for all Americans in the harsh days which will come upon the nation in the crisis of racism and poverty in the cities of the land.

Only that—and some word, too, about the theological significance of the hostility between the rich and the poor, and the alienation between the races, and how reconciliation is wrought.

In other words, I seek here only to describe the milieu of my own life and work during the years I have been in Harlem and, from that, to emphasize the moral ambiguity of social policy and legislation which intend to cope with slum housing and delinquency and deteriorated schools and racial discrimination and narcotics traffic and public welfare and unemployability and all the rest which characterize the internal life of urban ghettos.

—*MPE*, 2–4

FREEDOM IN PLACE—ISLAND

Stringfellow titled this section "An Island Is a Ghetto, Too." It makes connections, both in terms of community and colonization, to his experience of place in East Harlem. This is part of a graduation address he delivered to the Island high school. It is hopeful in its appeal to realism.

The consideration of my Island neighbors for my practical well-being in the time immediately after Anthony's death, conveyed to me in part through the episode of learning to drive, caused me to realize how similar, as a community, Block Island is to East Harlem. Superficially, of course, these seem to be very different places—the one still rural, underdeveloped, sparse, and, of course, at sea; the other a penultimate urban scene, ruined, congested, a slum. Yet the similarities, of a substantial character, are striking. Both are essentially villages, with high self-conscious inhabitants. Both nurture strong identities standing over against the rest of the world, Block Island as distinguished from the mainland or America, East Harlem as distinct from the rest of the city outside the ghetto. In both there is astonishing internal communication—grapevines—that informs more or less everyone about more or less everything more or less instantaneously.

Once accepted—though that may be a complex and subtle initiation—a person is safeguarded in many ways simply by being a member of the community. In both an ethic of privacy survives, along with a neighbor ethic sensitive to common needs. In short, according to my experience, both Block Island and East Harlem are communities that function as extended families.

Block Island and East Harlem share many problems, too, not the least being those associated with the economic dependence of each on the rest of American society and the extent to which both are exploited regions within American society. One cannot be optimistic about the future of either place, though I believe one may nonetheless live in hope. Hope means something quite different from optimism—in fact, hope is virtually the opposite of optimism. This is to say, simply, that optimism refers to the capabilities of principalities and human beings, while hope bespeaks the effort of the Word of God in common history. Moreover, that distinction signifies that hope includes realism, while realism undermines of refutes optimism.

One day, while I was loitering at the airport, I overheard a conversation of some people—mainlanders—as they awaited an airplane that was to fly them, as I gathered from what they were saying, into New York City. When the pilot summoned them to board the plane, one of them turned to his companions: "Oh, well," he exclaimed, "back to reality!"

I stifled my impulse to protest his remark, and allowed them all to depart the Island in ignorance. But, at the same time, I thought to myself: *Anyone who has ever received a bill from the Block Island Power Company knows where reality is.*

That visitor's sentiment concerning Block Island bespeaks a very common view among tourists and seasonal residents, and, I observe, it is as much an attitude of many Islanders and year-round folk.

The *real* world is over there—on the mainland—in America. *Reality* is in New York City and in Washington, D.C., and in Providence and Warwick, and (as it most assuredly *is*) in Westerly.

Block Island is somewhere else—in a different dimension of space or time or both. Block Island is like a residue from another century. I know someone here who tells me he came to the Island originally two dozen years ago, because he wanted to live in the eighteenth century and this was the nearest he could come to it. Anthony Towne suffered a somewhat similar exceptional nostalgia; at the least, he withheld his assent to the twentieth century.

The Block Island Chamber of Commerce, I notice, in its literature indulges this same attitude, which it considers, I suppose, an exploitable economic asset, though it refers to the nineteenth century—"a Victorian idyll"—as the ethos in which Block Island is found.

The *Providence Journal-Bulletin* nourishes impressions of this sort by its periodic reports, not about life here, but an image of life here construed as amusing or interesting, eccentric or quaint, when compared to the seriousness, importance, sophistication, and solemnity of mainland culture and society. And if one has noticed how condescending the *Journal-Bulletin* generally is in its stories of Block Island, I trust one will also realize that condescension is a form of exploitation.

Block Island is an escape from the tumult and complexity and congestion and anger and noise and overdevelopment and decay and pollution and motion and waste and babel and competition and fatigue and violence and harassment and conformity and danger of the mass, urbanized and suburbanized, American technocratic regime. Persist in this way of thinking of Block Island and Block Island becomes Fantasy Island.

Yet I say that reality is on Block Island, now, in the twentieth century, not in some facsimile of another era. Block Island is not a mythological realm. As a theologian, I treasure myth and know something about the significance of myth. Myth is helpful when it enables discernment of the truth, but myth is harmful and, even dehumanizing, when it inhibits coping with reality.

The reality of Block Island now is sobering, just as it is for the rest of America and for the rest of the world. That is, in part, because the essential issues here and elsewhere are profoundly similar. If matters vary here in scope compared to the mainland, the difference is compensated for in the intensity with which questions are focused on the Island.

The singularity of issues, as between the mainland and the Island, is most apparent in the imminence of nuclear calamity or apocalyptic scale in which all humanity and, indeed, the whole of Creation, now lives. That calamity is the penultimate shadow impending over everyone and everything. It portends a grotesque consummation of all war, plague, catastrophe, holocaust, and chaos that has ever happened. There are those in high offices who talk pompously of "limited nuclear strikes" and "acceptable risks" of tens of millions of casualties, but I suggest that anyone capable of such bizarre calculations is patently insane—in the old legal meaning of insanity as loss of conscience, or moral disability.

All of us may die as nuclear fatalities before madness has time to implement such wicked games, because the nuclear arms race—in which more than twenty nations are now entered—has a momentum of its own outside the control of technocrats, scientists, military professionals, or, perchance, the direction of governments—much less the influence of ordinary citizens. In any case, Block Island is no escape from nuclear reality; in fact, it is directly within high-priority targeted regions and is utterly vulnerable.

If Block Island is not decimated, its next most probable destiny is its depopulation and disappearance as a full-time community. And if the Island ceases to be a viable society year round and becomes merely a seasonal resort, then that manifestation of Block Island will predictably become, more and more, a façade or a replica—a put-on for the visitors—of the same genre, in principle, as Disneyland, Mystic Seaport, or, should the Island become classy enough, Williamsburg. But Block Island will disappear.

The seasonal commercial trade needs the civilizing basis of an authentic, historic, living community and of a viable year-round economy in order to have integrity, in order to be, humanly speaking, worthwhile, and in order to spare the ethos of the Island from raw exploitation. The threat of the expiration of the winter colony has been evident for some time and has been accentuated lately (since about the time that Block Island was rediscovered by the *New York Times*). Hardy as *we* are, the numbers who live here all year dwindle annually, and the human costs of winter survival become harsher each year.

Some causes of this situation can be identified, though they are not neat and, in reality, they are long-term, mixed up, complex, and interconnected with the demoralization of society on the mainland.

One fact is that Block Island has a desperate balance of payments problem. A huge volume of cash—profits, income, and taxes—is generated each summer on the Island, but most of it leaves the Island and prospers the mainland. A relatively modest amount remains to circulate here in the wintertime, to provide goods and services and jobs so much needed when the resort season ends. Every dollar that does remain here to circulate is actually worth six times as much because it is exchanged that often. In short, the economic relationship between the mainland and the Island is parasitical, and the Island is the victim.

A corollary to this is the Island's overdependence upon imports. At the turn of the century, the Island produced its own food and fuel and energy (or else it did without). If it was not self-sufficient, it was at least self-reliant. And it was able to support not only a thriving resort commerce, but a full-time community with thrice the population that there is now, employed in a diversified economy. Overdependence upon imports, both basic and superfluous, has been convenient, as long as imports were cheap and transport was inexpensive, but those days have passed, long since. If the Island cannot identify indigenous resources of food and fuel and energy, create jobs utilizing the Island's own resources, and begin to export Island products, the Island faces extinction as a year-round economy and community.

In the summer of 1980, an edition of the *Block Island Times*, with its accustomed hyperbole, announced that the Island was in the midst of a great economic boom. The truth is that "boom" is only a balloon—fragile, inflated, and vulnerable to a pinprick or a spark. The single most valuable asset of the Block Island economy is underdevelopment: the natural environment, the open spaces, the beachways, the wetlands, the bluffs, the Island's wild ecology. Such things have become so scarce in America, especially in the Northeast, that access to them becomes expensive here. So land values escalate, the land is bought and sold and developed, and each time that happens, though quick profits are taken, the Island's rudimentary asset is depleted and diminished. Moreover, the expenses of living on the Island increase for everyone as the demand for energy capacity and municipal services rises. That burden falls disproportionately on those who pay this overhead year round. At the same time, the full-time community does not grow because the escalation in land values makes homesteading prohibitive. Block Island is caught in the cyclical kind of development that squanders the future of the Island.

Yet I do not consider this a melancholy message. It is a plea for realism. As I was saying, hope is conceived in the truth, not in myth, fantasy, or fairy tale.   —*SF,* 94–100

DREAMING THE NIGHTMARE

On one of those steaming, stinking, stifling nights that each summer brings to Harlem tenements, I had a dream: *In the dream, I was walking to Harlem on 125th Street, in the broad daylight. I seemed to be the only white man in sight. The passers-by stared at me, ruefully. Then two Negroes stopped me and asked for a light. While I searched my pockets for a match, one of them sank a knife into my belly. I fell. I bled. After a while, I died.*

I woke quickly.

I felt my stomach; there wasn't any blood.

I smoked a cigarette and thought about the dream: *The assault in the dream seemed unprovoked and vicious. The death in the dream seemed useless and, therefore, all the more expensive. The victim in the dream seemed innocent of offense against those* who murdered him. Except, the victim was a white man. The victim was murdered by the black men because he was a white man. The murder was retribution. The motive was revenge.

No white man is innocent.

I am not innocent.

Then I cried.

—MPE, 102

CARING ENOUGH TO WEEP

What follows represents Stringfellow's response to the keynote address at the First National Conference on Religion and Race (Chicago, January 1963) delivered by the great Rabbi Abraham Heschel. The headlines next day were taken, however, by String-fellow, particularly for his scandalous suggestion that the conference was "too little, too late, and too lily white." The other scandals included the references to Malcolm X, his representation of racism as a demon or principality, and his comments on baptism. When he published it in The Witness, *it was represented as a transcript. However, this version is tightly edited, with omissions and even expansions.*

I will try to be brief. In fact, I can say what I have to say to and about this conference in a single sentence. In saying it, I raise no particular questions about the nice intentions, good will, or benign disposition of anybody at the conference, but instead, I make a straightforward plea for realism, for facing and stating the truth about the racial crisis in this country in the South and in the North, in relation to the churches and synagogues of this country.

The truth is—I fear—that this conference is too little, too late, and too lily white.

The truth is that this conference represents a mentality which still assumes that significant initiative in the racial crisis remains with the churches and synagogues of the land. Yet, in fact, the churches and synagogues are by and large and more often than not simply absent from the scenes of the racial crisis in both south and north. They are just, for the most part, not there.

Pronouncements of ecclesiastical authorities do not compensate for this absence or rationalize this absence, nor do they betray an immediate, intimate, firsthand familiarity with the scope, bitterness, complexity, pathology, and emergency of the racial crisis in this country.

Never mind the South—you cannot be very long in any of the Negro ghettoes of the Northern cities without hearing the acrid, mocking, redundant ridicule to which the name of the church is subjected. And then if one sees and reflects upon the extent and ingenuity of segregation and discrimination which still survives and thrives in the churches, there is little to refute the ridicule.

This conference purposes to issue a "Statement of Conscience" about race relations, but the situation in which we are is one in which the very idea of such a statement (such another statement) is obsolete and absurd.

The idea of such a statement—the notion that it amounts to anything at all—is made obsolete by the harsh realities which now emerge among American Negroes and which, now at last in the open, must be faced bluntly and truthfully and with some courage.

This conference, furthermore, represents a mentality which guilefully thinks that the initiative in the racial crisis resides with white folks.

But the initiative has passed in the racial crisis in this country from white to black, and white people are in a position of waiting to respond to whatever initiative comes from the Negroes. While waiting, they might well spend their time thanking God that, as yet, there has not emerged, to lead the Negroes in either North or South, a black General Walker.

Meanwhile, even in the North, perhaps especially there, the estrangement between the races has become almost complete, and, it now becomes the case that almost any public association of Negroes and white becomes suspect—is thought to be a guilty association in which one or the other is somehow selling out to his race.

The spirit which moves and acts in the racial crisis now, especially in the Northern cities, is a spirit of radical hostility and of revenge.

This conference will be protected from this news. This conference will not hear the voices of Malcolm X or even James Baldwin. And the temptation is that by not in fact hearing them the conference will suppose they did not exist.

This conference, finally, represents a mentality which stupidly supposes that there is power and efficacy in individual action. From the point of view of either biblical religion, the monstrous American heresy is in thinking that the whole drama of history takes place between God and human beings. But the truth, biblically and theologically and empirically is quite otherwise: the drama of this history takes place amongst God and human beings and the principalities and powers, the great institutions and ideologies active in the world. It is the corruption and shallowness of humanism which beguiles Jew or Christian into believing that human beings are masters of institution or ideology.

Or, to put it a bit differently, racism is not an evil in human hearts or minds; racism is a principality, a demonic power, a representative, image, and embodiment of death, over which human beings have little or no control, but which works its awful influence over their lives. This is the power with which Jesus Christ was confronted and which, at great and sufficient cost, he overcame.

In other words, the issue here is not equality among humanity, but unity. The issue is not some common spiritual values, not natural law, nor middle axioms. *The issue is baptism.* The issue is the unity of all humankind wrought by God in the life and work of Christ. Baptism is the sacrament of that unity of all people in God.

It is known already, from the life and work of Christ, that the reconciliation which Christ works among us means, among other things, the crucifixion: the design, sequence, structure, drama, and fulfillment of reconciliation is focused upon crucifixion. There is no reason to expect that it will be otherwise in the reconciliation of the races now in such great conflict and estrangement in this country.

But, we were supposed now to be practical: to say what could be done in the American racial crisis.

If you want to do something, the most practical thing I can tell you is: weep.

First of all, care enough to weep.

— *The Witness*, December 21, 1963

BETRAYING ONE'S RACE

I remember . . . being invited more than two years ago to lecture at Columbia on the racial crisis in the city, especially as it pertained to politics. I spoke before an audience of bright, young, white law students. They listened to the lecture, I thought, in a rather sullen way. The burden of the lecture is the burden of this chapter in my book—that one who becomes somehow immersed in some of the visceral and brutal realities of the racial crisis cannot escape a premonition of chaos and imminent disaster.

What I had to report that night was later to become the substance of an article, "Race, Religion and Revenge," published by the *Christian Century* in its issue of February 14, 1962. I gave the speech and said, I trust, what, as nearly as I could figure out as a white person, was and is the truth about the relations between races in the Northern cities. When I finished, there were a lot of comments from the law students. They fell, roughly, into two categories. The first alleged that I had been too harsh and "pessimistic" about the relations between the races in America, and these assertions were documented by the experiences of some of the students themselves, such as the fact that several of them had been exposed to Negroes in New York—taxi drivers and waiters and the like—and had been treated by them, in these situations, with civility and courtesy. After further discussion, it soon became apparent to the students that the casual contacts they had experiences with taxi drivers, elevator operators, waiters, and so on, did not constitute significant, nor even honest and honorable, communication with Negroes in the city. So that line of attack on my paper was abandoned. The line which took its place was much more revealing. They said, in effect, "Well, the trouble with you, Stringfellow, is that you have lived so long among *them* that you have begun to think like *they* do!" Their objection, finally, as far as I could comprehend it, was that I, by living and working those years in Harlem, had somehow ceased to be a white man, or at least had lost the capacity and authority to speak as a white man—through, I suppose, overexposure to Negroes.

If that be the case, let it be.

All this time I had thought that there is something unique about being a human being, something which transcends all of our human differences and diversities, whether of race or age or class or profession or sex or wealth or whatever. And if it must come to pass, in the agonizing tension and fears which characterize the racial crisis, that any white person regards me—or any one of a number of other white people—as a traitor to our race and heritage, *then let that be*. It can only prove how deep and pathetic the estrangement of the races has become in this society, so fond of boasting of its democracy and regard for humanity.

The estrangement *is* almost complete. The proof of that is in the so-called white liberals of the North, as much as, or perhaps more than, in the white segregationists of the South. For these white Northerners, in their professions of liberalism toward the Negroes, suffer from a mentality which still assumes that white people retain the initiative in the racial crisis and that white people have, and should continue to have, the prerogative of determining the pace of the Negro's emancipation and the terms of reception into full citizenship. "What would Negroes want?" they ask, not discerning that this very question embodies the essence of white supremacy, even though perhaps it be a more subtle and more genteel white supremacy than that characteristic of the irrational and crude segregationists of the Deep South.

That question—"What do the Negroes want?"—presupposes that what the Negroes want is for the whites to give, as if, in this society, the whites retain some right to dispense to the Negroes or to anybody else what is theirs by birthright and citizenship and, in truth, by their common humanity. Whites have no authority—legally or morally—to rule upon any demands of Negroes. White people have only to acknowledge and honor at last the same civil and human rights for Negroes that they treasure for themselves.

Yet the condescension among Northern whites is still conspicuous and, one might add, obnoxious. It is, in its own fashion, much more embittering and provocative, much more incitive and die-hard than the rabid, traditional, and sometimes pathological racism of the South. It not only assumes that whites hold the initiative in the resolution of the racial crisis, which is a fantasy, since the initiative has now conclusively passed into the hands of the Negroes, as the past years attest; but it also still treats participation by white citizens in the civil rights struggle as a "good cause"—as a cause that ought to be supported by people or principle and conscience, just as aid to refugees might also be supported with time and money, or just as the work of the United Nations might be upheld with words and occasional actions.

The only thing is that this is no "good cause." Not at least in the sense that refugee assistance or apologetics for the United Nations may be. The Negro revolution is no ordinary charity to which enlightened whites should give their donations and their names. The Negro revolution is, rather, an authentic *revolution*, in which the whole prevailing social order of the nation is being overturned in the face of three hundred years of slavery, segregation, discrimination, and de facto racism throughout the country. Every important institution in the public life of the nation—education, employment, unions, churches, entertainment, housing, politics, commerce, investment, welfare, transportation, public accommodations—is immediately affected by this revolution, and this revolution will not spend its course until every such institution surrenders to its objectives. The only real question is the means by which the inevitable integration of American public life will take place—peaceably or violently, realistically or obstinately, today or tomorrow.

This is no "good cause," in the conventional sense of the term. And to treat it as such—as so many Northern liberals still do— is in itself condescending and stupid. How, then, should white people, especially those in the North, treat this issue?

First of all, they must surrender their prerogatives of decision. *First of all*, they must face the fact that the real decisions determining how the racial crisis will be resolved are for the Negroes to make. *First of all*, they must give up their idea that they have and should continue indefinitely to have the prerogatives of white supremacy. *First*, white people must die to that mentality by suffering the hostility and rejection of Negroes and by risking their lives and the future of this society in the hands of the Negroes.

That is the preface to reconciliation between black and white people. —MPE, 125–29

DISCERNING SIGNS

The gift of discernment is basic to the genius of the biblical lifestyle. Discerning signs has to do with comprehending the remarkable in common happenings, with perceiving the saga of salvation within the era of the Fall. It has to do with the ability to interpret ordinary events in both apocalyptic and eschatological connotations, to see portents of death where others find progress or success but, simultaneously, to behold tokens of the reality of the Resurrection or hope where others are consigned to confusion or despair. Discerning signs does not seek spectacular proofs or await the miraculous, but, rather, it means sensitivity to the Word of God indwelling in all Creation and transfiguring common history, while remaining radically realistic about death's vitality in all that happens.

This gift is elemental to the work of prophetism as that is
known and practiced within the confessing community; indeed,
it is discernment which saves prophecy as a biblical vocation
from either predestinarianism on one hand, or occult prediction
on the other. At the same time, discerning signs is directly related
to the possibility of celebration in a sacramental sense, to the
vitality of the worship of the people and the quality of that worship for coherence and significance as the worship of God rather
than hoax or superstition.

Proximate to the discernment of signs is the discernment of
spirits. This gift enables the people of God to distinguish and
recognize, identify and expose, report and rebuke the power of
death incarnate in nations and institutions or other creatures,
or possessing persons, while they also affirm the Word of God
incarnate in all of life, exemplified preeminently in Jesus Christ.
The discernment of spirits refers to the talent to recognize the
Word of God in this world in principalities and persons despite
the distortion of fallenness or transcending the moral reality of
death permeating everything [sic].

This is the gift which exposes and rebukes idolatry. This is
the gift which confounds and undoes blasphemy. Similar to the
discernment of signs, the discernment of spirits is inherently
political while in practice it has specifically to do with pastoral
care, with healing, with the nurture of human life, and with the
fulfillment of all life.

The powers of discernment are held by Saint Paul to be those
most necessary to the receipt and effectual use of the many other
charismatic gifts (1 Cor. 12). Discernment furnishes the context
for other tasks and functions of the people of God. It safeguards
against covetousness, pride, trick, exploitation, abuse, or dissipation (1 Cor. 13, 14). Moreover, discernment represents the
fulfillment of the promise of Jesus Christ to his disciples that
they would receive authority *and* capability by the Holy Spirit to
address and to serve all humanity (John 15:18–26). Discernment
is bestowed upon them, and those gathered with them, in Pentecost, wherein the church is born and the Jerusalem vocation is

renewed. And discernment is thereafter always evident in practice wherever the church is alive (see Acts 2:14–21).

These are awesome gifts. They have seemed, perchance, all the more so because the powers of discernment are nowadays so seldom invoked, so little practiced, so erratically verified in the demeanor of the conventional American churches. As with other gifts of the Holy Spirit mentioned in the New Testament, discernment of both signs and spirits has somehow become regarded as something rare and unusual—bizarre, even esoteric, occult, or spooky. We admit discernment as an attribute of the primitive church but readily suppose that it has disappeared or has been so diluted in the succession of centuries since the Apostolic era that it can no longer be expected to be apparent in any but the most exceptional circumstances.

I have a quite different view of the gifts of God to the church and to the members of the church. I regard none of the charismatic gifts—least of all discernment—as fantastic or outlandish but, on the contrary, as commonplace and usual marks of the church. Pentecost, in other words, typifies the event of the church, and that not only during the Apostolic period, but thereafter. The manifestation of the multifarious charismatic gifts, including, most particularly, the exercise of the powers of discernment, is definitive of the church. No assembly, institution, or congregation professing to be of the Church of Christ can be regarded seriously in that profession if these powers and works are not evidenced. If today there is hesitance or inhibition in apprehending the practice of discernment within any of the American churches, it is not because the Holy Spirit has begrudged a gift, but, more likely, because there has been too much timidity in practicing discernment. The problem is not want of accessibility to the Holy Spirit, but rather that the gift has been rejected or abandoned. Indeed, as ancient baptismal affirmations declare, discernment is the elementary, common, and ecumenical gift, intrinsic to the authority which every Christian receives, essential to the efficient use of all other charismatic gifts, characteristic of the mature Christian witness in

the present day no less than long ago. There are, of course, risks
of vanity and temptations of abuse in the discernment of signs
and of spirits, as there are with respect to any of the charismatic gifts; but that does not absolve lassitude or excuse indifference or rationalize inaction or condone equivocation. What
chiefly hinders discernment in the contemporary churches is
not so much arrogance as it is ingratitude. It is not that church
people are too proud, but that they are not bold enough; it
is not even very pertinent to this issue that American Christians are apostate, since what is more relevant is that they are
adolescent in biblical faith.

Discernment of spirits and discernment of signs generally
coincide in the same circumstances or appear as particular versions or dimensions or emphases in the same event. Both have
to do with the recognition and exposure of the moral presence
of death in history and with the confrontation of the power of
death with the Word of God. Thus, to follow my own counsel
against timidity in practicing discernment, and to supply concrete examples, I must pose the question: what can the biblical
mind perceive in a society, in America now, overrun with the
violence of babel?   —EC, 138–40

DYING IN TRUTH: THE IMMOLATIONS

*William Stringfellow went to Vietnam early in 1966 en route to a
speaking tour in New Zealand and Australia. Later that year he
published* Dissenter in a Great Society, *from which the following is excerpted. Without a doubt the most thoughtful and lucid
discussion of self-immolation as a nonviolent witness against
war is the conversation between Daniel Berrigan and Thich
Nhat Hahn in* The Raft Is Not the Shore *(Beacon Press, 1975;
Orbis Books, 2001). Berrigan had stood at the bedside of Roger
Laporte, the young Catholic Worker who immolated himself
in 1965 and also preached at his memorial service. Nhat Hahn
knew personally the Buddhist monks and nuns, many of his own
order, who had undertaken the act in Vietnam. Stringfellow's*

attentiveness to Norman Morrison and Alice Herz is remarkable for its timely immediacy and the rare ethical affirmation. Exactly how these conversations nourished one another can at present only be guessed.

The right to protest has taken many forms in American history, but recently in this country there have been several instances of self-immolation—events for which we seem to have no precedent. Five citizens of the United States have—so far—committed suicide by burning their own bodies. Another has recovered, insofar as that is possible, from a clumsy attempt to perform the same act. Whether these examples will be further imitated by the time this is published is difficult to predict.

It is worth recalling that in 1963, at least twelve monks of the zealous political sects of Buddhism in Vietnam died of self-immolation in protest against the corruption, banality, and brutality of the regime of Ngo Dinh Diem. It is also worth remembering that this regime was installed, and for a long time subsidized and sanctioned, by the American government.

Despite the difficulty of making estimates on such matters, I do not recollect that at the time the Buddhist immolations had much impact, one way or the other, upon the sympathies of the American people. There were, of course, those ghastly Technicolor photographs in *Life* of some of the burnings, but I suspect that they were no more offensive to the sensibilities of most Americans than, say, the lurid Technicolor pictures of intestinal surgery which the same periodical has also published. Gory sights do not excite the American conscience.

Besides, the Buddhist immolations happened when Vietnam seemed much farther away than it now does, and Americans were even more desperately ignorant about that beleaguered country than they are today. The Buddhist "barbecues"—as Madame Nhu styled them—could be dismissed with facility by Americans as religious and political fanaticism, the sort of thing which is apt to happen in foreign and unsophisticated places with strange and unpronounceable names.

Actually there is ample evidence, as I learned in Vietnam, that the Buddhist burnings were actions chosen on the basis of a sophisticated ethical and tactical protest aimed at dramatizing the intolerability of the Diem dictatorship. So far as the majority of the South Vietnamese were concerned, this has been government by terrorism, torture, and mayhem, and, so far as the American presence in South Vietnam matters, by manipulation, guile, and obsequiousness.

The immolations were not impetuous acts but carefully staged events; those willing to be burned alive first volunteered, and then some were selected by their peers. Those selected endured pious preparation for their witness in prayer and fasting; they were administered medication to mitigate their agony; and, while burning, they were usually, though not always, successfully, shielded by their brothers from the interference of authorities or onlookers who might interrupt or halt the ritual. In death, the ashes of flesh and bones were carried in procession through the streets and accorded homage in the temples.

The Buddhist sectarians who advocated and practiced immolation as a form of profound social protest in 1963 are said to hold religion and politics to be so intermingled as to be indistinguishable. If their actions are to be regarded as extraordinarily extremist by Americans, it must at least be said of them that they fanaticized their patriotism. There are, after all, many in the United States who esteem *that* as the highest civic virtue, although they are for the most part Birchers and not Buddhists.

From the distance, it appears that the Buddhist immolations were instances of authentic martyrdom, not in the particular sense in which that word is occasionally used in the New Testament and in the subsequent history of the Gospel in the world to refer to some Christian who is put to death by others because he is a Christian, but in the other, ordinary, sense of a life which is surrendered to death in adherence to a cause thought to be of greater moral significance than the life sacrificed. Men may dispute about which causes have a dignity that rationalizes such martyrdom, but in the end this remains in the solitary discretion of the martyred, and nobody else at all has any basis by which to judge such commitment unto death.

What can be said, however, of these American immolations?

Buddhist fanatics in faraway places may burn themselves, but there seems something alien, peculiar, and, indeed, inherently unpatriotic in the self-immolation of an American citizen. But this does not mean that these American examples do not have something important to bespeak. Even if Americans can somehow be pardoned by other human beings for moral indifference to the Buddhist martyrs and the protest against American policy implicit in the Buddhist burnings, these American "barbecues" must not be dismissed too casually.

The impulse has been to explain them away as pathetic, precipitous, private acts, having no significance as social protest.

Thus, from the White House itself, the morning after the Quaker Norman Morrison had set himself ablaze outside the Pentagon, came the gratuitous suggestions that Morrison harbored a morbid personal death wish and had utilized the Vietnam war as an excuse to act out his pathological compulsion to suicide. Surely no citizen would dissent so profoundly from American policy as to burn himself to death right outside Secretary McNamara's window; *ergo*, Morrison must have been insane. Conceivably, Norman Morrison was insane; I do not know. For that matter, neither does anyone else, least of all anyone in the White House or any robots in the Pentagon or any propagandists in the State Department. It remains, however, a far more plausible explanation of Morrison's death that he wanted to surrender his life for a cause which he regarded as of greater moral significance than his own life.

He had, after all, for a long time been involved in other protests against the American military involvement in Vietnam, and it argues against the notion that his was some grisly personal act, that he selected an hour and a location for his immolation certain to attract attention. Maybe Morrison was insane, but it is much more likely that he was, in the same sense as the Buddhists, a martyr.

Much the same thing can be affirmed, I think, about the earliest known American immolation, even though it was not widely publicized nor regarded as of much social significance at the time it took place, March 16, 1965, on a street corner in Detroit. In that first immolation an old woman—eighty-two years of age, Alice Herz by name—ignited herself in protest against the war in Vietnam. She lingered for ten days in agony before she died. In moments of awful lucidity during those days she said that her purpose was not to document "despair but faith in the human spirit." It could, of course, be easily rationalized that such an old woman was near death, anyway, and that immolation was, as the authorities at the White House said to Morrison, not a social protest but a pathological act accounted for in merely personal terms. The record, however, does not support such an easy excuse, because Alice Herz had long been active in other forms of protest, especially about the Vietnam calamity, and, as with Morrison, her decision to burn herself took place in public and was calculated to be and to become a public protest.

In other words, the pathology most evident in the episodes of Alice Herz and Norman Morrison is not that of these immolations themselves—it appears that they both volunteered for martyrdom—but rather that of a nation which can understand radical dissent only as a sickness, and which so eagerly believes and so pathetically wants to believe that martyrdom is treason.
—*DGS*, 79–84

DECIDING VOCATIONALLY

Stringfellow made a number of decisions which he called vocational events: dying to career in London, moving to East Harlem and then resigning the Group Ministry, reordering his life in the wake of Anthony's death. But the one about which he was most theologically articulate was the decision to undergo surgery to remove his pancreas in 1968. Here is that discussion.

It is the ubiquity of God's judgment—extending to every time and place—and the universality of God's judgment—reaching every person and every principality or power—and the secrecy of God's judgment—which embraces all creation—taken together with such knowledge as there is of the character of God's judgment—namely that judgment is a facet of God's grace—that authorizes the emphasis of Saint Paul on the extraordinary freedom of the Christian, in making decisions, from anxiety about how those decisions are judged by God. Paul redundantly boasts that human beings are not the judges of one another, that the State is not the judge, that the company of the church is not the judge, that he as an Apostle is not the judge, that a person is, least of all, his or her own judge. And Paul considers the presumption to judge, on the part of institutions or persons, a moral dissipation. Genesis, incidentally, affirms the same truth. A nation that usurps God's office as judge vitiates its own authority as a nation. Human beings cannot play judge, even of themselves, without suffering profound corruption in their identities as a human beings.

Not to be judged and not to judge, and not to be subjected to judgment by others, or principalities, describes, as Paul well knew, the freedom to decide this or that in grace—in fear and trembling—in the audacity which takes the place of anxiety over one's moral justification. It is the maximal freedom that a human being can experience. It is, for human beings, the definitive freedom, showing both the most mature humanity and the proper limits of the institutional powers. And if there be complaint that such a remarkable freedom, when practiced, causes perpetual revolution in all things, then let the complaint stand as a fair designation of how the Gospel sets forth the vocation to be human.

That is, of course, what is really at the heart of decision. Decision is a vocational event. . . .

Biblically, vocation does not have any connotation limited to work. Vocation pertains to the whole of life, including work, of course, if and when there is work, but embracing every other use of time, every other engagement of body or mind, every other circumstance in life. In the Gospel, vocation does not mean being professionally religious, it has no special reference to the ecclesiastical occupations, it does not imply "full-time Christian service" (as some preachers still put it), it does not require extemporizing prayer into business and political situations—especially at breakfast time—it has nothing to do as such with philanthropy—tax deductible or otherwise; it is not about honesty, sobriety, thrift, loyalty or similar homely virtues on the job; it does not concern positive attitudes and is alien to the success ethic. Moreover, in the Gospel, vocation always bears an implication of immediacy—there is really no such thing as preparing to undertake one's vocation when one grows up or when one graduates or when one obtains a certain position or when one gets to a certain place. Vacation is always here and now, without anxiety where one might be tomorrow, what regard there is for tomorrow and tomorrow's issues are sufficiently anticipated, so far as vocation is concerned, in today's unconditional involvement in life as it is. Vocation has to do with recognizing life as a gift and honoring the gift in living. To that, the question of whether another day will be added to one's life, and, if that comes to pass, how the gift will be spent on the morrow, is a distraction or diversion from living of the gift today. Carried, as the Letter of James cautions, too far, a concern about how to live faithfully tomorrow causes infidelity in living today. Carried to its ultimate absurdity, the anxiety for tomorrow becomes a preoccupation with a fantasy afterlife, a notion without biblical support, albeit popularized in churches, at the cost of squandering or repudiating the immediate gift of life.

In the Gospel, vocation means being a human being, now, and being neither more, nor less than a human being, now. And, thus, is the vocation of other people illuminated and affirmed, and so also is the vocation of the institutional powers and the principalities of this world exposed and upheld. And, thus, each and every decision, whether it seems great or small, whether obviously or subtly a moral problem, becomes and is a vocational event, secreting, as it were, the very issue of existence.

My state of mind, when it became apparent that the therapy had failed and that the practical options open to me were limited and, in each case, both disagreeable and dangerous, was informed privately chiefly by the terms with which I had come to deal with the pain—that pain is not something extraordinary or abnormal but the same reality as work, the concrete experience of fallenness—and by my understanding of the vocational character of decision. It was a state of mind freed, in this way, from potential hang-ups of all sorts. That is to say, I knew that there was nothing traumatic, nothing heroic, nothing tragic, nothing stoic, nothing dramatic in my situation. In truth, mine was a commonplace experience, not only in relation to the circumstances of other human beings, but also in relation to my own history. I realized I had to make some decision, but it was as if I had already rehearsed that decision one million times whenever I had theretofore made any decision about anything. Moreover, I knew that it did not matter what my decision would be vocationally. The decision might well affect how long I survived, it certainly would affect the physiology of my survival, but neither of these matters altered the vocational issue, which is to live as a human being while one lives. Nor did survival, for whatever time and in whatever health, change the moral significance of my decision, since that pertains to God's own judgment, about which I could only confess ignorance, together with a confidence in God's mercy.

With this outlook, the decision was made, and quite matter-of-factly, without excitement, lucidly, unanxious about any future, almost casually. I would have surgery.

I felt like a human being. I felt free.   —SB, 91–92, 94–98

INSPIRING ETHICS: CONSCIENCE

There is a popular Christian commonplace which asks: If you were charged with being a Christian would there be enough evidence to convict you? Stringfellow and Towne were actually indicted for practicing the Gospel virtue of hospitality (so-called harboring a fugitive). This reflection on the nature and source of conscience was occasioned by the witness and actions of Daniel Berrigan, the guest to whom they gave succor.

Conscience, in the Gospel, as well as in the actual experiences of the early Christians, refers to the new or restored maturity of human life in Christ. A person who becomes a Christian—speaking of that event in its biblical connotations as distinguished from any particular church traditions—suffers at once a personal and a public transfiguration. One's insight into one's own identity as a person is, at the same time, an acceptance of the rest of humanity. One's reconciliation, that is, the experience of forgiveness, is profoundly private, but, simultaneously, this reconciliation is radically—even cosmically—political, incorporating one's own humanity into the whole of humanity, and, indeed, the whole of creation. . . .

Baptism, as practiced in the Apostolic Church, was the manner in which this corporate or political dimension of personal reconciliation was solemnized and publicized. The renewal of this person being baptized was understood to be relevant and good news for all persons everywhere, not just for others of the church. Each time a person was (is) baptized, the common life of all human beings in community was (is) affirmed and notarized.

The baptized, thus, lives in a new, primary, and rudimentary relationship with other human beings signifying the reconciliation of the whole of life vouchsafed in Jesus Christ. The discernment—about any matter whatever—which is given and exercised in that remarkable relationship *is* conscience. In truth, the association of baptism with conscience, in this sense, is that conscience is properly deemed a charismatic gift.

Though to various others, conscience may be a synonym for personal convenience, rationalization, eccentricity or even whim, as far as the Christian faith is concerned to deride or dismiss conscience in any such ways as these amounts to a denunciation of the Holy Spirit, a denial of its militancy, perhaps even a secret denial of its existence. To ignore or suppress conscience is to effectually gainsay the vitality of God's concern for human life in society here and now.

The inescapable issue in conscience for Christians is what has here been called the social or political context in which conscience is exercised; that social or political element in conscience refers concretely to the activity of the Holy Spirit historically upon the community of believers and the members of the community evoking their experience of renewed humanity for the sake and service of human life in the world. The initiative in conscience belongs to God; the authority of conscience is the maturity of the humanity of the Christian; the concern of conscience is always the societal fulfillment of life for all men. Still, the Christian community is diverse and dispersed, its members have different capabilities and locations, and the Holy Spirit is versatile, while the needs of the world, in the sense of humanizing life for mankind, are multifarious and cumulative and, not infrequently, contradictory. The exercise of conscience, therefore, is not the same thing as the arrival at consensus. In specific circumstances within a particular segment of the body of Christians, there may be a coincidence of conscience and consensus, but there may also be conscientious fitness not attended by consensus or there may even be many simultaneous voices of conscience, some of which seem inconsistent one with another. That conscience is not mechanical or narrow but free in its use and far-reaching we take to be a tribute to the vigor and versatility of the Holy Spirit, as well as a sign of the imagination and seriousness with which Christians are called to regard and become involved in history.

Pietists, among them some partisans of natural law, will complain that this comprehension of functioning conscience within the Christian witness makes evaluation of any particular action, which is said to be conscientious, difficult. That we readily concede; it is, in fact, impossible, and we gladly recall that the prerogative of judgment of conscience is vested in God, not in human beings, not in laws, not in the State, not in the ethics of culture, not in the church, and certainly not in the churches, sects, and denominations. What transpires, in decisions and

actions of conscience, on the part of a Christian or of some community of Christians or of many Christians positioned diversely,
is a living encounter between the Holy Spirit and those deciding
and acting in relation to human needs in society. If either those
who act or those who stand apart from the action presume judgment of what is said and done, they negate the viability of that
encounter. The practice of conscience, thus, is an extraordinarily
audacious undertaking, disdaining all mundane or conventional
prudential calculations and confessing the exclusivity of God's
judgment and trusting God's judgment as grace. Conscience
requires knowing and respecting one's self as no less, but no
more, than human. The exercise of conscience represents—as
First Peter remarks—living as a free human being.—*ST*, 99–101

PRAYING IDENTITY

*Once, when asked about the nature of his prayer life, String-
fellow replied, "Well, I pray more or less constantly." He was
reluctant about forms and postures and methods, so this attitude
is practically characteristic. Perhaps the closest one might come
to a discipline in his household was use of the Psalter, generally
from the 1928* Book of Common Prayer. *Such is briefly refer-
enced here, but the larger framing of prayer and vocation is set
in the context of the extreme and constant pain which he then
suffered.*

Any number of different exercises are deemed to be prayer which
do not possess the dignity of prayer and, in certain instances,
actually contradict the reality of prayer. The confusion and, as
the case may be, the corruption centers upon the alleged interest of God in prayer and, indeed, upon the matter of whether, in
some machinations men call prayer, God could possibly be privy
to the activity at all.

An illusion, at least, of reciprocity between human beings and
God is maintained where prayer is construed as a way in which
human beings "talk with God," or, otherwise, literally com-
municate with God, and where the presumption is that God

is, somewhere, passively implicated—listening to this talk. Often, with the same general conception of prayer, God's attributed role is enlarged: God is said not only to listen but also to answer in some manner. Some people boast that God speaks to them as if they really mean that they hear God verbalizing in direct address to themselves; others are content to assign to selected events subsequent to prayer answers besought of God; still others find prayer to be an effort to persuade God to permit what they desire, and the attainment of the goal or gain desired becomes God's answer, while a failure in such attainment can either be blamed on a deficient zeal in the arts of persuasion or upon God's well-known inscrutability.

What is suspect in each of the foregoing styles of prayer, what they share in common, is the definitive emphasis upon human initiative in prayer. In each of them, prayer is a primary act of human beings, as to which either God is a passive object or, one might say, a victim, or else God is a mere respondent of some sort. Whatever the case, the initiative—that which constitutes and characterizes and consummates the happening—is never with God, but always with human beings. That makes God, in prayer, of all things, dependent upon human attentions and overtures. And that makes a mockery of God as biblically known—as God is beheld and esteemed, for one notable example, when Jesus utters the Lord's Prayer.

What is offensive in each of these arts which usurp prayer to biblical experience—remembering that the biblical experience embraces both the saga of the people of God in the biblical times and the sojourn of biblical men in the present day—is their debasement of God. "Prayer" which relegates God as passivism or to mechanical and magical responses to human maneuvering and manipulating issues in a denial of God's godliness—of God's otherness, as Karl Barth put it—of God's freedom as God. Such a humiliation of God, even though it is not accomplished by human beings self-consciously, points to a real profanity rampant in this land, especially in churches, and also in the precinct of what some have called America's civic religion, where, quite literally, God's name is taken in vain.

What is further suspect about practices called prayer such as these is that God, in any meaningful sense in which the name of God may be used, is not an essential party to what transpires at all, but that the invocation of God's name provides a suitably vague and aptly euphoric concealment of some other transaction, which may range from autosuggestion to the motivational manipulation to hallucination to astrological calculation to voodoo incantation to sorcery, which bears a general characteristic as an act of self-generation.

Notice that I do not deny that any of these indulgences—they were so condemned by Saint Paul in Galatians—may yield the results sought, or be somehow efficacious so far as the practitioner is concerned, and I repeat that I do not raise now, at all, any doubt about the sincerity of anyone. The query I have concerns whether what is involved in prayer as prayer has meaning in the Gospel of Jesus Christ. At the heart of *that* issue is the fact that in these varieties of alleged prayer, God turns out to be a projection of the will or whim (or lust or delusion) of the one who "prays."

Yet if what has been performed in white Protestantism, and to some extent elsewhere, as prayer is not prayer, in a sense which is conscientious about the Gospel, but instead witchcraft or hypnosis or positive thinking or some similar hocus-pocus, then, what is prayer?

Prayer is a relationship which God initiates and constitutes between God and human beings. It is God's action in prayer which is definitive: God enables us to pray. Prayer is not something which, so to speak, begins with us and ends with God, but throughout prayer, we are respondents and, more than that, the possibility of the human response to God called prayer is bestowed by God's initiative.

The substance of that initiative is God's incessant, patient, and ubiquitous affirmation of God's own creation, including, concretely, human beings in relation to the rest of creation and, now, the particular person—who prays—in this relation to creation. The latter should be emphasized: there is an integrity in God's affirmation of the creation, which requires that the affirmance of the specific person always places that person at the interstices of the whole of creation. There is no way in which a specific person can suffer the affirmation of their own life by God in a void, without connection to all other people and all other things and, indeed, all of time, which is why incidentally, the Book of Common Prayer makes reference to praying in the company of the Communion of Saints. It is also why a radically individualistic conception of prayer—such as Norman Vincent Peale merchandises—oriented towards personal success (an occurrence which can *never* happen except at the expense of other human beings) is not prayer in accordance with biblical experience and is accurately classified as sorcery.

The essential response of human beings in prayer is always the same, regardless of how, in an instance, it may be symbolized verbally or actively; the response is always a confession of human creatureliness. Prayer originates in God's affirmation of life for the one who prays in the context the totality of existence, and prayer is consummated in participation of the one who prays in that very same affirmation. Because prayer has such dimensions as these, it is not superstitious or otherwise nonsensical to speak of God already knowing all our needs and desires before we ask, or of prayer being answered even before a prayer is uttered. Because prayer has its consistent focus, for both God and men, in God's affirmation of particular life, and of all of life, prayer (rather than being a technique for bolstering willpower, generating willfulness or aggrandizing ambition—as Dr. Peale advertises) always entreats the perfection of God's will by the fulfillment of your will or my will in the acceptance of our humanity as such. Thus the biblical archetype of prayer sums up all that transpires in such a phrase as "nevertheless, thy will be done, O Lord," and these words are then not some way of tricking ourselves or trying to con God.

One of the implications of prayer construed as human participation in God's affirmation of life is that prayer is not inherently verbal. In a culture which is verbally adept, not to mention one which is verbose, like America, it is to be expected that the verbalization of prayer would be common and customary. I do not doubt that putting prayer into words can be edifying. I also believe that the redundant use of verbal formularies in prayer can help maintain a sense of continuity in what I have here named the biblical experience of prayer. Besides, contemporary Christians ought to feel at home amidst the Communion of Saints and, where the ritual verbalization of prayer assists that, I am glad. A problem arises, however, where words are taken as so specialized and important in themselves that their mere use is equated with prayer or where the words are supposed to be intrinsically efficacious. That is one of the points at which the line is traversed between prayer and the practice of sorcery.

Without discounting a legitimate verbal usage in prayer, but remembering that words are perhaps the most elementary symbols that can be appropriated in prayer, it remains basic that prayer designates a state of being of the one who prays or of the company which prays that, in given circumstances, may or may just as well not be verbalized. That prayer is not inherently verbal is disclosed more fully where such a state of being becomes and is, with more or less intensity from day to day, the continuing disposition of a person. Then, of course, where there is verbalization, the vocabulary of prayer becomes marvelously versatile and literally any words may be appropriate: familiar or novel, traditional or spontaneous, solemn or silly. Indeed, ecstatic speech, speaking in tongues incomprehensible to either speaker or hearer, can then be a means of prayer.

When I write that my own situation in those months of pain and decision can be described as prayer, I do not only recall that during that time I sometimes read the Psalms and they become *my* psalms, or that, as I have also mentioned, I occasionally cried "Jesus" and that name was my prayer, but I mean that I also at times would shout "Fuck!" and that was no obscenity, but a most earnest prayerful utterance.

In the final analysis, no matter what the vocabulary of prayer, or where muteness displaces words in prayer, the content—what is communicated by a person in the world before God—in prayer is in each and every circumstance the same and it can be put plainly in one word: *Help!* That is the word of Gethsemane's prayer; that is the word of the Lord's Prayer; that is the prayer when Christ repeats the Twenty-second Psalm from the cross.

It is the prayer of Christ interceding for all people, and it is the prayer of a human being as creature acknowledging God's vocation in affirming the life which God has called into being. It has been and is my prayer: it was, in the autumn of 1968, my prayer, that is to say, my condition, at once pathetic and glorious.   —*SB*, 102–9

LIVING HOLY, LIVING WHOLLY

Dorothy Day is reputed to have said, "Don't call me a saint. I don't want to be dismissed so easily." Hence it is a bizarre coincidence that she is now becoming official canon fodder. One supposes Jesus might have said, "Don't call me divine," for similar reasons. Stringfellow applied this logic when he saw Dan Berrigan being written off as a " poet" following his capture by the FBI in 1970. There is no cause to render his witness extraordinary and so beyond ethical reach. But it is equally important to add that, as an aspect of his vocation, as a charism of his humanity, Berrigan's poetness may actually be understood to be transfigured in much the same way as St. Paul's zeal in the following account of holy wholeness, or sanctification.

While I do not wish to magnify semantic or rhetorical issues, or to dwell much on them, both sanctification and holiness bring freight and are often subject to inflated connotations. In any case, by sanctification I mean the endeavor by which a person is sanctified or rendered holy. The endeavor is not one of the person so affected but, quite the contrary, is an effort of the Word of

God, which *elects* the one made holy and which, I believe, offers similar election freely to every person. To be more precise about it, *sanctification is a reiteration of the act of creation in the Word of God.* Thus sanctification refers to the activity of the historic Word of God renewing human life (and all of created life) in the midst of the era of the fall, or during the present darkness, in which the power of death apparently reigns. Holiness designates the essential condition of a person who confesses that he or she has suffered the renewal of his or her being, or selfhood, in the Word of God and is restored to wholeness as a human being. While there *is* an implication, in being holy, of incessant repentance, there is no implication of perfection or of any superior moral status. Among humans, holiness may involve a relatively more profound experience of being human, but it does not indicate as such the exceptional or the extraordinary. To the contrary, holy connotes the holistic in human life and, in that connection, the normal, the typical, the ordinary, the generic, the exemplary.

I am aware, of course, that sanctification is ridiculed and holiness is belittled—and the saints are defamed and scandalized—when especial moral worth or purity or achievement is imputed to being holy. This is in reality a condescension of those conformed to the world, their form of dismissal, an excuse for others to cop out in a manner which pretends to recognize and flatter the saints.

Within my own memory, probably the outstanding incident of this pretentiousness happened on the day in 1970 when Daniel Berrigan (the Jesuit who had become both celebrated and notorious for his resistance to the war in Southeast Asia), then being sought by the federal authorities as a fugitive (as Dan puts it) from injustice, was seized by the FBI at the home of Anthony Towne and myself on Block Island. The event was heavily covered by television and other media, and that evening, on one of the Providence TV newscasts, an interview was conducted, about Dan's capture, with another prominent Jesuit who was in the jurisdiction. He was John J. McLaughlin, a candidate in the Republican Party for the United States Senate. This was, of course, before strictures against priests in public office were widely pronounced by the Pope. (McLaughlin lost and later achieved some prominence on the White House staff as casuist for President Nixon, but after a while he quit the Jesuit order.) In the interview on television the day that Dan was seized, Father McLaughlin delivered a long and verbose comment about those who work for change from within the system and those who work for change from outside the system. But then, as if summing up the contrast, he declared, "Of course, you must remember that Dan is a poet!" With that accusation, he not only dismissed the Berrigan witness against the Vietnam war but also banished Dan from the company of ordinary folk. Dan is different from other people: Dan is a poet; Dan is eccentric; what applies to Dan does not have relevance or weight for other persons. More than that, at the conclusion of this sophistry is the notion that because a poet is considered idiosyncratic, an ordinary human (i.e., a nonpoet) is excused from the claims of conscience which may be thought to influence the poets.

McLaughlin's evasion of conscience aside, as I have stressed being holy, becoming and being a saint does not mean being perfect but being whole; it does not mean being exceptionally religious, or being religious at all; it means being liberated from religiosity and religious pietism of any sort; it does not mean being morally better, it means being exemplary; it does not mean being godly, but rather being truly human; it does not mean being otherworldly, but it means being deeply implicated in the practical existence of this world without succumbing to this world or any aspect of this world, no matter how beguiling. Being holy means a radical self-knowledge; a sense of who one is, a consciousness of one's identity so thorough that it is no longer confused with the identities of others, of persons or of any creatures or of God or of any idols.

For human beings, relief and remedy from such profound confusion concerning a person's own identity and the identity and character of the Word of God becomes the indispensable and authenticating ingredient of being holy, and it is the most crucial aspect of becoming mature—or of being fulfilled—as a human in this world, in fallen creation. This is, at the same time, the manner through which humans can live humanly, in sanity and with conscience, in the fallen world as it is. And these twin faculties, sanity and conscience—rather than some sentimental or pietistic or self-serving notion of moral perfection—constitute the usual marks of sanctification. That which distinguishes the saint is not eccentricity but sanity, not perfection but conscience.

These are all considerations which impinge upon why I commonly use, herein, and have used, for more that a decade, in other books or public utterances, the *Word of God* as the name of God, in preference to the mere term *God*.

In American culture, and, I suspect, everywhere else, the name of God is terribly maligned. For one thing the name *God* is seldom any longer used as a name, and that in itself is a literal curse addressed to God. To take a very obvious and familiar example, when Ronald Reagan, in his pronouncements on the school prayer issue and otherwise says "God," it is difficult to fathom what he may be fantasizing, though it would appear, at most, that he is imagining some idea of god. Sometimes he himself clarifies that by inserting a prefix and speaking "his god" or "our god" or, also, "their god," while mentioning, as Reagan perceives the situation, an alien or enemy people.

Yet *no* idea of god is God; no image of god is God; no conception of god, however appealing or, for that matter, however true, coincides with the living God—which the biblical witness bespeaks—present, manifest, militant in common history, discernible in the course of events through the patience and insight of ordinary human beings. The living God, whose style and character the Bible reports, is subject now, as in the biblical era, to the witness of human beings, to their testimony describing what they have beheld of the intent, involvement, self-disclosure, effort, and concern of the Word of God in this world. And so, with as much standing or authority as our predecessors in the faith had long ago, biblical people in this day attest to God as he is revealed in this history, as the *Word of God*, the very same One to whom the biblical witness refers and in which the biblical witness so much rejoices.

When, therefore, I use here this name of God, it is deliberately intended to invoke the scriptural saga of the Word of God active in common history from the first initiative of creation. Simultaneously I refer (as, so to say, both Isaiah and John insist), the selfsame Word of God incarnate in Jesus Christ. At the same time, I mean to recall the Word of God permeating the whole of creation and ready to be discerned in all things whatsoever in the fallenness of this world; and, again, the Word of God as the Holy Spirit, at work contemporaneously, incessantly agitating change in this world (as the event of Pentecost and the Acts of the Apostles each verify).

The restoration of the original identity of a person—in all its particularities and all its relationships, in the totality of its political significance—the renewal of a person's wholeness, which is the initiation into holiness, is utterly the effort of the Word of God. There is no interpretation which is attributable to a person's ambition, attainment, discipline, works, or merit. The renewal of creation, including the restoration of integrity to persons, is a matter of the grace of the Word of God. It is a generous gift indeed, as I have already mentioned, encompassing the restoring of relationships within a person and between that person and all other persons, all principalities and powers, nature, and the residuum of creation. The gift is also precocious because it is offered *now*, in the midst of the fall, in a way that disrupts, challenges, and resists the apparent sovereignty of the power of death in this world. That means, in turn, that this is an experience which shatters time and liberates people from the confinement of time by at once recalling all that has gone before and anticipating all that is to come.

Instead of being somehow transported "out of this world," rather than indulging abstinence, evasion, or escapism, rather than fabricating some isolation or separation or privatism, the irony in being holy is that one is plunged more fully into

the practical existence of this world, as it is, than in any other
way. . . .

Holiness is not an attainment, in any sense of the term, but
is a gift of the Word of God. Holiness is not a badge of achievement for a saint but is wrought in the life, in the very being, of an
ordinary person by the will of the Word of God. Holiness, from
the vantage of the person who may truthfully be said to be holy,
is, in the most elementary meaning, the restoration of integrity
and wholeness to a person. That inherently involves, for that
person, repentance—utter repentance, encompassing and comprehending the whole of that person's existence, even recollect-
ing one's creation in the Word of God by the Word of God. It
involves, as well, a prospective or continuing living in repentance unto the very day of the Judgment of the Word of God in
the consummation of the history of this world. But such radical
repentance does not imply, much less require, self-denial or any
sort of suppression or sublimation of self. Quite the contrary:
In becoming and being sanctified, *every* facet, feature, attribute,
and detail of a person is exposed and rejuvenated, rendered new
as if in its original condition again, and restored. Thus, instead
of self-denial, what is taking place is more nearly the opposite of
self-denial: in place of denial there is fulfillment.

The experience of Saint Paul is edifying in this respect, particularly since Paul has furnished us with more news of his
experience in becoming and being a saint than any other New
Testament character. To take a straightforward example, Paul in
his early career boasted that he was the most zealous of those
who persecuted the Gospel and confessors of the Gospel. From
that we know that Paul had a quality, perchance even talent,
which is described as *zeal*. Later on, Paul becomes the most
zealous apologist for the Gospel, even aspiring to confront the
emperor with his advocacy. Lo! Paul retains this quality of zeal,
save now, when he has become the great apologist, this aspect
of his personhood is turned around, renewed, matured, restored
to him in something like its original integrity in his own creation in the Word of God. The zeal of Paul does not have to be

excised in order for him to become and be a saint, although he had engaged this zeal of his to harass and harm and inhibit the Gospel. Had his zeal been somehow suppressed or extinguished, it would then have been less than the person Paul implicated in conversion and in becoming holy. And *that* becomes a self-contradiction: It is only the whole person, fully repentant, without anything withheld, denied, secreted, who can be holy.

—*PS*, 30–35, 41–42

SOJOURNING WITH THE
ESCHATOLOGICAL CIRCUS

Among Stringfellow's earliest toys as a child was a circus wagon filled with wooden animals. A newspaper photo in his scrapbook shows "Billy Stringfellow of this city" astride an elephant, just blocks from his home where the travelling circuses set up their tents. His love of the circus was lifelong. He always intended a full book of theological reflection upon it. Alas, what follows, luminous and passionate, is all he actually produced.

Eschatology impinges incessantly upon ethics. A biblical person in one who lives within the dialectic of eschatology and ethics, realizing that God's Judgment has as much to do with the humor of the Word as it does with wrath.

Anthony understood this, on his own authority, and that is why he abided my attraction to the circus. My most vivid memory, that night after the requiem, was of the year when Anthony and I spent most of the summer weeks traveling with the Clyde Beatty–Cole Bros. Circus through New England and part of New York State.

It was 1966, and there were already signals that the trouble with my health was impending. That may have had something to do with our decision to spend the summer the way we did. In any case, we outfitted a station wagon so that it could be used for sleeping, and joined the circus company en route, booked in a new city each day, traveling late each night in the circus convoy to the next day's stand. As Anthony had foreseen, the experience did not satiate my fascination with the circus as a society, but only whetted it.

It is only since putting aside childish things that it has come to my mind so forcefully—and so gladly—that the circus is among the few coherent images of the eschatological realm to which people still have ready access, and that the circus thereby affords some elementary insights into the idea of society as a consummate event.

This principality, this art, this veritable liturgy, this common enterprise of multifarious creatures called the circus, enacts a hope, in an immediate and historic sense, and simultaneously embodies an ecumenical foresight of radical and wondrous splendor, encompassing, as it does both empirically and symbolically, the scope and diversity of Creation.

I suppose some—ecclesiastics or academics or technocrats or magistrates or potentates—may deem the association of the circus and the Kingdom scandalous or facetious or bizarre, and scoff quickly at the thought that the circus is relevant to the ethics of society. Meanwhile, some of the friends of the circus may consider it curious that during intervals when Anthony and I have been their guests and, on occasion, confidants, that I have had theological second thoughts about them and about what the corporate existence of the circus tells and anticipates in an ultimate sense. To either I only respond that the connection seems to me to be at once suggested when one recalls that biblical people, like circus folk, live typically as sojourners, interrupting time, with few possessions, and in tents, in this world. The church would likely be more faithful if the Church were similarly nomadic.

In America, during the earliest part of this century, the circus enjoyed a "golden age." It was the era of P. T. Barnum, Adam Fourpaugh, and the Ringling Brothers, to name but a few of the showmen who assembled extraordinary aggregations of performers, animals and oddities. It was then that the circus was most lucidly an image of the Kingdom in its magnitude, versatility and logistics. There were, for example, few permanent zoological collections in those days, and the circus menagerie was the opportunity for people to see rare birds and reptiles, exotic animals and mammals, wild beasts and other marvelous creatures. Indeed, when the Ringling Brothers advertised their "mammoth millionaire menagerie" as the "greatest gathering since the deluge" it was not a much exaggerated boast. It was similar with the "sideshows" or "museums" traditionally associated with the American circus. A separate feature from the main circus performance, the side show originated with Barnum. It assembled and exhibited human "oddities" and "curiosities"—giants, midgets, and the exceptionally obese; Siamese twins, albinos, and bearded ladies; those who had rendered themselves unusual like fire eaters, sword swallowers, or tattooed people. If the side show seems macabre because "freaks" were sometimes exploited, it must also be mentioned that in those days little medical help and few other means of livelihood were available to such persons and that the premise of these exhibits was educational. In any case, so long as they continued they symbolized the circus as an eschatological company in which all sorts and conditions of life are congregated.

It is in the performance that the circus is most obviously a parable of the eschaton. It is there that human beings confront the beasts of the earth and reclaim their lost dominion over other creatures. The symbol is magnified, of course, when one recollects that, biblically, the beasts generally designate the principalities: the nations, dominions, thrones, authorities, institutions, and regimes (see Daniel 6).

There, too, in the circus, humans are represented as freed from consignment to death. There one person walks a wire fifty feet above the ground, another stands upside down on a forefinger, another juggles a dozen incongruous objects simultaneously, another hangs in the air by the heels, one upholds twelve in a human pyramid, another is shot from a cannon. The circus performer is the image of the eschatological person—emancipated from frailty and inhibition, exhilarant, militant, transcendent over death—neither confined nor conformed by the fear of death any more.

The eschatological parable is, at the same time, a parody of conventional society in the world as it is. In a multitude of ways in circus life the risk of death is bluntly confronted and the power of death exposed and, as the ringmaster heralds, defied. Clyde Beatty, at the height of his career, actually had *forty* tigers and lions performing in one arena. The Wallendas, not content to walk the high wire one by one, have crossed it in a pyramid of seven people. John O'Brien managed sixty-one horses in the same ring, in what a press agent called "one bewildering act." Mlle. La Belle Roche accomplished a double somersault at great speed and height in an automobile at the time when autos were still novelties.

Moreover, the circus performance happens in the midst of a fierce and constant struggle of the people of the circus, especially the roustabouts, against the hazards of storm, fire, accident, or other disaster, and it emphasizes the theological mystique of the circus as a community in which calamity seems to be always impending. After all, the Apocalypse coincides with the Eschaton.

Meanwhile, the clowns make the parody more poignant and pointed in costume and pantomime; commenting, by presence and performance, on the absurdities inherent in what ordinary people take so seriously—themselves, their profits and losses, their successes and failures, their adjustments and compromises—their conformity to the world.

So the circus, in its open ridicule of death in these and other ways—unwittingly, I suppose—shows the rest of us that the only enemy in life is death, and that this enemy confronts everyone, whatever the circumstances, all the time. If people of other arts and occupations do not discern that, they are, as Saint Paul said, idiots (cf. Rom. 1:20–25; Eph. 4:17–18). The service the circus does—more so, I regret to say, than the churches do—is to openly, dramatically, and humanly portray that death in the midst of life. The circus is eschatological parable and social parody: it signals a transcendence of the power of death, which exposes this world as it truly is while it pioneers the Kingdom.

—*SF*, 87–91

A Stringfellonian
Lexicon

Antichrist bluntly designates the power of death incarnate institutionally or in some other principality or, sometimes, in a person associated with and possessed by demonic power (i.e., Rev. 19:17–20). In the New Testament, the Antichrist is beheld in the emperor or, again, in the throne or the office of the emperor, or, again, in the empire as such, or, again, in the state and its agencies of violence like the army. . . . The Antichrist, remember, means antihuman as much as it means anti-God. . . . A human being cannot be an idolator of the Antichrist without negating his or her humanity, which at the same time means indulgence in a travesty of worship.　　—EC, 112, 113; see above, p. 157

Babel means the inversion of language, verbal inflation, libel, rumor, euphemism and coded phrases, rhetorical wantonness, redundancy, hyperbole, such profusion in speech and sound that comprehension is impaired, nonsense, sophistry, jargon, noise, incoherence, a chaos of voices and tongues, falsehood, blasphemy. And, in all of this, babel means violence. . . . By the 1970s in America, successive regimes had been so captivated by babel that babel had become the means of ruling the nation, the principal form of coercion employed by the governing authorities against human beings.　　—EC, 106–7; see above, pp. 165, 169

Baptism is often profoundly misunderstood. It is widely thought to be the sacrament of the unity of the church. But that is not what baptism is; just as it is not mere membership or initiation ritual. Baptism is the assurance—accepted, enacted, verified, and represented by Christians—of the unity of all humanity in Christ. . . . The oneness of the church is the example and guarantee of the reconciliation of all humankind to God and of the unity of all humanity and all creation in the life of God.

211

The church, the baptized society, is asked to be the image of all humanity, the one and intimate community of God.
                                        —*ID,* 111; see above, pp. 29, 81

Biblical Ethics. Biblically speaking, the singular, straightforward issue of ethics—and in the elementary topic of politics—*is how to live humanly during the Fall.* Any viable ethics—which is to say, any ethics worthy of human attention and practice, any ethics which manifests and verifies hope—is both individual and social. It must deal with human decision and action in relation to the other creatures, notably the principalities and powers in the very midst of the conflict, distortion, alienation, disorientation, chaos, decadence of the Fall.   —*EC,* 55; see above, p. 102

Biblical Politics. The biblical topic *is* politics. The Bible is about the politics of fallen creation and the politics of redemption; the politics of the nations, institutions, ideologies, and causes of this world and the politics of the Kingdom of God; the politics of Babylon and the politics of Jerusalem; the politics of the Antichrist and the politics of Jesus Christ; the politics of the demonic powers and principalities and the politics of the timely judgment of God as sovereign; the politics of death and the politics of life; apocalyptic politics and eschatological politics.
                                        —*EC,* 14–15; see above, p. 44

Blasphemy denotes wanton and contemptuous usurpation of the very vocation of God, vilification of the Word of God and persecution of life as life originates in the Word of God, preemptive attempt against the sovereignty of the Word of God in this world, brute aggression against human life which confesses or appeals to the Word of God.   —*CO,* 69; see above, pp. 11, 166

Charismatic vs. Demonic. I am using these terms, let it be clear immediately, in a generic sense: demonic refers to any, and every, agency of death, in whatever guise or form, however subtle or ingenious, howsoever vested or manifested; charismatic refers to each and every gift, talent, capability and limitation of persons, within the whole body of humankind in this world, as these are bestowed and renewed in the Word of God. As shorthand, with all its imprecision, one might think of the demonic as anything whatever which dehumanizes life for human beings, while the charismatic is that which rehumanizes life for human beings within the context of the whole of fallen Creation.[25]

Christian. A Christian is distinguished by radical esteem for the Incarnation—to use the traditional jargon—by a reverence for the life of God in the whole of Creation, even, and in a sense especially, Creation in the travail of sin.

—*PPF*, 43; see above, pp. 39, 215

Church. The vocation of the Church of Christ in the world, in political conflict and social strife, is inherently eschatological. The church is the embassy of the eschaton in the world. The church is the image of what the world is in its essential being. The church is the trustee of the society which the world, now subjected to the power of death, is to be on the last day when the world is fulfilled in all things in God. To the world as it is, then, the Church of Christ is always, as it were, saying both Yes and No simultaneously. They are, in fact, the same word, for they each say that the end of the world is its maturing in Christ. It is that maturity of human life in society which the church as the reconciled community foreshadows in the world. Thus, also, the church is constantly engaged, in and through her actual existence as the new society, in beseeching the end of the world; therefore, the church is always authorized to complain, for the sake of this world, about everything in this world.

—*DGS*, 142; see above, p. 106

Circus. This principality, this art, this veritable liturgy, this common enterprise of multifarious creatures called the circus, enacts a hope, in an immediate and historic sense, and simultaneously embodies an ecumenical foresight of radical and wondrous

---

25. Preface to "Grieve Not the Holy Spirit," manuscript toward a book; published in *AKW*, 317–18; see above, p. xxx.

splendor, encompassing, as it does both empirically and symbolically, the scope and diversity of Creation. . . . One recalls that biblical people, like circus folk, live typically as sojourners, interrupting time, with few possessions, and in tents, in this world. The church would likely be more faithful if the church were similarly nomadic. . . . It is in the performance that the circus is most obviously a parable of the eschaton. It is there that human beings confront the beasts of the earth and reclaim their lost dominion over other creatures. The symbol is magnified, of course, when one recollects that, biblically, the beasts generally designate the principalities: the nations, dominions, thrones, authorities, institutions, and regimes (see Daniel 6). . . . The circus performer is the image of the eschatological person—emancipated from frailty and inhibition, exhilarant, militant, transcendent over death—neither confined nor conformed by the fear of death any more.   —*SF,* 88, 89; see above, p. 207

Communion of Saints. I refer, when I use that curious and venerable title, to the entire company of human beings (inclusive of the church, but transcending time and place and thereby far more ecumenical than the church has ever been) who have, at any time, prayed and who will, at any time, pray; and whose occupation, for the time being, is intercession for each and every need of the life of this world. As the Communion of Saints anticipates, in its scope and constituency, the full assemblage of created life in the Kingdom of God at the end of time, so prayer emulates the fullness of worship when the Word of God is glorified eternally in the Kingdom.   —*SF,* 68; see above, p. 32

Conscience. The most notable mention of conscience is in the First Epistle of Peter. That epistle expounds the meaning of baptism as the sacrament of the new and mature humanity of persons in Christ, of the new citizenship in Christ compared to the old citizenship under Caesar. . . . Similarly, Romans 12 hinges the chapter's discourse on the life of the Body of Christ in the world upon not being conformed to the world but being transformed by the renewal of the mind. In Christian faith, conscience does not mean a private, unilateral, self-serving, morally superior opinion held by an individual disconnected from the community, but it bespeaks the freedom to transcend self, to expand life, to share in suffering, to risk death for the sake of others and on behalf of the world which is integral to becoming a member of the corpus of the church. Conscience for Christians, rather than being solitary or esoteric, bespeaks the church's witness of advocacy. —CO, 101–2; see above, p. 193

Constantinian Arrangement. [The] Accommodation, which has shaped Christendom in the West since the fourth century, by which the church, refuting precedent, acquired a radical vested interest in the established order and became culpably identified with the institutional status quo in culture and society, in economics and politics, in warfare and imperialism, in racism and sexism (*The Witness*, September 1975). . . . The Constantinian mentality which afflicts the church equivocates contemplation of the judgment of the Word of God. Within the Constantinian ethos, the church even seeks, in the name of the Word of God, to broker compromises of that judgment with princes and presidents, regimes and systems. The capacity of God for anger is gainsaid, though it be in the face of the chaos—the war and hunger and famine and disease and tyranny and injustice—over which the rulers of this age in truth preside.

—CO, 80; see above, pp. 13, 142

Conversion. The event of becoming a Christian is the event at which human beings utterly and unequivocally confront the presence and power of death in and over their own existence. . . . During conversion a person has total recall of their history. All that one is and has been, all that one has done, everything that one has said, all whom one has met, every place where one has been, every fragment and facet of one's own awareness that one has been and is consigned to death, bonded to death, in fact dying. Conversion is the event during which persons find themselves radically and absolutely helpless. In becoming

Christians, persons see that they are naked, exposed, and trans-
parent in every respect—completely vulnerable. . . . Conversion
is an ultimate and radically personal exposure to death, but it
is also the ultimate and immediately personal exposure to the
power of God overcoming death. Conversion is death in Christ.

—*ID*, 107–8

Death is so great, so aggressive, so pervasive and so militant a
power that the only fitting way to speak of death is similar to
the way one speaks of God. Death is the living power and presence in this world which feigns to be God (*CAJ*, 52). Death is
a mystery quite inexhaustible, as to which there will forever be
more to notice, more to learn, more to say. . . . When the name
of death is used, I intend that it bear *every* definition and nuance,
every association and suggestion, *every* implication and intuition that *anyone* has *ever* attributed to death, and I intend that
the name of death, here, bear all meanings simultaneously and
cumulatively. . . . The name of death refers to clinical death and
to biological extinction and includes the event of the undertaker,
but, much more than that, the moral reality of death involves
death comprehended sociologically and anthropologically, psychologically and psychically, economically and politically, societally and institutionally. Death as a moral power means death
as social purpose.   —*EC*, 69–70; see above, pp. 115, 150

Devil. Terms which characterize are frequently used biblically
in naming the principalities: "tempter," "mocker," "foul spirit,"
"destroyer," "adversary," "the enemy." And the privity of the
principalities to the power of death incarnate is shown in mention of their agency to Beelzebub or Satan or the Devil or the
Antichrist (*EC*, 78). Do not laugh or scoff at the venerable
images of the power of death named the "Devil" or the "Angel
of Death," for they are ways in which human beings have recognized that death is a living, active, decisive reality.

—*ID*, 21; see above, pp. 53, 159

Eschatological hope, biblically speaking, anticipates an end of time which is simultaneously time's redemption. That hope neither abolishes nor repudiates time; on the contrary, the eschaton means the moral completion or perfection of time. Moreover, the biblical hope, eschatologically, is no disembodied abstraction, no ethereal notion, no antiworldly vision, but a hope recurrently foreshadowed and empirically witnessed in events taking place now, and all the time, in the common history of persons and nations in this world.   —*EC*, 44; see above, p. 166

Eschatological Ethics. See "Church" or "Circus."

Evangelism in the Gospel of Christ, means the affirmation of the Word of God in the life of each and every human being in relation to all of creation. Evangelism, in the Gospel is an enthusiastic expression of the love that Christ bears for the whole of the world, which is authorized by that same love which the evangelist has himself suffered (*CAJ*, 43). The evangelist merely calls upon the one addressed to recollect his or her own creation in the Word of God, to remember who he or she truly is, to recover one's own life. Thus evangelism is an act of love by the church, or by a member of the church, for the world or some person. Evangelism is the act of proclaiming the presence of the Word of God in the life of another, the act of profoundly affirming that person's essential identity and being. And such an affirmation given by one to another is love.   —*ID*, 106

Fall refers to the profound disorientation, affecting all relationships in the totality of creation, concerning identity, place, connection, purpose, vocation. The subject of the fall is not only the personal realm, in the sense of you or me, but the whole of creation and each and every item of created life. The fall means the reign of chaos throughout creation now, so that even that which is ordained by the ruling powers as "order" is, in truth, chaotic. The fall means the remarkable confusion which all beings—principalities as well as persons—suffer as to who they are and why they exist. The fall means the consignment of all created life, and of the realm of time, to the power of death.

—*PS*, 38; see above, p. 158

Glossolalia. At Pentecost, ecstatic utterance means the emancipation of human beings from the bonds of nation, culture, race, language, ethnicity. At Pentecost, speaking in tongues is the sublime and notorious worship of God. . . . And this, in turn, points to a more profound meaning of speaking in tongues today in America, which is that tongues parody babel. In an American atmosphere heavy-laden with babel, *glossolalia* bespeaks the rebuke of the Word of God. . . . Within the surveillance of the Antichrist, this spontaneous, unpredictable, unconformable, liberated witness can only be heard as the sound of revolution, though, indeed it be a much greater portent than that. This speaking in tongues heralds the doom of Babylon, warns of the judgment impending upon the Antichrist, joins in the jubilation of the heavenly chorus when the great city falls.

—*EC*, 147, 148; see above, p. 27

Gospel vs. Religion. The Gospel of Jesus Christ ends all religious speculation; demolishes all merely religious ceremonies and sacrifices appeasing unknown gods; destroys every exclusiveness which religion attaches to itself in God's name; attests that the presence of God is not remote, distant, and probably out-of-reach—but here, now, and with us in this world, already. This Gospel means that the very life of God is evident in this world, in this life, because Jesus Christ once participated in the common life of humanity in the history of our world. The Christian faith is distinguished, diametrically, from mere religion, in that religion begins with the proposition that some god exists; Christianity, meanwhile, is rejoicing in God's manifest presence among us. . . . Religion is the attempt to satisfy the curiosity of human beings in this world about God; Jesus Christ is the answer to the human curiosity in this world about what it means to be truly human in this world which God created.   —*PPF,* 15

Hardness of heart. I mean by "moral impoverishment" what the Bible often cites as "hardness of heart" or as the impairment or loss of moral discernment; the incapacity to hear, though one has ears; or to see, though one has eyes (e.g., Mark 8:14–21). I refer, thus, not so much to an evil mind as to a paralyzed conscience; not so much to either personal or corporate immorality as to a social pathology possessing persons and institutions; not so much to malevolence, however incarnate, as to the literal demoralization of human life in society. —*EC*, 29

Heaven is not a site in the galaxies any more than "hell" is located in the bowels of the earth. Rather, it is that estate of self-knowledge and reconciliation and hope—that vocation, really; that blessedness—to which every human being and the whole of creation is called to live *here* in this world, aspires to live *here*, and by virtue of Christ is enabled to enter upon *here*.
—*EC*, 43–44; see above, p. 208

Hell. The recital in the Apostles' Creed, *He descended into Hell*, has a significance similar to that of Hell. Hell is the realm of death; Hell is when and where the power of death is complete, unconditional, maximum, undisguised, most awesome and awful, unbridled, most terrible, *perfected*. That Jesus Christ descends into Hell means that as we die (in any sense of the term "*die*") our expectation in death is encounter with the Word of God, which is, so to speak, already there in the midst of death.
—*SF*, 110; see above, p. 75

Holiness does not mean that you are any better than anyone else; holiness is not the same as goodness; holiness is not common piety. Holiness is not about pleasing God, even less about appeasing God. Holiness is about enjoying God. Holiness is the integrity of greeting, confessing, honoring, and trusting God's presence in all events and in any event, no matter what, no matter when, no matter where. —*ID*, 35; see above, p.202

Holy Spirit denotes the living, acting presence and power of the Word of God in the history of this world: the presence and power which lives and acts now in unity and integrity with the works of the Word of God in creation, redemption, and judgment, as well as in solidarity and identification with the advent, birth, ministry, death, descent, resurrection, and Lordship of Jesus Christ in this world. In plain language, the Holy Spirit is the power and presence of God's Word seen and heard in the world.   —*FO*, 100; see above, p. 79

Hope vs. Optimism. Hope means something quite different from optimism—in fact, hope is virtually the opposite of optimism. That is to say, simply, that optimism refers to the capabilities of principalities and human beings, while hope bespeaks the effort of the Word of God in common history. Moreover, the distinctions signifies that hope includes realism, while realism undermines and refutes optimism.   —*SF*, 95; see above p. 172

Idolatry. All idols are imposters of God. Whatever its specific character, an idol is a person or a thing or an abstract notion enshrined as God. Idolatry is the worship of what humanity has turned into such an imposter. In other words, idolatry means honoring the idol as that which renders the existence of the idolater morally significant, ultimately worthwhile.   —*IG*, 23

Incarnational theology regards this world in the fullness of its fallen estate as *simultaneously* disclosing the ecumenical, militant, triumphant presence of God. It esteems that which is most characteristic of Jesus Christ as the incarnate Word of God as also inherent in the whole of creation.

—*EC*, 41; see above, p. 117

Intercession. As I understand it, the one who intercedes for another is confessing that his or her trust in the vitality of the Word of God is so serious that he or she volunteers risks sharing the burden of the one for whom intercession is offered even to the extremity of taking the place of the other person who is the subject of the prayer. Intercession takes its meaning from the politics of redemption. Intercession is a most audacious witness to the world.   —*PS*, 84; see above, p. 33

Jerusalem vs. Babylon. What Babylon means theologically and, hence, existentially for all nations or other principalities in the dimensions of fallenness, doom, and death, Jerusalem means to each nation or power in the terms of holiness, redemption, and life. Babylon describes the apocalyptic while Jerusalem embodies the eschatological as these two realities become recognizable in the present, common history of the world. . . . Babylon is concretely exemplified in the nations and the various other principalities—as in the Roman Empire, as in the U.S.A.—but Jerusalem is the parable for the Church of Jesus Christ . . . visibly exemplified as an embassy among the principalities—sometimes secretly, sometimes openly—or as a pioneer community—sometimes latently, sometimes notoriously—or as a prophetic society—sometimes discreetly, sometimes audaciously. And the life of Jerusalem, institutionalized as Christ's Church (which is never to be uncritically equated with ecclesiastical structures professing the name of the church) is marvelously dynamic. Constantly changing in her appearance and forms, she is incessantly being rendered new, spontaneous, transcendent, paradoxical, improvisational, radical, ecumenical, free.

—EC, 48, 50; see above, pp. 122, 144

Loneliness is the specific apprehension of a person of his or her own death in relation to the impending death of all persons and all things. . . . Loneliness does not deny or negate the existence of lives other that the life of the one who is lonely, but loneliness vividly anticipates the death of such other lives that they are of no sustenance or comfort to the life and being of the one who suffers loneliness. Loneliness is the most caustic, drastic, and fundamental repudiation of God. Loneliness is the most elementary expression of original sin. There is no one who does not know loneliness. Yet there is no one who is alone.

—ID, 24–25; see above, p. 75

Lordship of Christ. This is not, as is sometimes erroneously supposed, a title designating the divinity of Christ; it, rather, explicitly explains the humanity of Jesus as the one who epitomizes the restoration of dominion over the rest of creation vested in human life by the sovereignty of the Word of God during the epoch of the fall. Jesus Christ as Lord signifies the renewed vocation of human life in reconciliation with the rest of creation.

—*CO*, 31; see above, pp. 37, 77

Mourning vs. Grief. I understand grief to be the total experience of loss, anger, outrage, fear, regret, melancholy, abandonment, temptation, bereftness, helplessness suffered privately, within one's self, in response to the happening of death. By distinction and contrast, I comprehend mourning as the liturgies of recollection, memorial, affection, honor, gratitude, confession, empathy, intercession, meditation, anticipation for the life of the one who is dead. Empirically, in the reality of someone's death, and in the aftermath of it, grief and mourning are, of course, jumbled. It is, I think, part of the healing of mourning to sort out and identify the one from the other.   —*SF*, 22

Pain, manifestly, is not the ultimate idol, but only a demigod representing death. The same is true of other varieties of works, but with pain, as contrasted with charities or rituals or pietism or whatnot, surrogation to the power of death is the more obvious since pain is literally a symptom of the advent of death. To endure pain is to suffer anticipation of death, in both mind and body. The experience of pain is a foretaste of the event of death. Pain is an ambassador of death. Pain is one of death's disguises, though not one of the more subtle ones. It is the surrogate, really, servant relationship evident between pain and death which causes me to write of pain so much in personified terms . . . pain as an acolyte of the power of death.

—*SB*, 53–54; see above, pp. 33, 200

Prayer is nothing you do; prayer is someone you are. Prayer is not about doing, but being. Prayer is about being alone in God's presence. Prayer is being *so* alone that God is the only witness to your existence. The secret of prayer is God affirming your life (*ID*, 31). . . . More definitively, prayer is *not* personal in the sense of a private transaction occurring in a void, disconnected with everyone and everything else, but it is *so* personal that it reveals (I have chosen this verb conscientiously) every connection with everyone and everything else in the whole of Creation throughout time. A person in the estate of prayer is identified in relation to *Alpha* and *Omega*—in relationship to the inception of everything and to the fulfillment of everything (cf. Rom. 1:20; 1 Cor. 12:12–13; Rev. 22:12). In prayer, the initiative belongs to the Word of God, acting to identify, or to reiterate the identity of, the one who prays. —*SF,* 67–68; see above, p. 196

Preaching vs. Prophetism. [The preacher's] task is the responsible utterance of the Word of God within the congregation—so that the Word may be acknowledged and admired there, and so that those who gather as the congregation may be identified by the Word of God in their corporate life as the Body of Christ, and so that they may be so enlightened by the Word of God in the congregation that they will become sensitive to and perceptive of the . . . Word in the common life of the world in which their various ministries as lay people take place. But it is out in the world, not within the congregation, that the prophetic task is exercised. The prophet is characteristically not priest or preacher, but lay person. The task is to represent and expose the Word of God in the world, and particularly in the posture of the Word which stands over against the world's existence and the world's disregard of and arrogance toward the Word of God. And sometimes this task is to declare and convey the Word of God as it stands against the worldliness of the church.

—*PPF,* 52

Principalities. The realities to which the biblical terms "principalities and powers" refer are quite familiar to modern society, though they may be called by different names. What the Bible calls "principalities and powers" are called in contemporary language "ideologies," "institutions," and "images." A principality, whatever its particular form and variety, is a living reality, distinguishable from human and other organic life. It is not made or instituted by human beings, but, as with humans and all creation, made by God for God's own pleasure. . . . Like all people and all things, the angelic powers and principalities are fallen and are become demonic powers. . . . To put it another way, that dominion which human beings receive from God over the rest of creation (including their dominion over the principalities) is lost to them in the fall and, as it were, reversed, so that now the principalities exercise dominion over human beings and claim in their own names and for themselves idolatrous worship from human beings.   —FO, 52, 62, 63; see above, pp. 14, 152

Providence. Perhaps that is the clue to the biblical context of providence: grace. Perhaps we err or become confused about what providence means because we dwell upon only some particular event, an occasional occurrence that seems outstanding; we tend to think of the providential as rare and exceptional; we make selections, among all the things that happen to us, calling some matters of providence and treating the rest as having nothing to do with providence. Perhaps there just is no discrimination at all, in the concern of God for this life in this world, beyond one happening and another. *Perhaps everything is providential.* If everything is providential, then providence means the constant and continual renewal of God's grace in all situations for everyone throughout time. . . . If everything is providential, then the issue in living is the patience and ingenuity of God's grace, and human beings need never live bereft of hope.

—*SB*, 121

Racism is not an evil in human hearts or minds; racism is a principality, a demonic power, a representative image, an embodiment of death, over which human beings have little or no control, but which works its awful influence over their lives. This is the power with which Jesus Christ was confronted and which, at great and sufficient cost, he overcame.

—*The Witness*, Feb. 21, 1963, 14; see above, pp. 177, 180.

Reconciliation is the event, as 2 Corinthians testifies, of a new order of corporate life of persons and institutions inaugurated in the world in Christ. In view of this order, it is impossible to consider the reconciliation of one person outside of, or separate from, the estate of all other human beings and institutions, this is, *politically*. No person speaks truthfully of being reconciled to God who has suffered reconciliation to God, who is not, in other words, now reconciled with themselves, with all other persons, and with all things in the whole of creation.   —*DGS*, 131

Resurrection. To become and be a beneficiary of the Resurrection of Jesus Christ means to live here and now in a way that upholds and honors the sovereignty of the Word of God in this life in this world, and that trusts the Judgment of the Word of God in history. That means freedom *now* from all conformities to death, freedom *now* from fear of the power of death, freedom *now* from the bondage of idolatry to death, freedom *now* to live in hope while awaiting the Judgment.

—*SF,* 113; see above, p. 25

Resurrection v. Immortality. The most radical confusion about afterdeath, however, has to do with the transliteration of the resurrection as some idea of immortality. . . . In my view, immortality, essentially, is no more than an elaborate synonym for remembrance of the dead, though there are attached to it multifarious notions of spiritual and/or material survival of death. Resurrection, however, refers to the transcendence of the power of death, and of the fear or thrall of the power of death, here and now, in this life, in this world. Resurrection, thus, has to do with life, and indeed, the fulfillment of life, *before* death. . . . Where confusion reigns and the distinction between resurrection and immortality is lost or suppressed, it is common to find people, frantic in their embrace of one or another versions of survival after death, rejecting life in this world, including, typically, the gift of their own lives.   —*SF,* 138–39; see above, p. 75

Sacrament. I had gone out in the afternoon, when it was warmer, dressed only in a shirt, chinos, and sneakers, but now that the weather had changed, I was shivering from the cold. About two blocks from my tenement, a boy I knew, who had been loafing on the corner, called out that he wanted to ask me something. As we talked he saw that I was freezing to death and so he took off his jacket and gave it to me to wear. The boy is an addict and I happened to know that the clothes on his back were virtually the only ones he had—he had pawned everything else. Sometimes, when his clothes were being laundered, he would have to stay in the house because he had nothing else to wear, unless he could borrow something from someone. But he saw that I was cold and gave me his jacket. That is what is known as a sacrament.

—*MPE*, 42; see above, p. 84

Sanctification. I mean the endeavor by which a person is sanctified or rendered holy. The endeavor is not one of the person so affected but, quite the contrary, is an effort of the Word of God, which *elects* the one made holy and which, I believe, offers similar election freely to every person. . . . Thus sanctification refers to the activity of the historic Word of God renewing human life (and all of created life) in the midst of the era of the fall, or during the present darkness, in which the power of death apparently reigns. It designates the essential condition of a person who confesses that he or she has suffered the renewal of his or her being, or selfhood, in the Word of God and is restored to wholeness as a human being. While there *is* an implication, in being holy, of incessant repentance, there is no implication of perfection or of any superior moral status. Among humans, holiness may involve a relatively more profound experience of being human, but it does not indicate as such the exceptional or the extraordinary. To the contrary, holy connotes the holistic in human life and, in that connection, the normal, the typical, the ordinary, the generic, the exemplary.   —*PS*, 30; see above, p. 201

Sin is not essentially the mistaken, inadvertent, or deliberate choice of evil by human beings, but the pride into which they fall in associating their own self-interests with the will of God. Sin is the denunciation of the freedom of God to judge humans as it pleases God to judge them. Sin is the displacement of God's will with one's own will. Sin is the radical confusion as to whether God or the human being is morally sovereign in history.

—*ID*, 20

State names the functional paraphernalia of political authority in a nation, which claims and exercises violence within a nation. The precedence of the State hierarchically among the principalities is related to the jurisdiction asserted by the State over other institutions and powers within a nation. Practically it is symbolized by the police power, taxation, licensing, regulation of corporate organization and activity, the military forces, and the like. The paramountcy of the State among the demonic powers is probably most readily recognized in tyrannical regimes, ancient or modern. —*EC*, 109; see above, p. 25

State vs. Nation. In the Bible where the State is designated as a principality of particular dignity or apparent superiority, the historical realities to which allusions are made are authoritarian or totalitarian (Rev. 13:18). In such a regime any substantive distinctions between the principality of the nation and the principality of the State are lost. The ethos of the nation is absorbed into the apparatus of authority. Or, to put it a bit differently, the spirit and tradition of the nation are abolished by the administration of the State or displaced by a fabricated version of tradition furnished by the State. For all practical purposes, in a totalitarianism, the nation and the State become merged. By contrast (though, from a human point of view, it be a very relative matter) in nonauthoritarian societies, the distinguishable but related principalities of the nation and the State remain separated to the extent that the identity and character of the nation are embodied in tradition and inheritance, sometimes expressed constitutionally, or sometimes as common law. This represents and attempts some restraint or discipline upon the exercise of authority and the functioning of the State.

—*EC*, 109–10; see above, p. 45

Technocracy. The political development of technology has produced a form of government which virtually abolished that familiar tension by its destruction of human rights, its coercion of human life, its domination of human beings; in short, by its undoing of that part of the constitutional fabric which values human life in society. Technology has installed a counter-revolutionary regime—a technocratic totalitarianism—which has set aside, if not literally overturned, the inherited constitutional institutions thereby creating a vested ruling authority outside the law and beyond accountability to people.

—*ID*, 90; see above, pp. 139, 146

Theology is dissimilar from both philosophy and religion: theology is not speculative, on the one hand, theology is not self-justifying, on the other, and theology is not so eminent as to be aloof from life as it is, as are those other two exercises. Theology is concerned with the implication of the Word of God in the world's common life. In this context, it must be recognized and affirmed that everyone, *if* they reflect upon the event of their own life in this world, is a theologian. It is only in this sense that I tolerate being sometimes called a theologian myself.

—*SB*, 21; see above, p. 3

Vocation is the name of the awareness of [the] significance of one's own biography. To have a vocation or to be called in Christ means to discern the coincidence of the Word of God with one's own selfhood, in one's own being, in its most specific, thorough, unique, and conscientious sense (*SF*, 21). Persons and principalities, all the creatures, all realities or elements of creation are named by the Word of God. Each is beneficiary of an identity, capacity, purpose, and place in conjunction with that of everyone and everything else. In other words, in creation, *vocation* issues from the Word of God. Still more precisely, in the biblical description of creation, the vocation of God becomes definitive of the vocation of human life and that of institutions and nations and other creatures and of all things whatever.

—CO, 29; see above, pp. 36, 190

Word of God. I intend this to be understood as a name. Thereby, I refer not only to the Bible as the Word of God, but, simultaneously to the Word of God incarnate in Jesus Christ and, also, to the Word of God militant in the life of the world as the Holy Spirit, and, further, to the Word of God inhering in the whole of creation.   CO, 14; see above, p. 204

Work is described in the Bible as the broken relationship between humanity and the rest of creation. . . . Work (as distinguished from humanity's charge to "fill the earth and have dominion over it," "to till the garden and keep it") refers to the reality, in the Fall (that is, in this history), of the enslavement of human beings to institutions and similar principalities.   —DGS, 55

Worship is the celebration of life in its totality. Worship is the sacramental appropriation of all of life in celebration. Worship is the festival of creation. Organized public corporate worship is a theatrical restoration of creation in which each and all of the participants symbolically and ritually enjoy their own selves and one another and all things. Liturgical worship, which is inherently a communal event, whether formal or spontaneous, whether traditional or extemporaneous, is an esoteric portrayal of the reconciliation of the whole world. Worship is the celebration of life in its ultimate expectancy. Sacramental worship is always, hence, profoundly ethical and specifically and self-consciously eschatological in its ethics, exposing contemporary society—whatever it happens to be—to the Gospel's eagerness for the end and fulfillment of history in God. In turn, that means that worship is explicitly a political and social happening of the most radical dimensions, illuminating every falsity and offense,

every vanity and need of the prevailing social order while notoriously, passionately, incessantly calling for the overturning—or, more literally, the transfiguring—of the incumbent order of society. Much more may be affirmed of worship, but suffice it to say . . . that worship has its most telling analogues in common life in revolution, on the one hand, and in play, on the other.
—*SB*, 101–2; see above, p. 86

Wry Post-Script. I realize that some who are reading this book, if they have persevered to this page, would have preferred a book on "spirituality" which pronounced some rules, some norms, some guidelines, some rubrics for a sacred discipline that, if pursued diligently, would establish the holiness of a person. I do not discern that such is the biblical style, as admirable as that may happen to be in a worldly sense.   —*PS*, 90

A Homiletic Afterword

To Celebrate the Death and Life of William Stringfellow

Daniel Berrigan, S.J.

On March 5, 1985, Daniel Berrigan gave the following homily at the Block Island funeral for William Stringfellow. Although the precise phrase does not appear in his remarks, this is the source for what has become synonymous with Stringfellow's notorious vocation: Keeper of the Word.

A sophisticated people is struck by a shortage of words adequate to describe a bad time and how one might meet it. So we grope with negatives—non-violence, non-compliance, non-betrayal. In such a time, friendship is reduced to the bone. It becomes a matter of non-betrayal.

Stringfellow saw betrayal on all sides (as indeed all but the purblind must see)—the large betrayal of public trust, public monies, the public compact. He went around the world, having come on another way than this. He was non-violent, non-cooperative, non-betraying.

He began his professional life in a good place, among the poor, who according to his faith were non-expendable. So he succored them.

When one president (among many) flagrantly betrayed the public trust, Stringfellow was the first who urged he be removed from office, to the enforced status of non-betrayer.

In the wake of the womens' outcry, he understood immediately the injustice of exclusive male order in his church. He urged non-compliance and stood among the first in the church courts demanding justice for women.

He was elected to public office in his beloved Block Island. Here he railed against the betrayal of public trust, the waste of public land, the degradation of the sublime ecology, the greed of

carving the Island into a freehold of the absentees and the irre-
sponsibles. He thundered against the contempt leveled at Island
folk, as the elderly, the workers, the productive and hopeful were
reduced to a landless servant class by the high and mighty who
live beyond accountability.

He came to believe that the betrayal of the Island and its
people was probably irreversible. He may well be right. In any
case, money and self-interest served him a hard lesson—he was
swept from office. The lesson of the times was brutally clear;
there was less and less room for conscience in public life in
Washington, Providence, or New Shoreham.

He retired. But hardly to nurse his wounds.

His political career on the Island had been brief, stormy, and
electric with hope. Who will ever forget the Town Meetings, how
people came alive under the lash of his rhetoric, how issues long
buried were laid out and perfidious deals made accountable? He
spoke for the powerless; he enraged the powerful. The burning
clarity of his mind pierced the smog of sophisticated betrayal.

The times were hostile to such fervent public civility. The
servile, the violent, the wheelers and dealers owned America.
Betrayal had become a credential for public office, high and low.
In such times, what could Stringfellow offer?

What was manifestly impossible in public life he created
and cherished up close. He was skilled in ways to define non-
betrayal, non-concession, non-surrender. He would bide his time
and explore those ways. There could exist in such a world a
community of non-betrayal, non-cooperation, non-surrender. It
required that the members enter a covenant, say their prayers,
gather and then scatter to their work and above all, the first of
all, cherish one another.

Whether they (or he) affected the course of events in the mad
world, freed as they were from lust after power or prestige, was
manifestly beside the point. They were to keep the Word of God,
in a time when very few kept any word. Keeping one's word,
making the work of God one's own was the point.

My encounter with this spirit of Stringfellow and his non-betraying friendship dates notoriously from 1970 and events that occurred up the road from this chapel. I was lifted from the home of Stringfellow and trundled off the Island into prison. From that vantage, I learned of the subsequent indictment of William and Anthony for the crime of harboring a fugitive (a strange foretaste of the present sanctuary movement within the church). But for those few days, Stringfellow's home was the only church I knew. It was the only safe place in the universe.

And this was the aspect of Christ that this Christian kept opening before his friends. Christ was our friend, in such a world, in such a lifetime as ours, precisely because He does not betray. He keeps covenant. He keeps His Word, even with us, even when we break covenant, break our word, betray. Christ keeps his Word with the poor, with the blacks, with the women, with the gays, even when all these are betrayed by the church, betrayed by the State, betrayed by racists and sexists and power-brokers and money-grubbers and militarists and office-seekers and property-owners and real-estate-developers and weapons-researchers. Betrayed by those who know with overmastering cynicism that the business of America is not justice or peace or bread for the poor or housing for the indigent or land for the landless or compassion for the powerless, who know, in the words of a classic political entrepreneur, that the business of America is business.

And further—since the business of America is business, it follows ineluctably that its business is also violence and war and racism. And it follows that such as Stringfellow (or you or I) are simply irrelevant to the main chance. Or if indeed we are determined to be relevant, we had best get in line, get into the business of America—the business of words without substance, claims without honor, promises broken, covenants betrayed. For those are the tools and skills of America and knowledge of the tools grants passage—from the estate of the betrayed to the exalted status of betrayer. And the passage, and its attendant rites, might be described as entrance into the American dream.

But there are other rites, another passage. We think today of the Word of God, the word of Stringfellow. I scarcely can distinguish between the two, as we celebrate a rare non-betrayal, the man who kept his word. It is to his supreme honor I mean this, that in his life, the Word of God and his own word, merged, and were one. He kept the Word of God so close, so jealously, with such fervor and attention and acute irony and sense of judgment and anger and reverence and fear and so much more—he kept that Word in such wise that the Word of God and its keeping became his own word and its keeping.

For thousands of us, he became the honored keeper and guardian of the Word of God, that is to say, a Christian who could be trusted to keep his word, which was God's Word made his own. To keep that close, to speak it afresh, to make it new.

Thus for me, a single notorious example of non-betrayal became an ikon of understanding. He could act honorably and courageously on occasion, in the breach, because he lived that way, over the long haul. In public and private, in good times and ill, in health and sickness, he kept his word.

And that Word he kept and guarded and cherished now keeps him. This is the way with the Word, which we name Christ. The covenant keeps us who keep the covenant.

And if we are assured that He keeps even those who betray the covenant, that God is not bound even by our betrayals, does not cast us off, what shall we say of the reward of this good and faithful servant for whom the keeping of the Word was a simple definition of life itself?

I think we must rejoice that his reward is exceeding great. The "small matters" (to which the Bible reduces in all sobriety the inflation and fury of this world) have yielded in death to something else. Stringfellow has entered into "great matters," matters of great and pressing moment.

He would like that—a vocation consonant with his great talents. "Well done good and faithful servant; because you have been faithful over small matters, I shall place you over great ones."

His vocation has just begun.

MODERN SPIRITUAL MASTERS
Robert Ellsberg, Series Editor

This series introduces the essential writing and vision of some of the great spiritual teachers of our time. While many of these figures are rooted in long-established traditions of spirituality, others have charted new, untested paths. In each case, however, they have engaged in a spiritual journey shaped by the challenges and concerns of our age. Together with the saints and witnesses of previous centuries, these modern spiritual masters may serve as guides and companions to a new generation of seekers.

Already published:

Simone Weil (edited by Eric O. Springsted)

Dietrich Bonhoeffer (edited by Robert Coles)

Henri Nouwen (edited by Robert A. Jonas)

Charles de Foucauld (edited by Robert Ellsberg)

Pierre Teilhard de Chardin (edited by Ursula King)

Anthony de Mello (edited by William Dych, S.J.)

Oscar Romero (by Marie Dennis, Rennie Golden, and Scott Wright)

Eberhard Arnold (edited by Johann Christoph Arnold)

Thomas Merton (edited by Christine M. Bochen)

Thich Nhat Hanh (edited by Robert Ellsberg)

Mother Teresa (edited by Jean Maalouf)

Rufus Jones (edited by Kerry Walters)

Edith Stein (edited by John Sullivan, O.C.D.)

John Main (edited by Laurence Freeman)

Mohandas Gandhi (edited by John Dear)

Mother Maria Skobtsova (introduction by Jim Forest)

Evelyn Underhill (edited by Emilie Griffin)

St. Thérèse of Lisieux (edited by Mary Frohlich)

Flannery O'Connor (edited by Robert Ellsberg)

Clarence Jordan (edited by Joyce Hollyday)

G. K. Chesterton (edited by William Griffin)

Alfred Delp, S.J. (introduction by Thomas Merton)

Bede Griffiths (edited by Thomas Matus)

Karl Rahner (edited by Philip Endean)

Pedro Arrupe (edited by Kevin F. Burke, S.J.)

Sadhu Sundar Singh (edited by Charles E. Moore)

Romano Guardini (edited by Robert A. Krieg)

Albert Schweitzer (edited by James Brabazon)

Caryll Houselander (edited by Wendy M. Wright)

Brother Roger of Taizé (edited by Marcello Fidanzio)

Dorothee Soelle (edited by Dianne L. Oliver)

Leo Tolstoy (edited by Charles E. Moore)

Howard Thurman (edited by Luther E. Smith, Jr.)

Swami Abhishiktananda (edited by Shirley du Boulay)

Carlo Carretto (edited by Robert Ellsberg)

Pope John XXIII (edited by Jean Maalouf)

Modern Spiritual Masters (edited by Robert Ellsberg)

Jean Vanier (edited by Carolyn Whitney-Brown)

The Dalai Lama (edited by Thomas A. Forsthoefel)

Catherine de Hueck Doherty (edited by David Meconi, S.J.)

Dom Helder Camara (edited by Francis McDonagh)

Daniel Berrigan (edited by John Dear)

Etty Hillesum (edited by Annemarie S. Kidder)

Virgilio Elizondo (edited by Timothy Matovina)

Yves Congar (edited by Paul Lakeland)

Metropolitan Anthony of Sourozh (edited by Gillian Crow)

David Steindl-Rast (edited by Clare Hallward)

Frank Sheed and Maisie Ward (edited by David Meconi)

Abraham Joshua Heschel (edited by Susannah Heschel)

Gustavo Gutiérrez (edited by Daniel G. Groody)

John Howard Yoder (edited by Paul Martens and Jenny Howells)

John Henry Newman (edited by John T. Ford, C.S.C.)

Robert McAfee Brown (edited by Paul Crowley)

John Muir (edited by Tim Flinders)